NO MATTER HOW I IT'S YOU GUYS' FAU POPULAR! ❷

NICO TANIGAWA

Translation/Adaptation: Krista Shipley, Karie Shipley
Lettering: Lys Blakeslee

WATASHI GA MOTENAI NOWA DOU KANGAETEMO OMAERA GA WARUI! Volume 2 © 2012 Nico Tanigawa / SQUARE ENIX CO., LTD. All rights reserved. First published in Japan in 2012 by SQUARE ENIX CO., LTD. English translation rights arranged with SQUARE ENIX CO., LTD. and Hachette Book Group through Tuttle-Mori Agency, Inc.

Translation © 2014 by SQUARE ENIX CO., LTD.

Yen Press
Hachette Book Group
237 Park Avenue, New York, NY 10017

www.HachetteBookGroup.com
www.YenPress.com

Yen Press is an imprint of Hachette Book Group, Inc. The Yen Press name and logo are trademarks of Hachette Book Group, Inc.

First Yen Press Edition: January 2014

ISBN: 978-0-316-32204-1

10 9 8 7 6 5 4 3 2 1

BVG

Printed in the United States of America

TRANSLATION NOTES ·

PAGE 1
The Belly I Want to Kick is a reference to a book called *Keritai Senaka (The Back I Want to Kick)* by Japanese novelist Risa Wataya, which won the 2003 Akutagawa Prize.

PAGE 17
Translated here as **Boaroscope**, this was originally a bad pun on *uranai* ("fortune, horoscope") and *uribou* ("wild boar piglet").

PAGE 30
The book title *Instill* is a reference to *Install*, another book by Risa Wataya — her first one, in fact, written when she was only seventeen years old.

PAGE 35
Kafcat on the Shore is a reference to the Haruki Murakami novel *Kafka on the Shore*.

PAGE 46
Toⓑbo refers to Tombo from the Studio Ghibli film *Kiki's Delivery Service (Majou no Takkyuubin)*, directed by Hayao Miyazaki, that Mokocchi is watching.

PAGE 46
Similar to **Otome Style**, there is an actual otome magazine called *Girls' Style*.

PAGE 46
Uta no Ouji-sama is a reference to the pop idol otome game franchise *Uta no☆Prince-sama♪*. The title translates literally to "Princes of Song" in Japanese.

PAGE 55
Mart 7/24 is a reference to the 7-Eleven convenience store chain.

PAGE 63
Fashion Center Mura-Mura is a reference to Fashion Center Shimamura, a store chain that sells cheap clothes, accessories, and shoes.

PAGE 73
The **poster** behind Mokocchi is of the protagonist from the popular *Shin Megami Tensei Persona 4* video game (aka. Yuu Narukami in the anime adaptation).

PAGE 78
Botchan is a classic novel by Japanese author Natsume Soseki.

PAGE 89
LoLo is a nod to the *shoujo* (girls') manga magazine *LaLa*, published by Hakusensha.

PAGE 90
In Japanese, the candy store is known as a *dagashiya*, a small-time store that sells cheap candy, snacks, toys, stickers, etc., primarily targeted at kids.

PAGE 90
Potato Stakes (chanko flavor) is a reference to the snack Potato Sticks. *Chanko* is a rich, nutritious stew that sumo wrestlers eat to gain weight.

PAGE 90
Ue●●ibou, the snack Mokocchi offers to buy Kii-chan, is Umaibou, a puffed cylindrical corn snack that comes in a variety of flavors and sells individually for ¥10 each.

PAGE 90
ChocoBunt is a reference to the actual chocolate snack ChocoBat.

PAGE 90
Super Bal Assortment is an altered version of the same brand name known in the United States. This is a mix of different types and sizes of Super Balls to use as prizes in drawings, etc.

PAGE 91
Sono Manma is from a line of bubble gum with liquid centers, where one in three pieces is sour instead of sweet.

PAGE 91
The original name for **Lil' Eely** is *Kabayaki-kun*, and the actual product name is *Kabayaki-san*. *Kabayaki* is loach or eel dipped and broiled in a soy-based sauce.

PAGE 91
Tomoko's honorary title of **Queen** may be a reference to the Queen rank given to the best female player in *karuta*, a traditional Japanese card game. *Karuta* is currently experiencing greater popularity thanks to the manga *Chihayafuru* and its anime adaptation.

PAGE 100
The original title of the (fake) otome game **Sagess Time** is *Seijo* ("holy woman") *Time*. This is a spin on the slang phrase "*kenja* ('sage's') time," which refers to the time of calm after a man has masturbated.

PAGE 117
Tomoko mentions two East Asian **cicada** species that are well-known in Japan for being evocative of dusk — higurashi (Tanna japonensis) — and late summer — *tsuku-tsuku-boushi* (Meimuna opalifera).

PAGE 118
The Kappa **Cygnids** is an actual meteor shower that occurs in late summer.

PAGE 119
I LOHA Water is a take on the actual brand name I LOHAS Water.

PAGE 128
Butt-Naked Butlers is based on an actual indie Japanese boys love game from 2011 called *Naked Butler (Hadaka Shitsuji)*.

PAGE 128
Boys Love, also known as BL, is a genre of man-on-man romance mostly by and for women.

EVEN RHINO BEETLES DO IT...

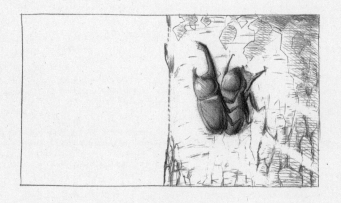

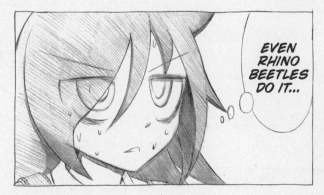

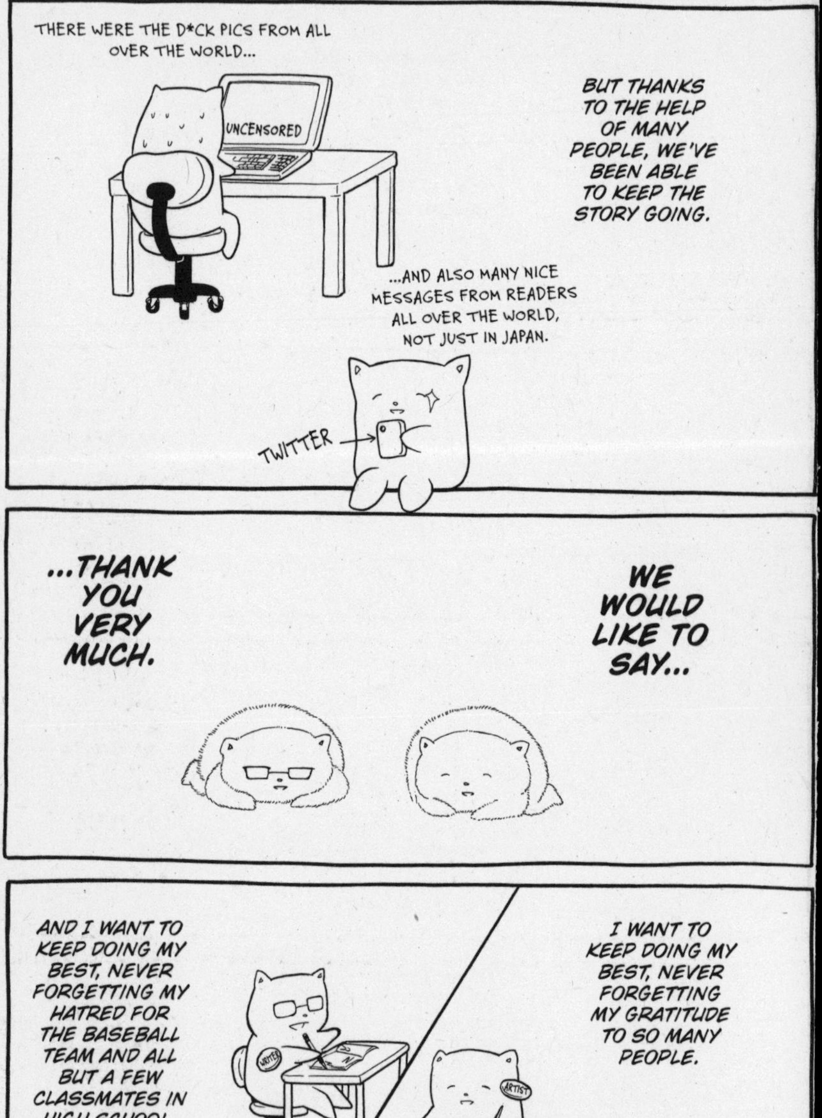
BUT THANKS TO THE HELP OF MANY PEOPLE, WE'VE BEEN ABLE TO KEEP THE STORY GOING.
THERE WERE THE D*CK PICS FROM ALL OVER THE WORLD...
UNCENSORED
...AND ALSO MANY NICE MESSAGES FROM READERS ALL OVER THE WORLD, NOT JUST IN JAPAN.
TWITTER
WE WOULD LIKE TO SAY...
...THANK YOU VERY MUCH.
I WANT TO KEEP DOING MY BEST, NEVER FORGETTING MY GRATITUDE TO SO MANY PEOPLE.
ARTIST
AND I WANT TO KEEP DOING MY BEST, NEVER FORGETTING MY HATRED FOR THE BASEBALL TEAM AND ALL BUT A FEW CLASSMATES IN HIGH SCHOOL.
WRITER

WITH THE HELP OF ASSISTANT YUUJI ASAKURA-SAN

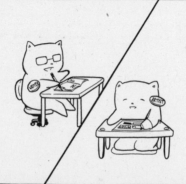

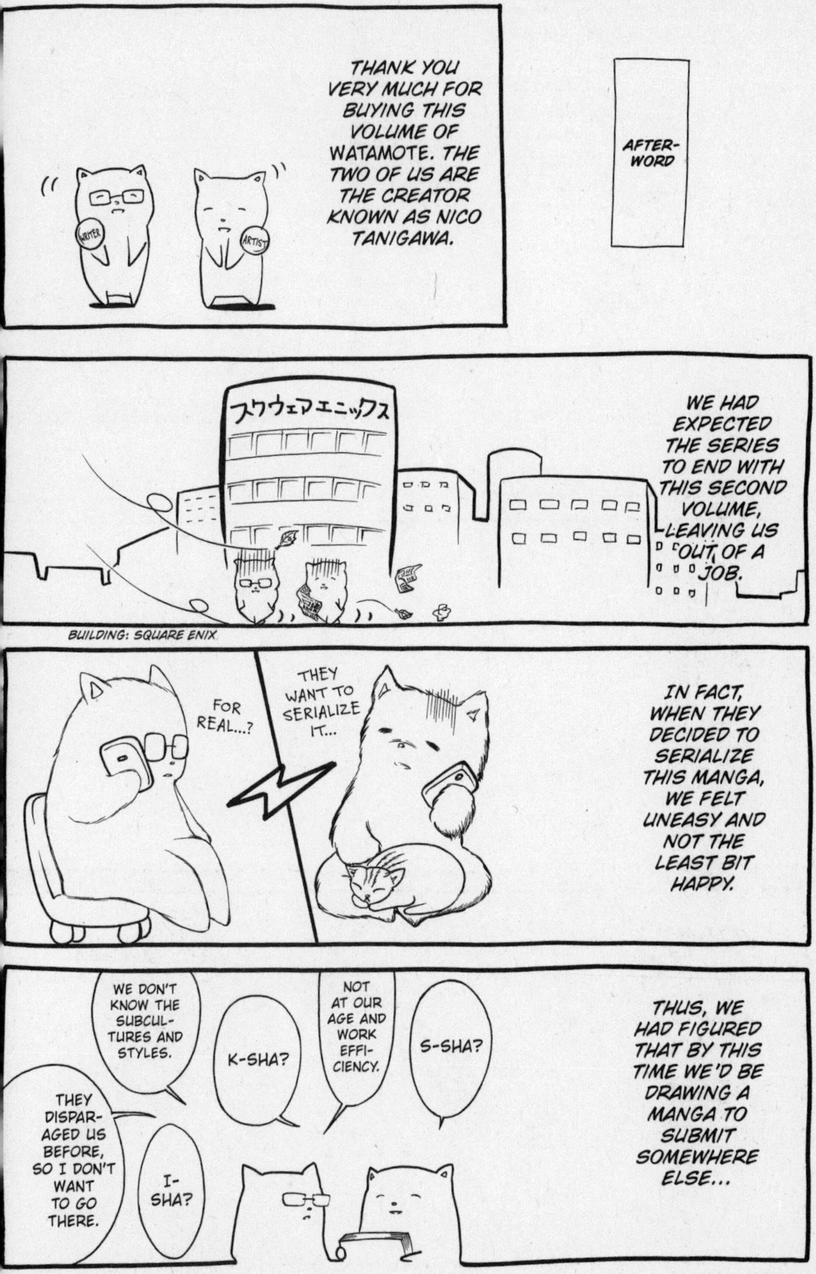
AFTER-WORD
THANK YOU VERY MUCH FOR BUYING THIS VOLUME OF WATAMOTE. THE TWO OF US ARE THE CREATOR KNOWN AS NICO TANIGAWA.
WRITER
ARTIST
WE HAD EXPECTED THE SERIES TO END WITH THIS SECOND VOLUME, LEAVING US OUT OF A JOB.
スクウェアエニックス
BUILDING: SQUARE ENIX
IN FACT, WHEN THEY DECIDED TO SERIALIZE THIS MANGA, WE FELT UNEASY AND NOT THE LEAST BIT HAPPY.
THEY WANT TO SERIALIZE IT...
FOR REAL...?
THUS, WE HAD FIGURED THAT BY THIS TIME WE'D BE DRAWING A MANGA TO SUBMIT SOMEWHERE ELSE...
S-SHA?
NOT AT OUR AGE AND WORK EFFI-CIENCY.
K-SHA?
WE DON'T KNOW THE SUBCUL-TURES AND STYLES.
I-SHA?
THEY DISPAR-AGED US BEFORE, SO I DON'T WANT TO GO THERE.

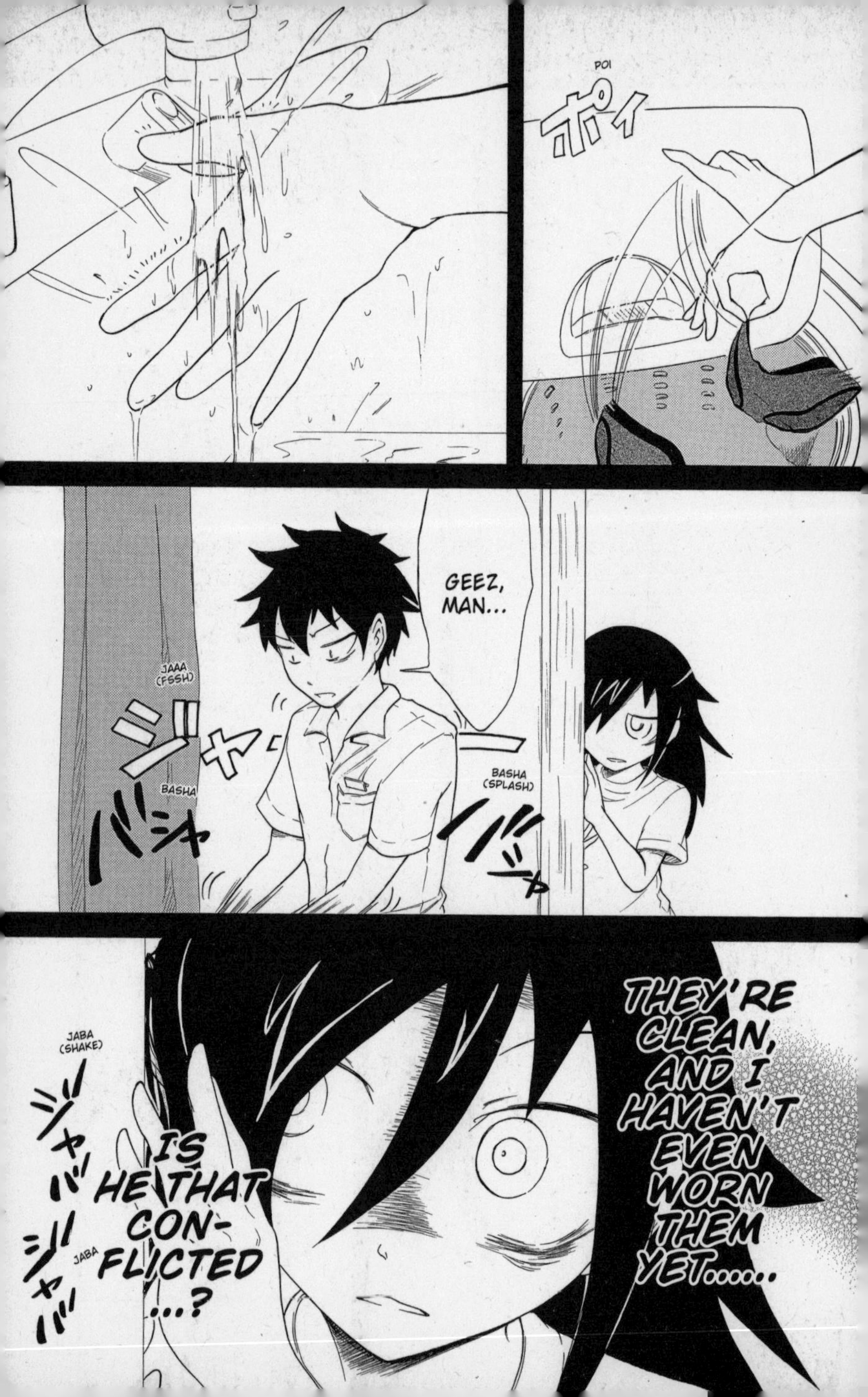
POI
ポイ
GEEZ, MAN...
BASHA (SPLASH)
バシャ
JAAA (FSSH)
ジャー
BASHA
バシャ
THEY'RE CLEAN, AND I HAVEN'T EVEN WORN THEM YET......
IS HE THAT CON-FLICTED ...?
JABA (SHAKE)
ジャバ
JABA
ジャバ

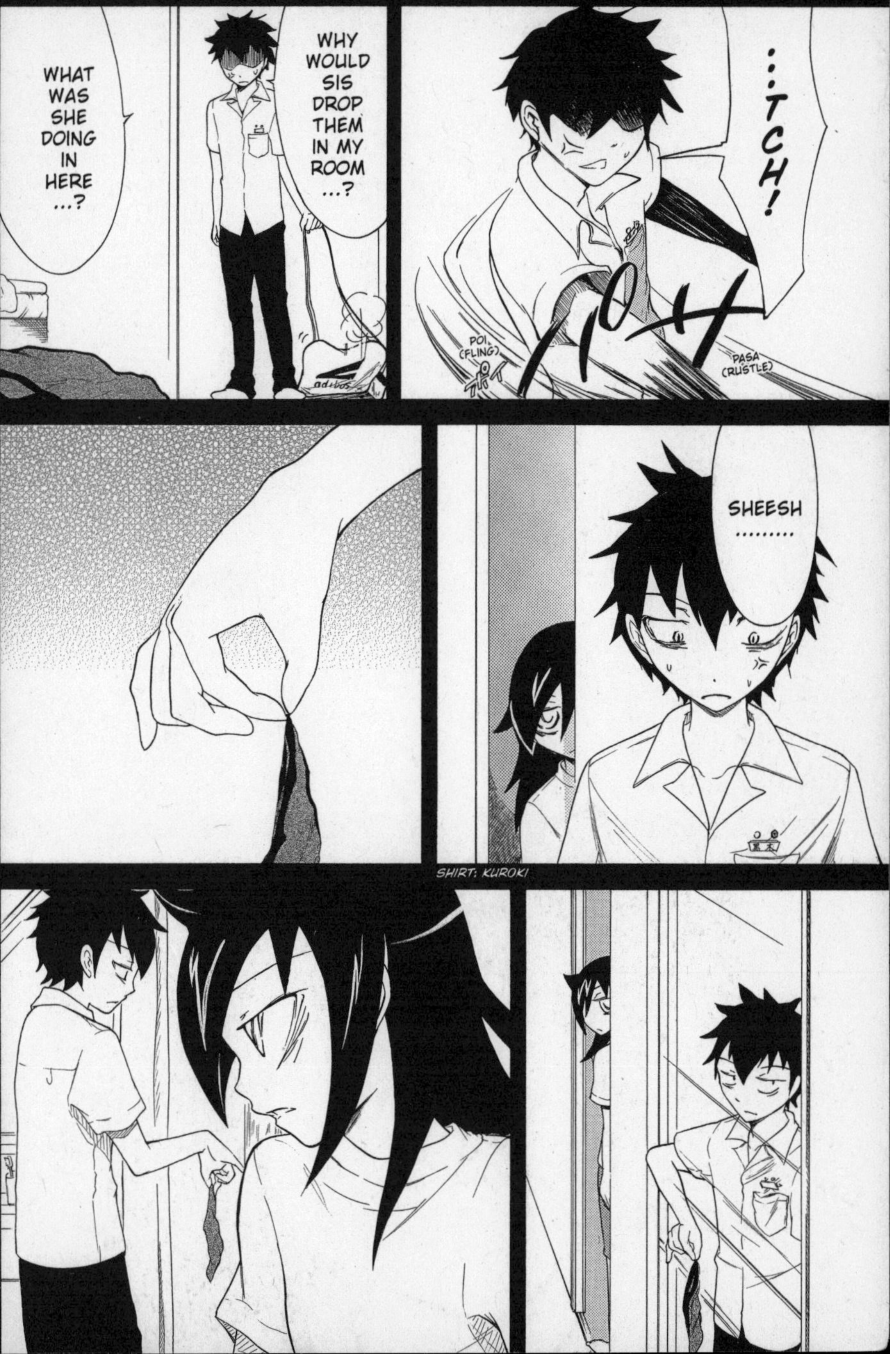
...TCH!
POI (FLING)
PASA (RUSTLE)
WHY WOULD SIS DROP THEM IN MY ROOM ...?
WHAT WAS SHE DOING IN HERE ...?
SHEESH ....
SHIRT: KUROKI

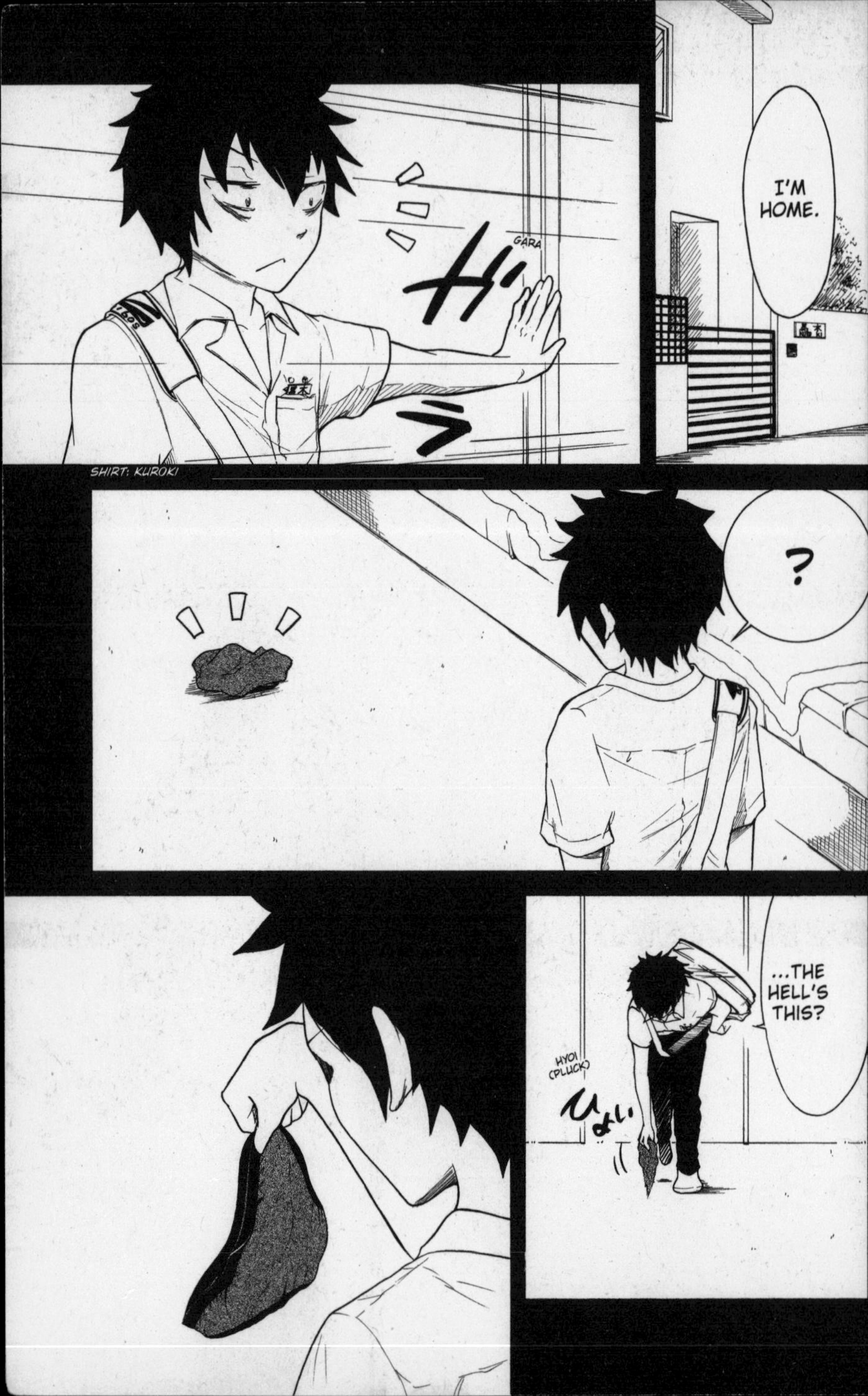
I'M HOME.
GARA
ガラ
SHIRT: KUROKI
?
...THE HELL'S THIS?
HYOI (PLUCK)
ひょい

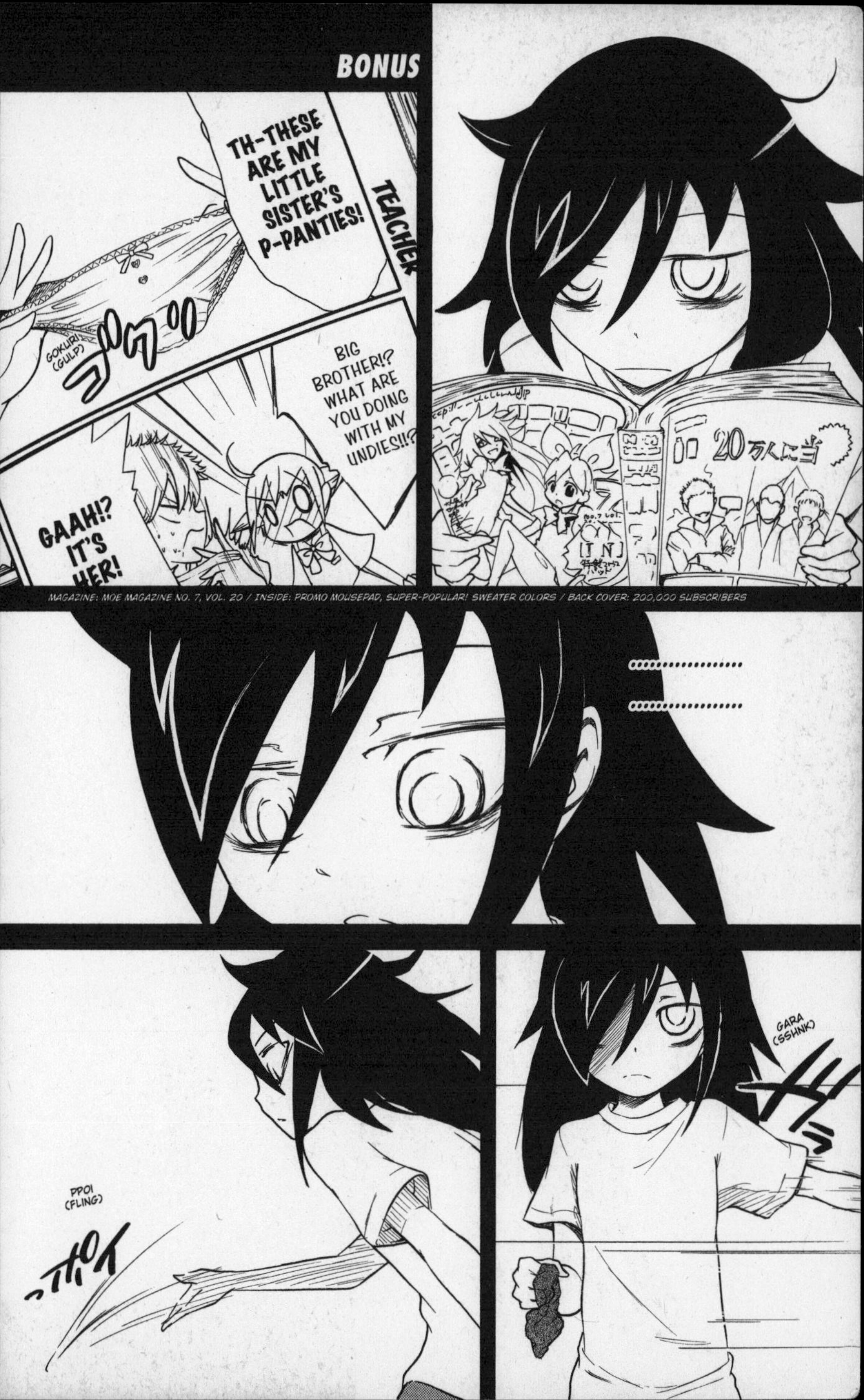
BONUS
20万人に当
TH-THESE ARE MY LITTLE SISTER'S P-PANTIES!
TEACHER
GOKURI (GULP)
BIG BROTHER!? WHAT ARE YOU DOING WITH MY UNDIES!!?
GAAH!? IT'S HER!
MAGAZINE: MOE MAGAZINE NO. 7, VOL. 20 / INSIDE: PROMO MOUSEPAD, SUPER-POPULAR! SWEATER COLORS / BACK COVER: 200,000 SUBSCRIBERS
....
....
GARA (SSHNK)
PPOI (FLING)

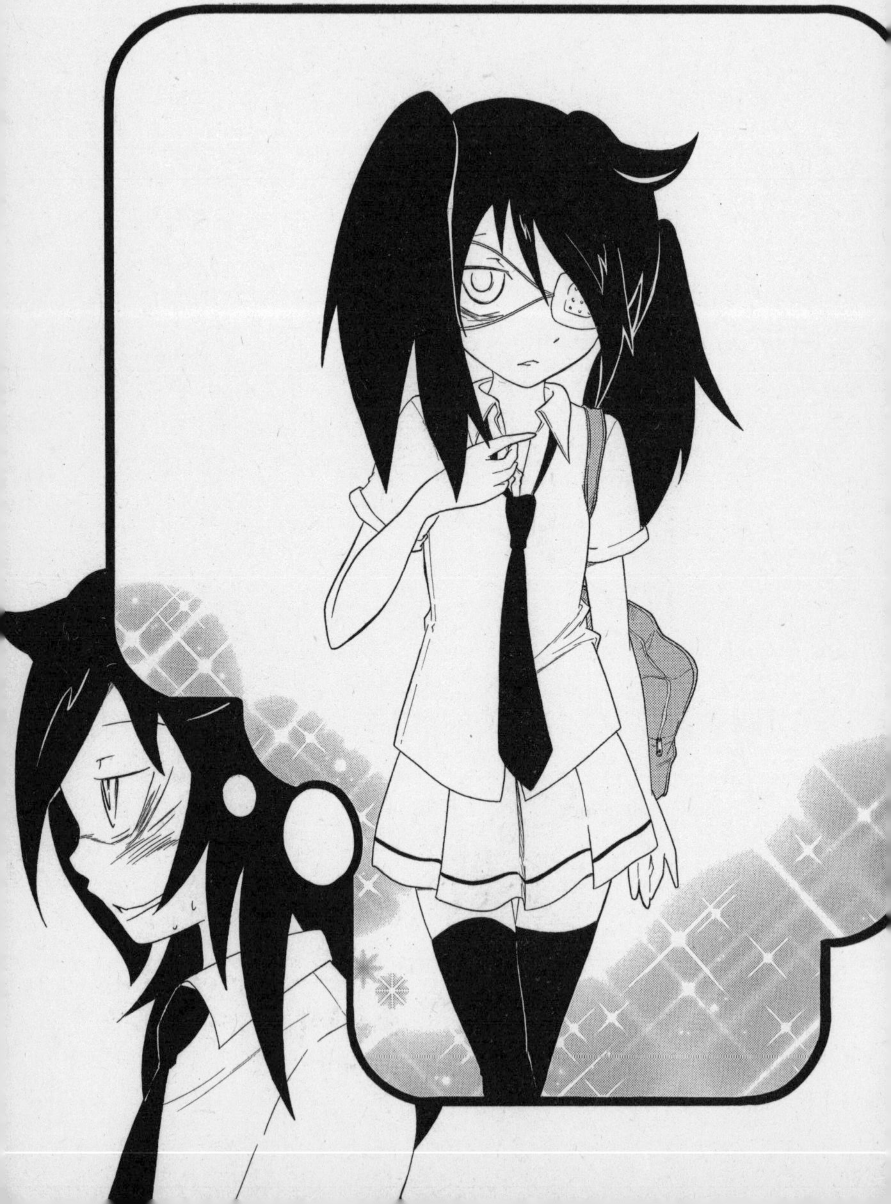

No Matter How I Look at It, It's You Guys' Fault I'm Not Popular!

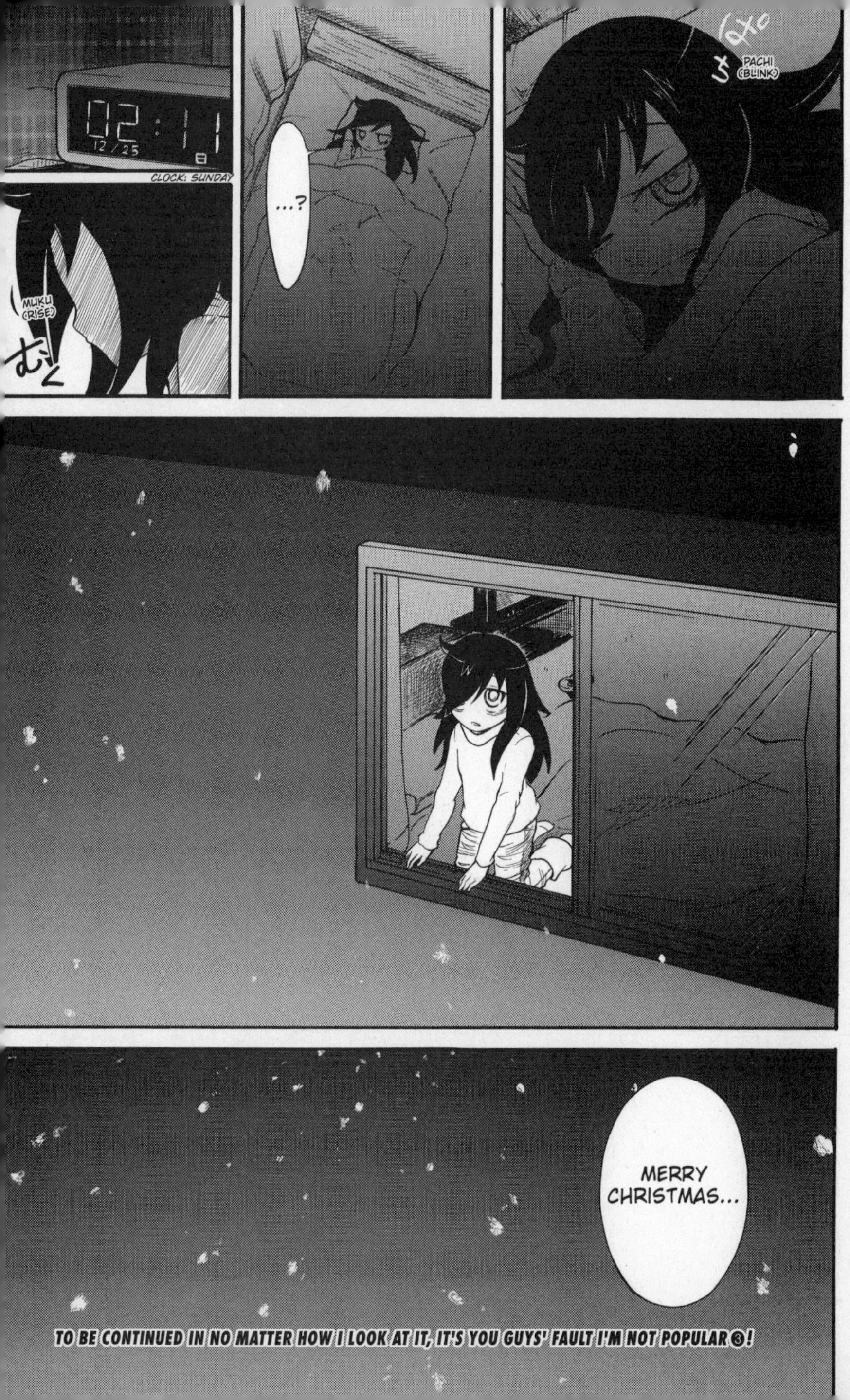
PACHI (BLINK)
...?
02:11
12/25
CLOCK: SUNDAY
MUKU (RISE)
MERRY CHRISTMAS...
TO BE CONTINUED IN NO MATTER HOW I LOOK AT IT, IT'S YOU GUYS' FAULT I'M NOT POPULAR ③!

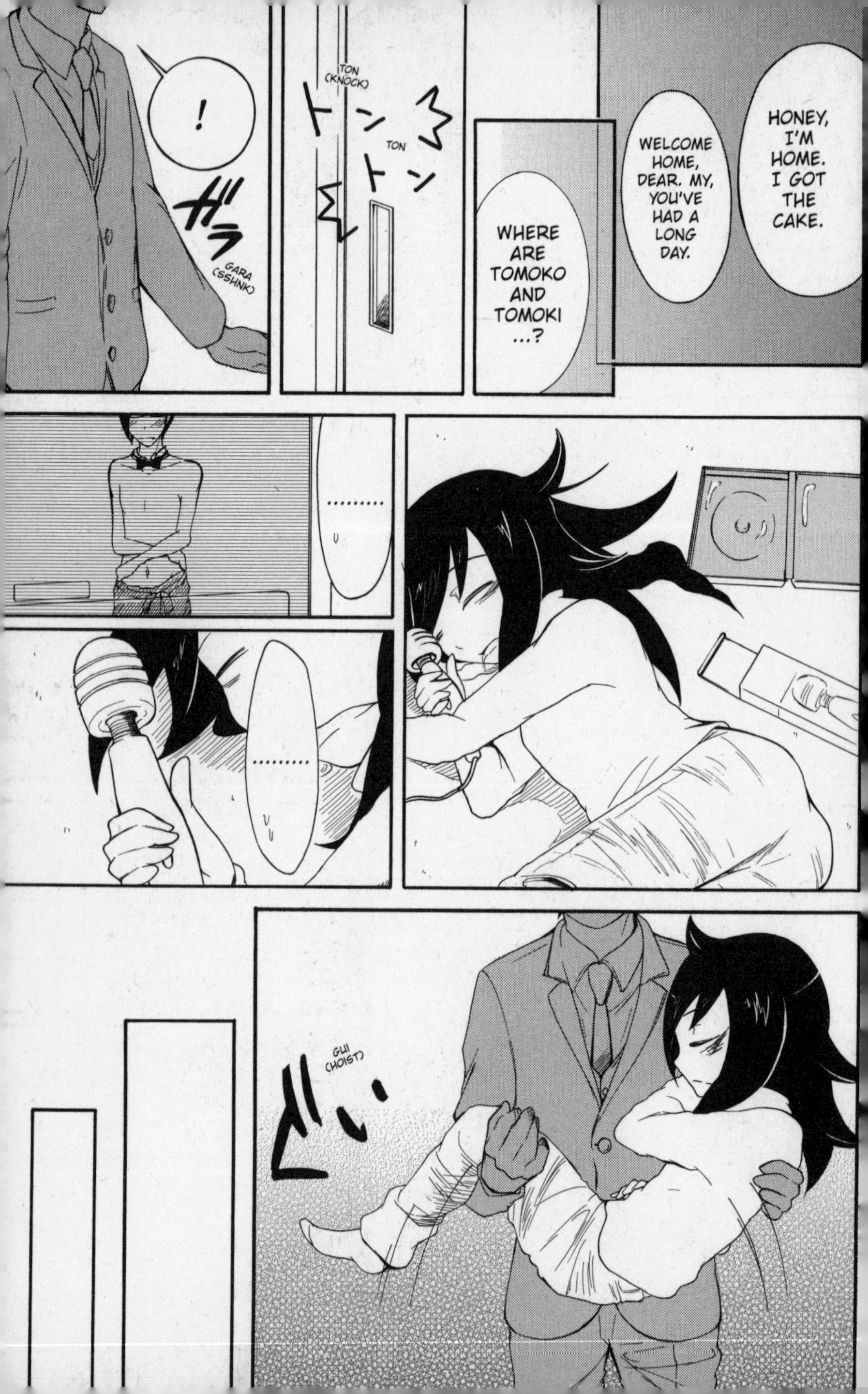
HONEY, I'M HOME. I GOT THE CAKE.
WELCOME HOME, DEAR. MY, YOU'VE HAD A LONG DAY.
WHERE ARE TOMOKO AND TOMOKI ...?
TON (KNOCK)
トン
TON
トン
!
ガラ
GARA (SSHNK)
....
....
GUI (HOIST)
ぐい

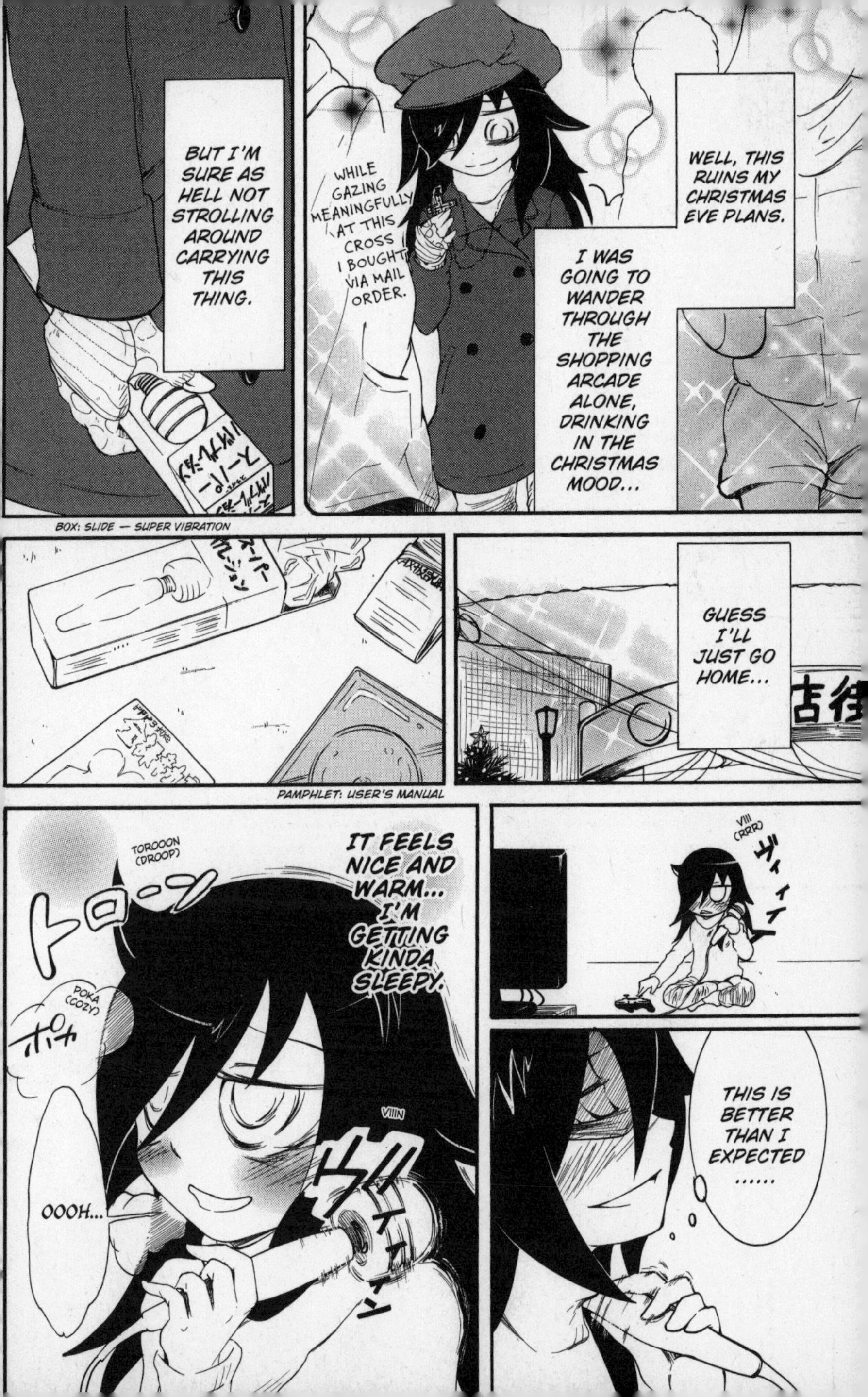
WELL, THIS RUINS MY CHRISTMAS EVE PLANS.
I WAS GOING TO WANDER THROUGH THE SHOPPING ARCADE ALONE, DRINKING IN THE CHRISTMAS MOOD...
WHILE GAZING MEANINGFULLY AT THIS CROSS I BOUGHT VIA MAIL ORDER.
BUT I'M SURE AS HELL NOT STROLLING AROUND CARRYING THIS THING.
BOX: SLIDE — SUPER VIBRATION
GUESS I'LL JUST GO HOME...
PAMPHLET: USER'S MANUAL
VIII (RRR)
THIS IS BETTER THAN I EXPECTED ......
IT FEELS NICE AND WARM... I'M GETTING KINDA SLEEPY.
TOROOON (DROOP)
POKA (COZY)
VIIIN
OOOH...

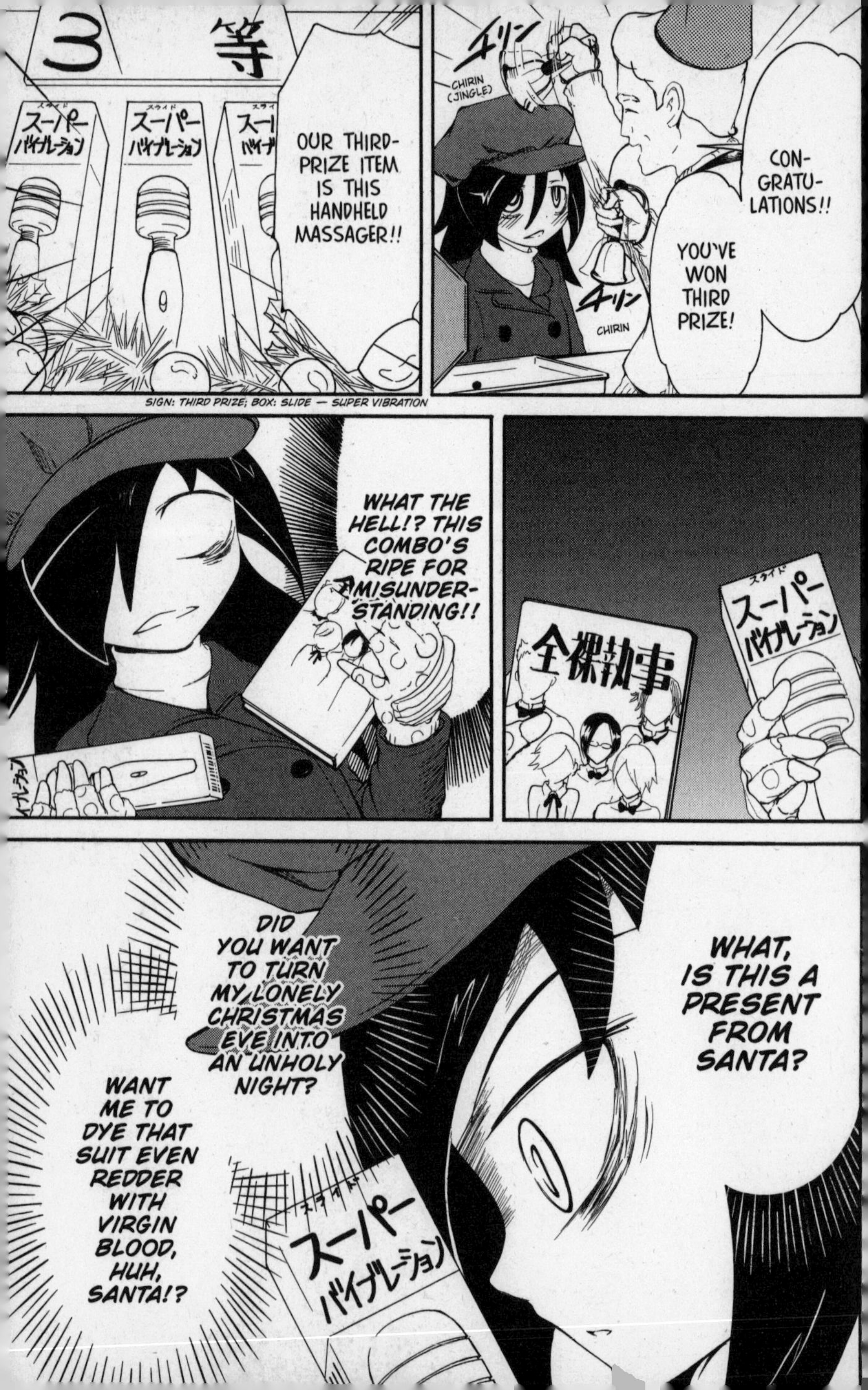
チリン
CHIRIN (JINGLE)
CON-GRATU-LATIONS!!
YOU'VE WON THIRD PRIZE!
チリン
CHIRIN
3等
スライド スーパーバイブレーション
OUR THIRD-PRIZE ITEM IS THIS HANDHELD MASSAGER!!
SIGN: THIRD PRIZE; BOX: SLIDE — SUPER VIBRATION
スライド スーパーバイブレーション
全裸執事
WHAT THE HELL!? THIS COMBO'S RIPE FOR MISUNDERSTANDING!!
WHAT, IS THIS A PRESENT FROM SANTA?
DID YOU WANT TO TURN MY LONELY CHRISTMAS EVE INTO AN UNHOLY NIGHT?
WANT ME TO DYE THAT SUIT EVEN REDDER WITH VIRGIN BLOOD, HUH, SANTA!?
スライド スーパーバイブレーション

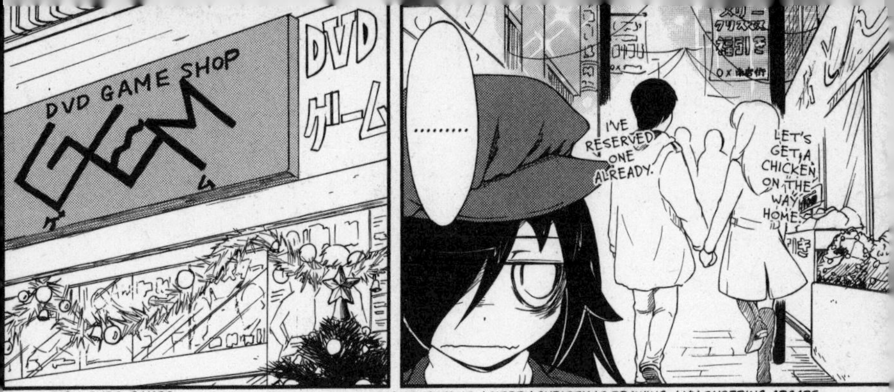
....
LET'S GET A CHICKEN ON THE WAY HOME.
I'VE RESERVED ONE ALREADY.
DVD
ゲーム
DVD GAME SHOP

SIGN: DVDS, GAMES

SIGNS: FUTONS / MERRY CHRISTMAS DRAWING / XY SHOPPING ARCADE

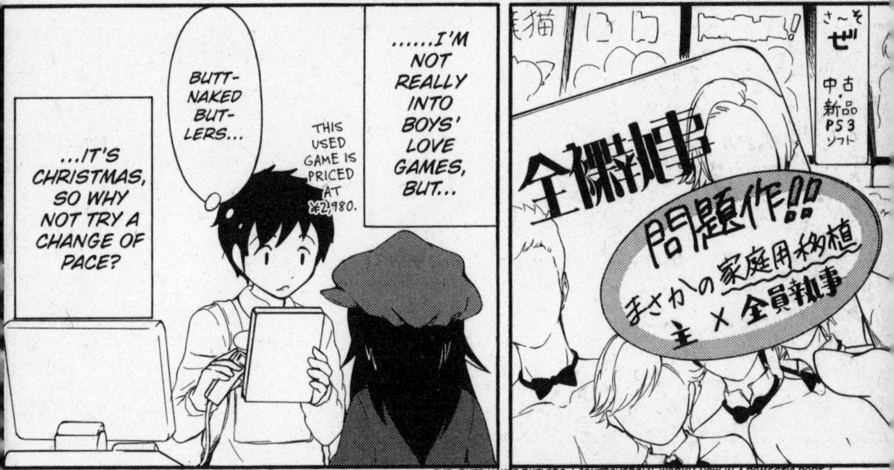
さ～そ
ゼ
中古
新品
PS3
ソフト
全裸執事
問題作!!
まさかの家庭用移植
主×全員執事
......I'M NOT REALLY INTO BOYS' LOVE GAMES, BUT...
BUTT-NAKED BUTLERS...
THIS USED GAME IS PRICED AT ¥2,980.
...IT'S CHRISTMAS, SO WHY NOT TRY A CHANGE OF PACE?

DVD: BUTT-NAKED BUTLERS / CONTROVERSIAL WORK!! NOW IN A DOMESTIC PORT / MASTER AND ALL OF HIS BUTLERS / LABEL: B, USED & NEW PS3 SOFTWARE / FAR DVD: CUTEY-CAT

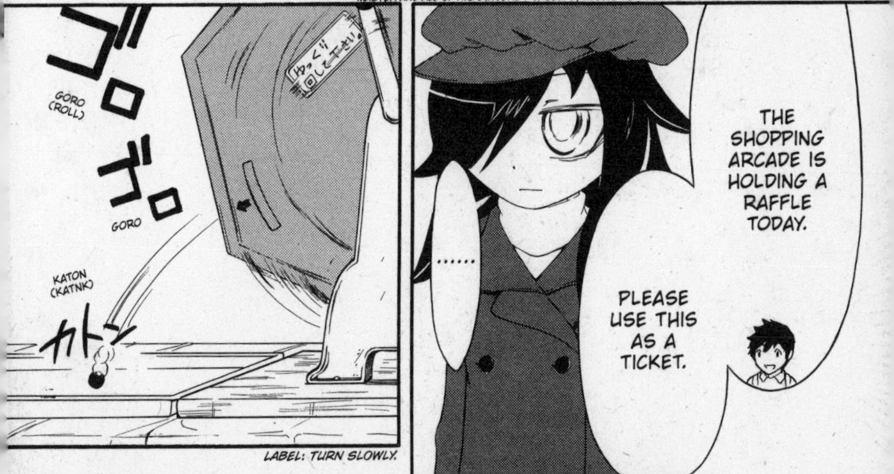
THE SHOPPING ARCADE IS HOLDING A RAFFLE TODAY.
PLEASE USE THIS AS A TICKET.
......
ゆっくり回して下さい。
ゴロ
GORO (ROLL)
ゴロ
GORO
カトン
KATON (KATNK)

LABEL: TURN SLOWLY.

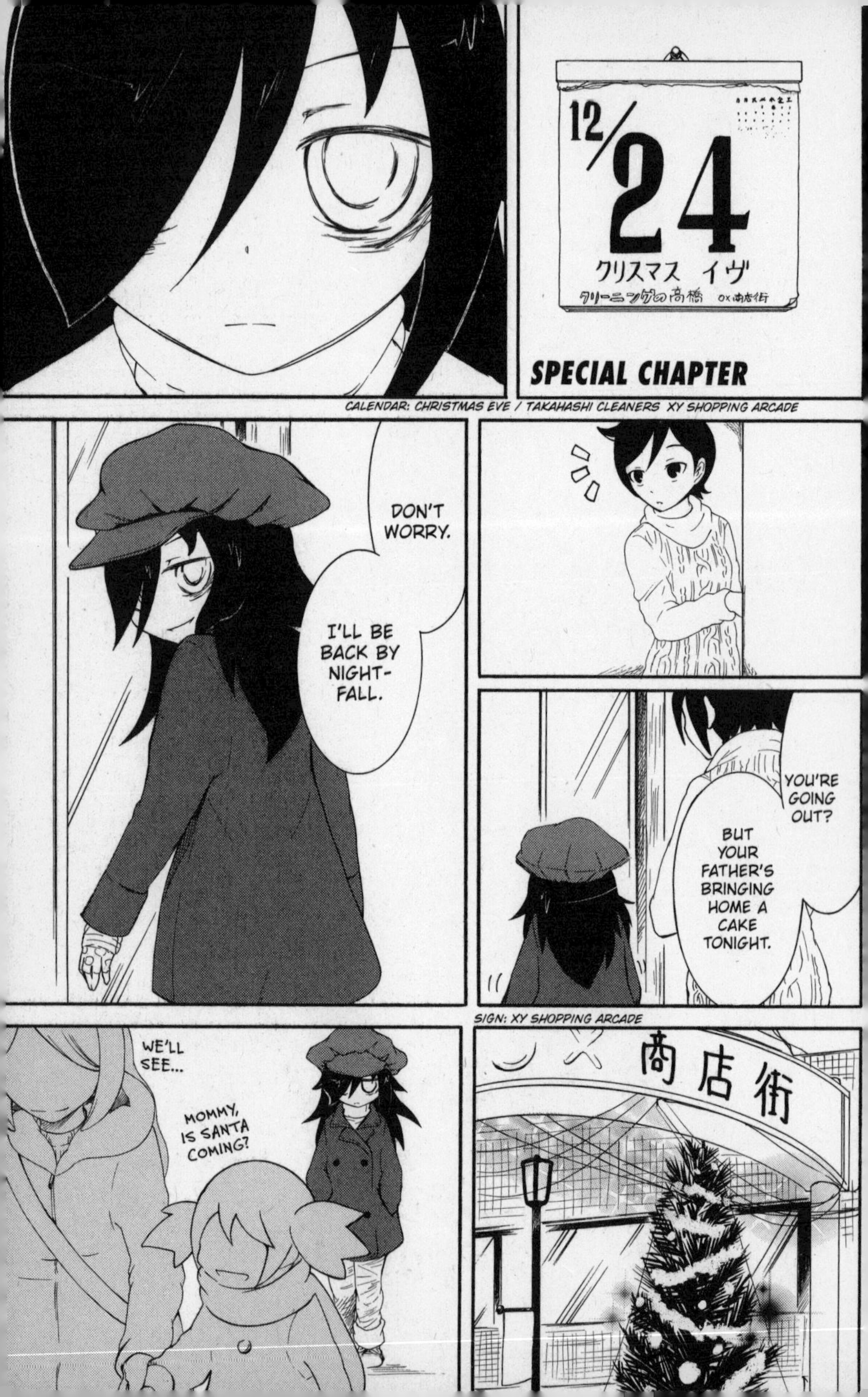
12/24
クリスマス イヴ
クリーニングの高橋 ○×商店街
SPECIAL CHAPTER
CALENDAR: CHRISTMAS EVE / TAKAHASHI CLEANERS XY SHOPPING ARCADE
YOU'RE GOING OUT?
BUT YOUR FATHER'S BRINGING HOME A CAKE TONIGHT.
DON'T WORRY.
I'LL BE BACK BY NIGHT-FALL.
SIGN: XY SHOPPING ARCADE
商店街
MOMMY, IS SANTA COMING?
WE'LL SEE...

No Matter How I Look at It, It's You Guys' Fault I'm Not Popular!

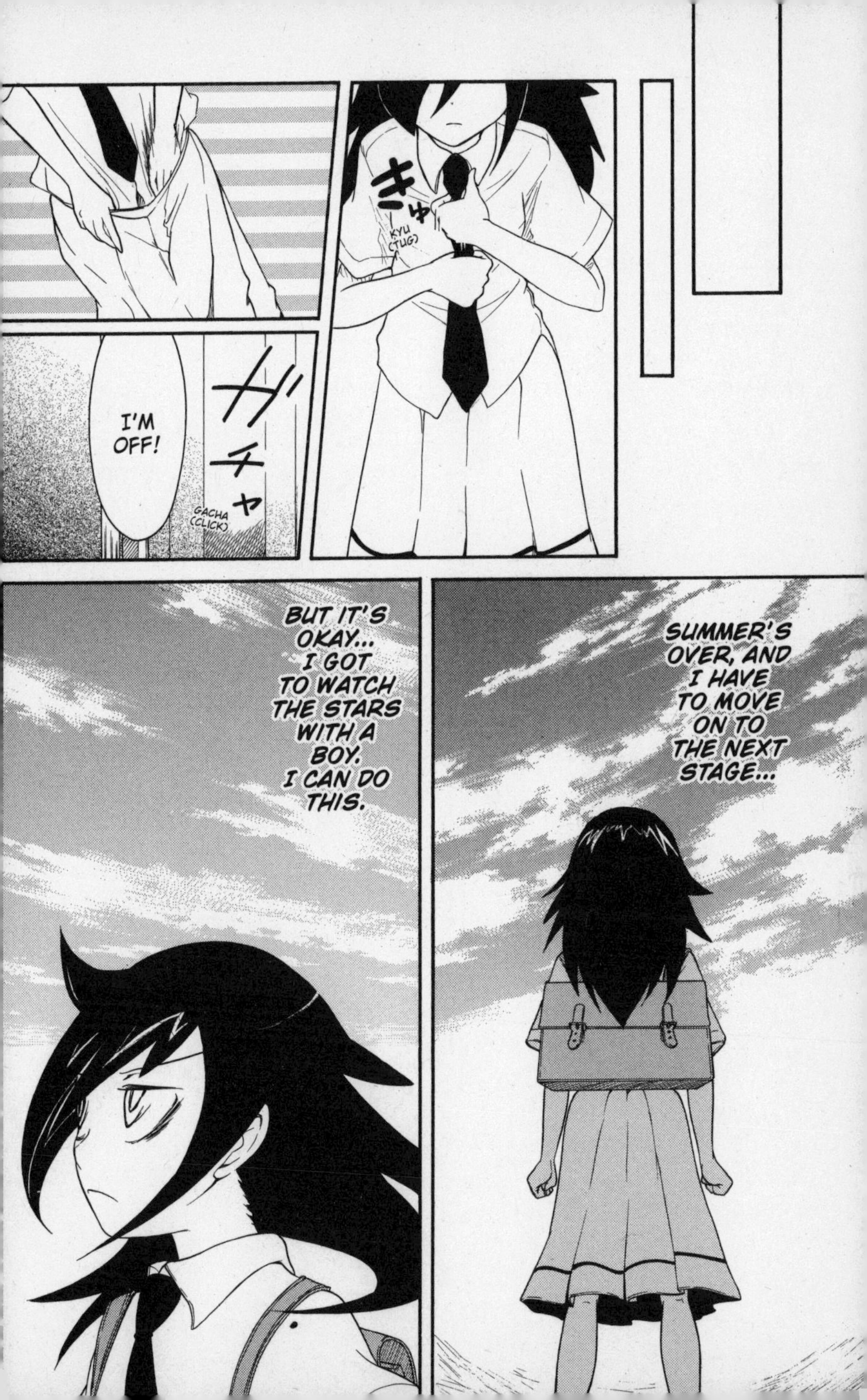
きゅ
KYU (TUG)
I'M OFF!
ガチャ
GACHA (CLICK)
SUMMER'S OVER, AND I HAVE TO MOVE ON TO THE NEXT STAGE...
BUT IT'S OKAY... I GOT TO WATCH THE STARS WITH A BOY. I CAN DO THIS.

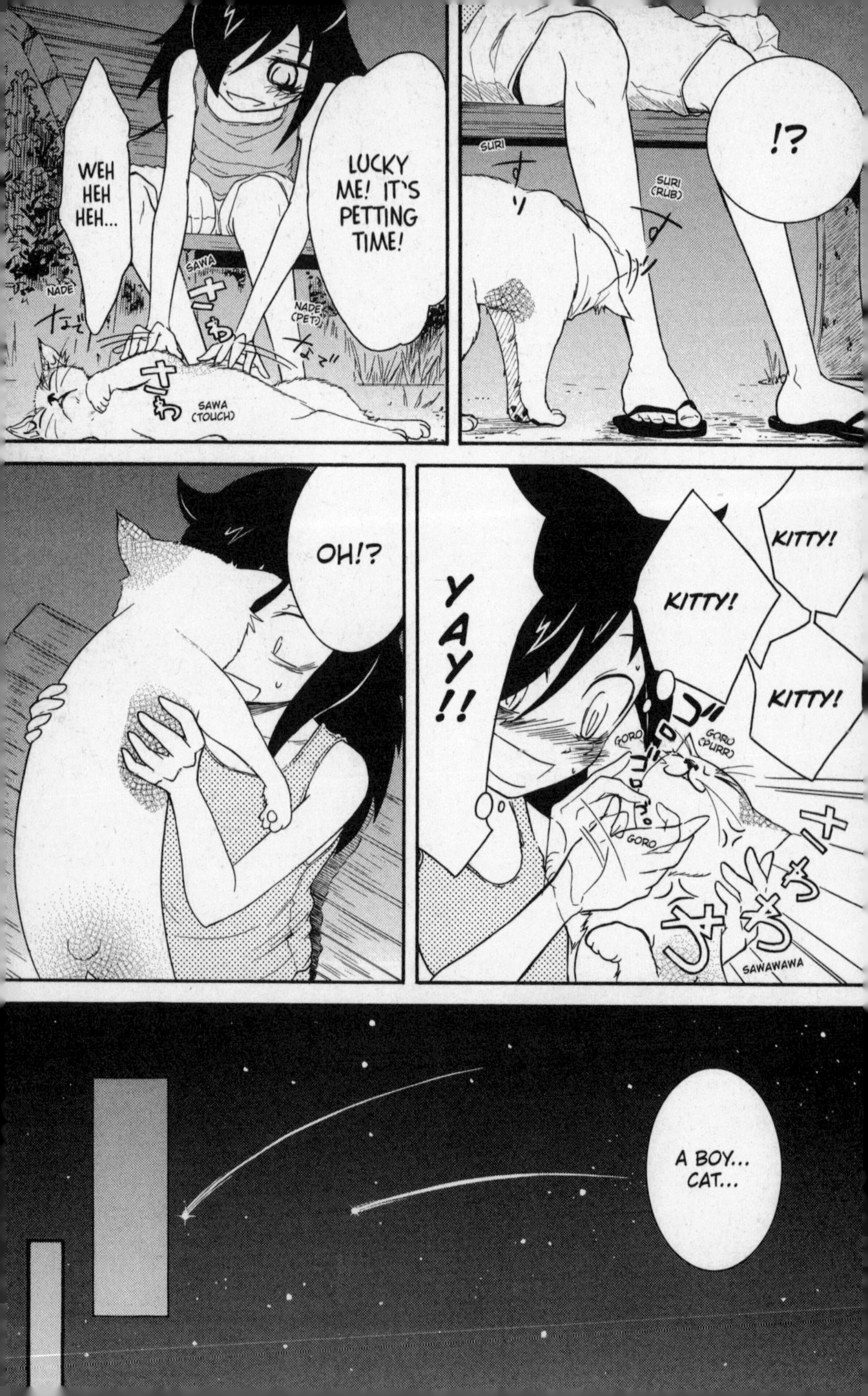
!?
SURI (RUB)
SURI
LUCKY ME! IT'S PETTING TIME!
WEH HEH HEH...
SAWA
NADE (PET)
NADE
SAWA (TOUCH)
KITTY!
KITTY!
KITTY!
YAY!!
GORU (PURR)
GORO
GORO
SAWAWAWA
OH!?
A BOY... CAT...

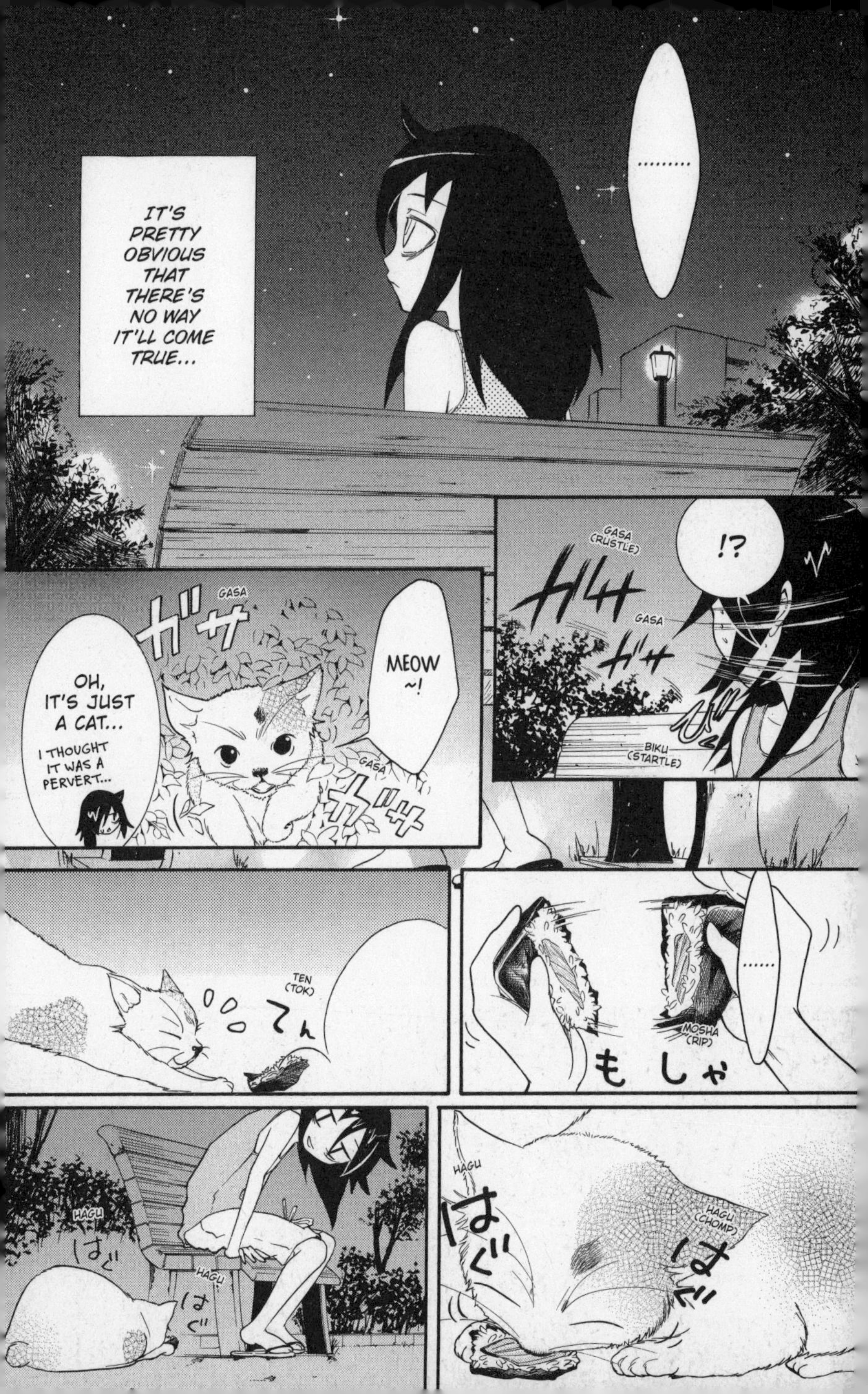
....
IT'S PRETTY OBVIOUS THAT THERE'S NO WAY IT'LL COME TRUE...
!?
GASA (RUSTLE)
ガサ
GASA
ガサ
BIKU (STARTLE)
MEOW ~!
GASA
ガサ
OH, IT'S JUST A CAT...
I THOUGHT IT WAS A PERVERT...
GASA
ガサ
......
MOSHA (RIP)
もしゃ
TEN (TOK)
てん
HAGU
はぐ
HAGU (CHOMP)
はぐ
HAGU
はぐ
HAGU
はぐ

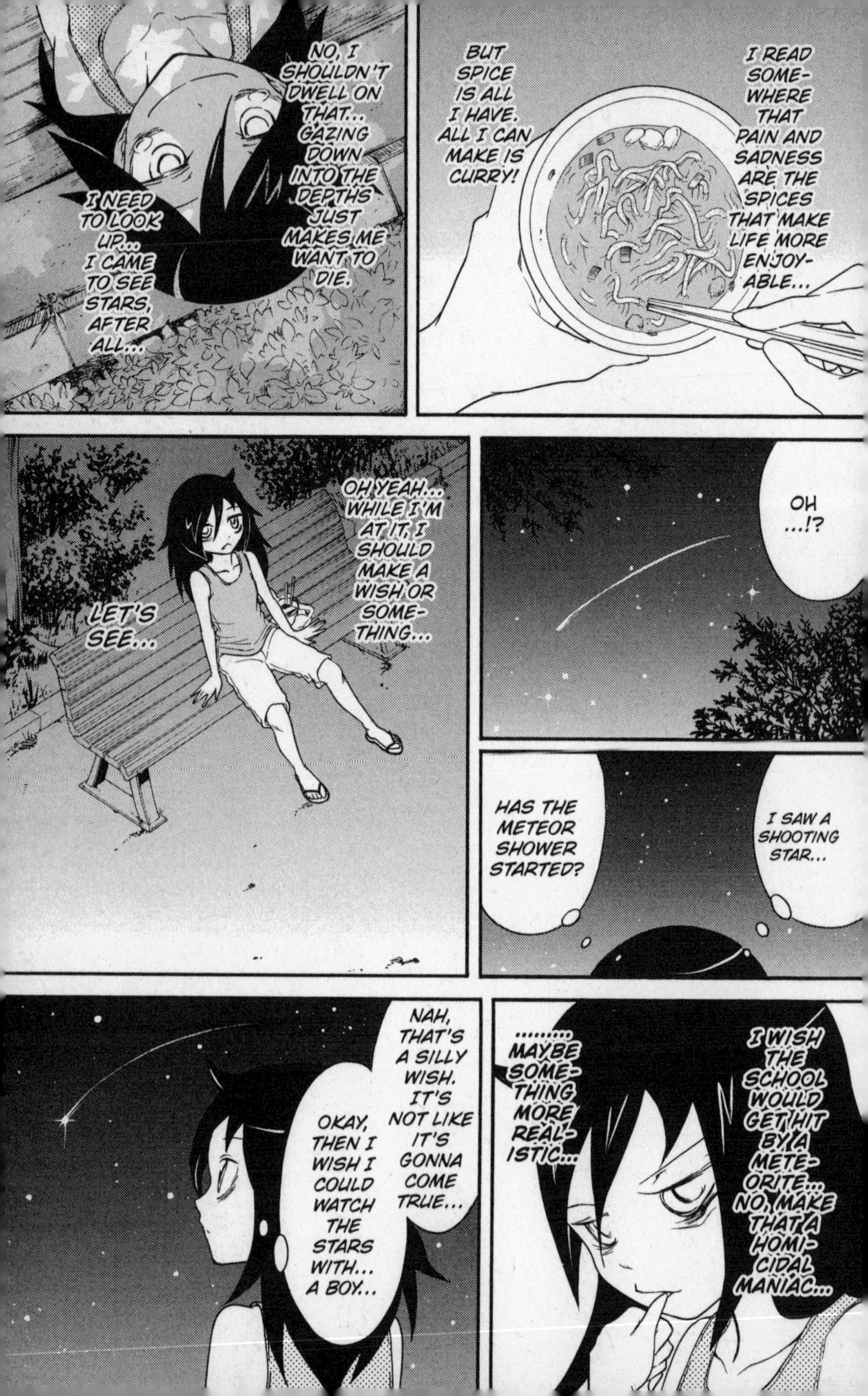
I READ SOMEWHERE THAT PAIN AND SADNESS ARE THE SPICES THAT MAKE LIFE MORE ENJOYABLE...
BUT SPICE IS ALL I HAVE. ALL I CAN MAKE IS CURRY!
NO, I SHOULDN'T DWELL ON THAT... GAZING DOWN INTO THE DEPTHS JUST MAKES ME WANT TO DIE.
I NEED TO LOOK UP... I CAME TO SEE STARS, AFTER ALL...
OH ...!?
I SAW A SHOOTING STAR...
HAS THE METEOR SHOWER STARTED?
OH YEAH... WHILE I'M AT IT, I SHOULD MAKE A WISH OR SOMETHING...
LET'S SEE...
I WISH THE SCHOOL WOULD GET HIT BY A METEORITE... NO, MAKE THAT A HOMICIDAL MANIAC...
.........MAYBE SOMETHING MORE REALISTIC...
NAH, THAT'S A SILLY WISH. IT'S NOT LIKE IT'S GONNA COME TRUE...
OKAY, THEN I WISH I COULD WATCH THE STARS WITH... A BOY...

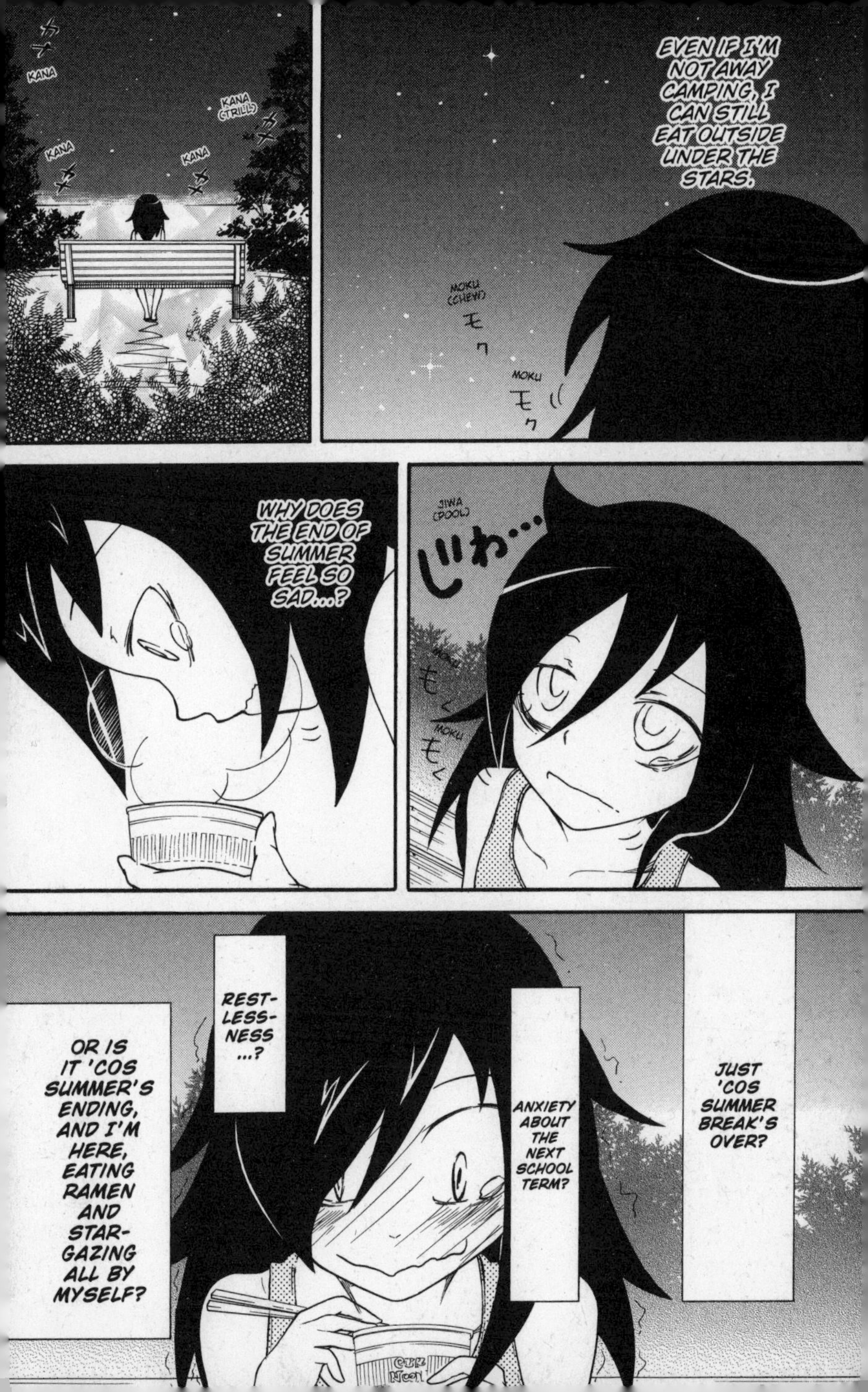
EVEN IF I'M NOT AWAY CAMPING, I CAN STILL EAT OUTSIDE UNDER THE STARS.
MOKU (CHEW)
モク
MOKU
モク
KANA
KANA
KANA
KANA
JIWA (POOL)
じわ…
MOKU
もく
MOKU
もく
WHY DOES THE END OF SUMMER FEEL SO SAD...?
JUST 'COS SUMMER BREAK'S OVER?
ANXIETY ABOUT THE NEXT SCHOOL TERM?
REST-LESS-NESS ...?
OR IS IT 'COS SUMMER'S ENDING, AND I'M HERE, EATING RAMEN AND STAR-GAZING ALL BY MYSELF?

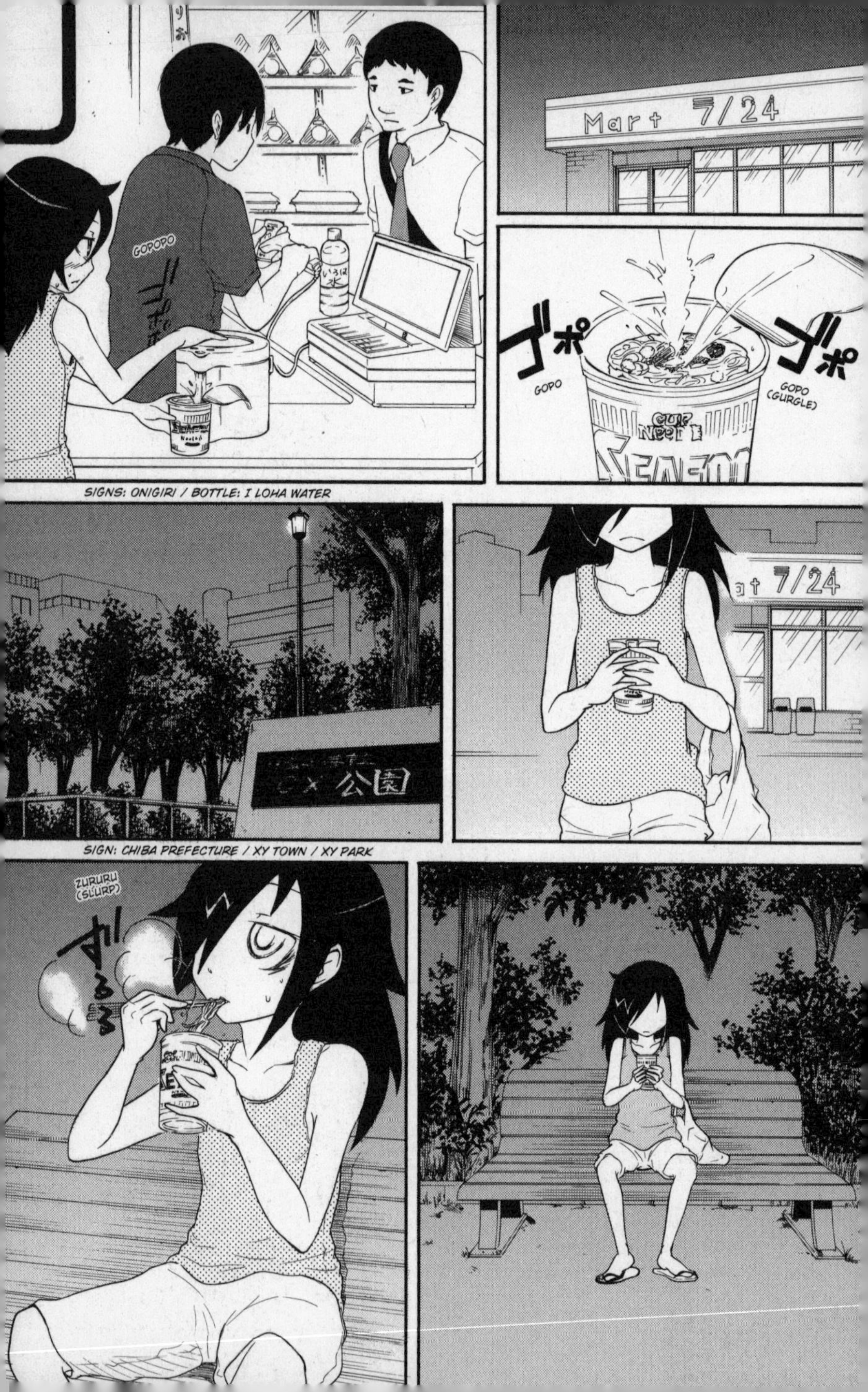

Mart 7/24
ゴポ
GOPO (GURGLE)
ゴポ
GOPO
CUP NEET
GOPOPO
SIGNS: ONIGIRI / BOTTLE: I LOHA WATER
7/24
公園
SIGN: CHIBA PREFECTURE / XY TOWN / XY PARK
ZURURU (SLURP)

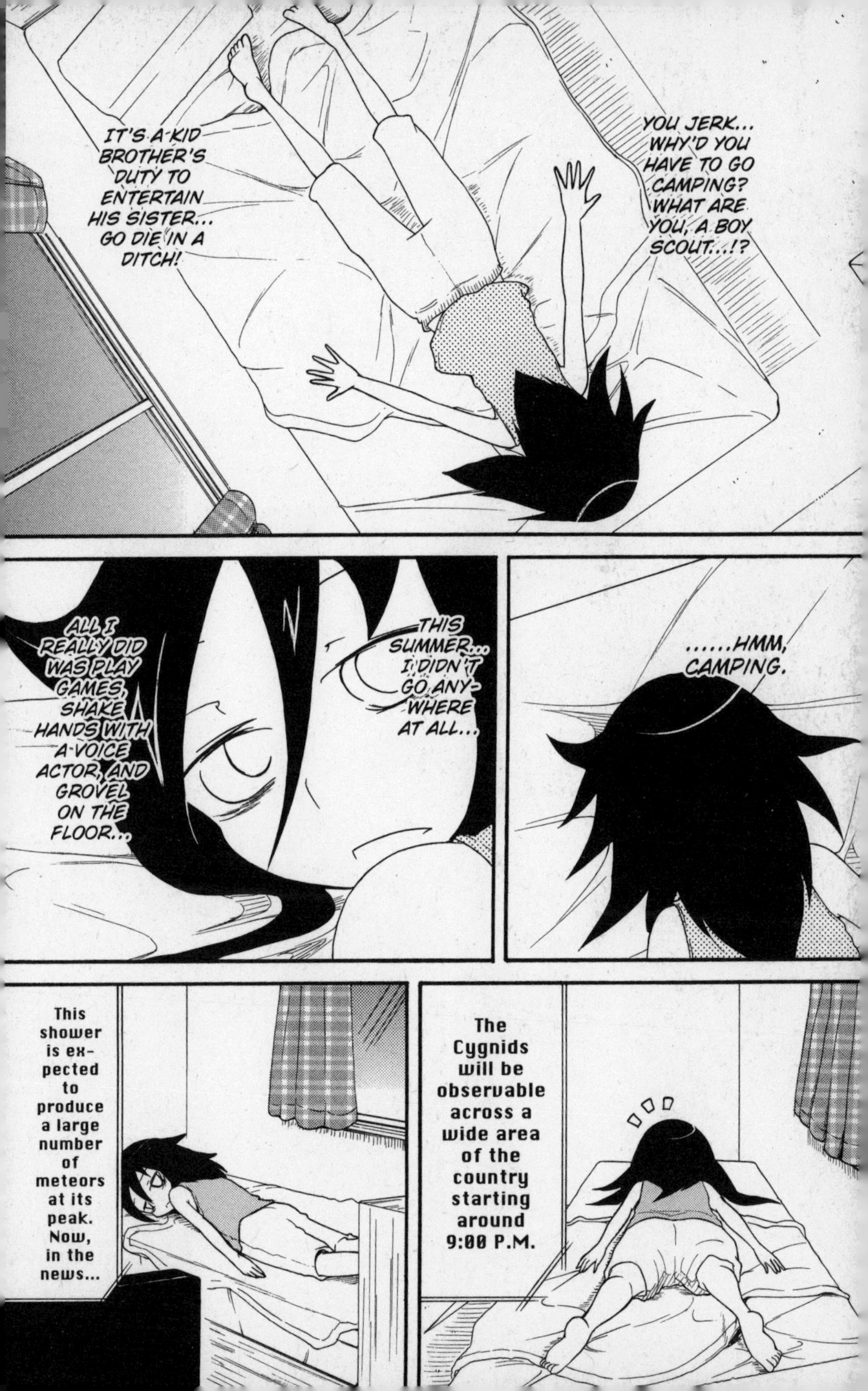
YOU JERK... WHY'D YOU HAVE TO GO CAMPING? WHAT ARE YOU, A BOY SCOUT...!?
IT'S A KID BROTHER'S DUTY TO ENTERTAIN HIS SISTER... GO DIE IN A DITCH!
......HMM, CAMPING.
THIS SUMMER... I DIDN'T GO ANYWHERE AT ALL...
ALL I REALLY DID WAS PLAY GAMES, SHAKE HANDS WITH A VOICE ACTOR, AND GROVEL ON THE FLOOR...
The Cygnids will be observable across a wide area of the country starting around 9:00 P.M.
This shower is expected to produce a large number of meteors at its peak. Now, in the news...

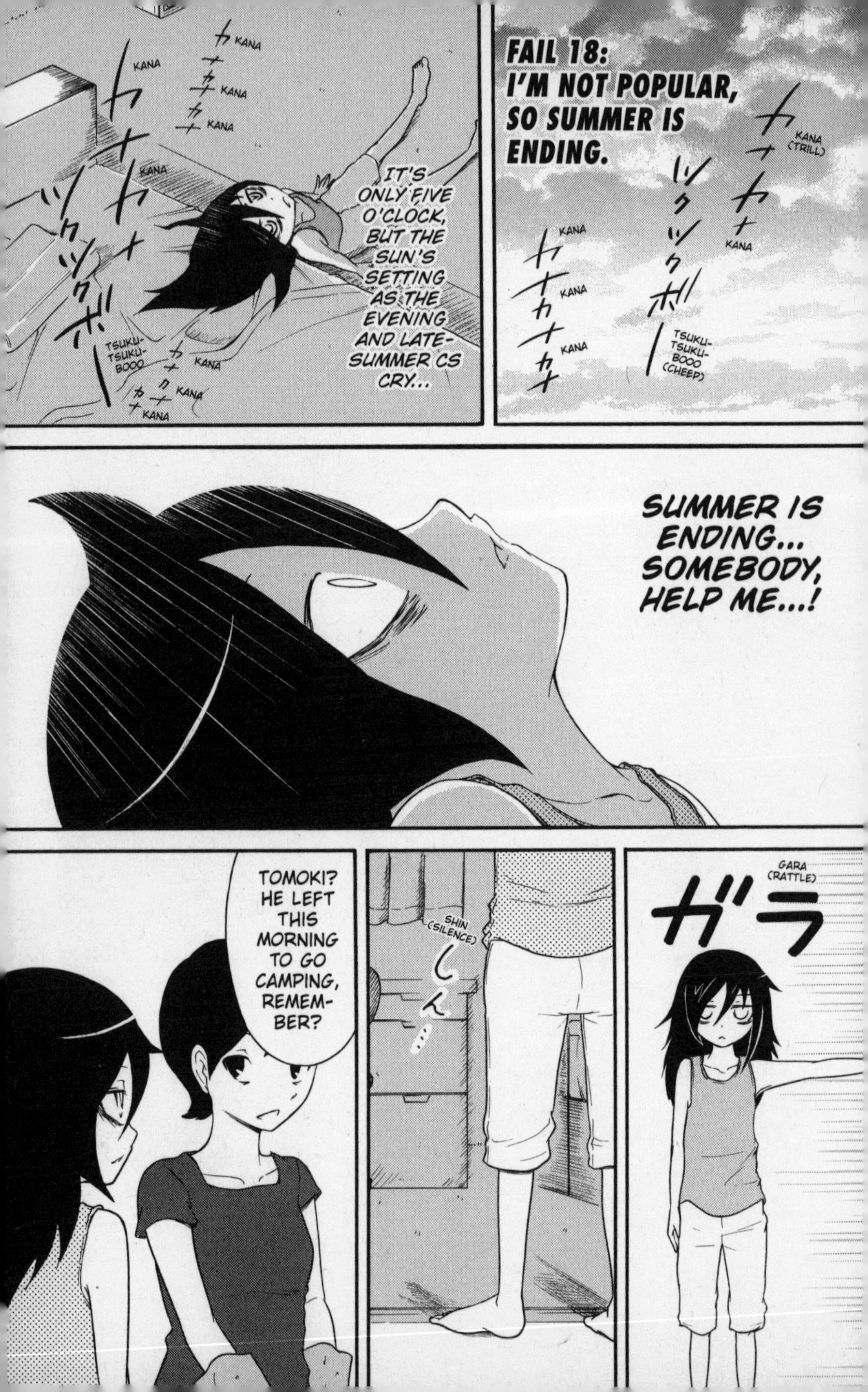
FAIL 18: I'M NOT POPULAR, SO SUMMER IS ENDING.
KANA (TRILL)
KANA
KANA
KANA
KANA
TSUKU-TSUKU-BOOO (CHEEP)
KANA
KANA
KANA
KANA
KANA
IT'S ONLY FIVE O'CLOCK, BUT THE SUN'S SETTING AS THE EVENING AND LATE-SUMMER CS CRY...
TSUKU-TSUKU-BOOO
KANA
KANA
KANA
SUMMER IS ENDING... SOMEBODY, HELP ME...!
GARA (RATTLE)
ガラ
SHIN (SILENCE)
しん…
TOMOKI? HE LEFT THIS MORNING TO GO CAMPING, REMEMBER?

NoMatter **How** I **Look** at It, **It's** You **Guys' Fault** I'm **Not Popular!**

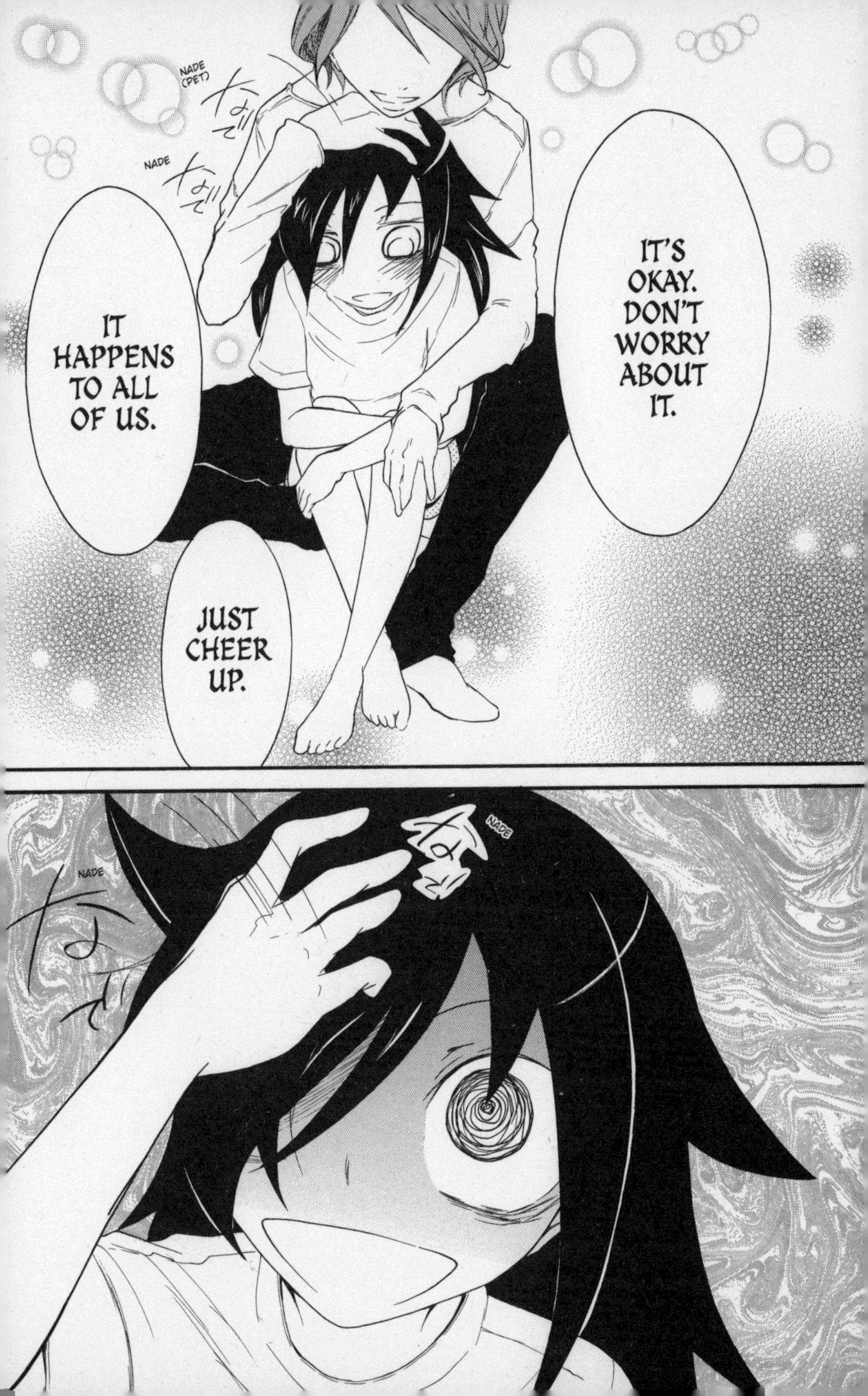
IT'S OKAY. DON'T WORRY ABOUT IT.
NADE (PET)
NADE
IT HAPPENS TO ALL OF US.
JUST CHEER UP.
NADE
NADE

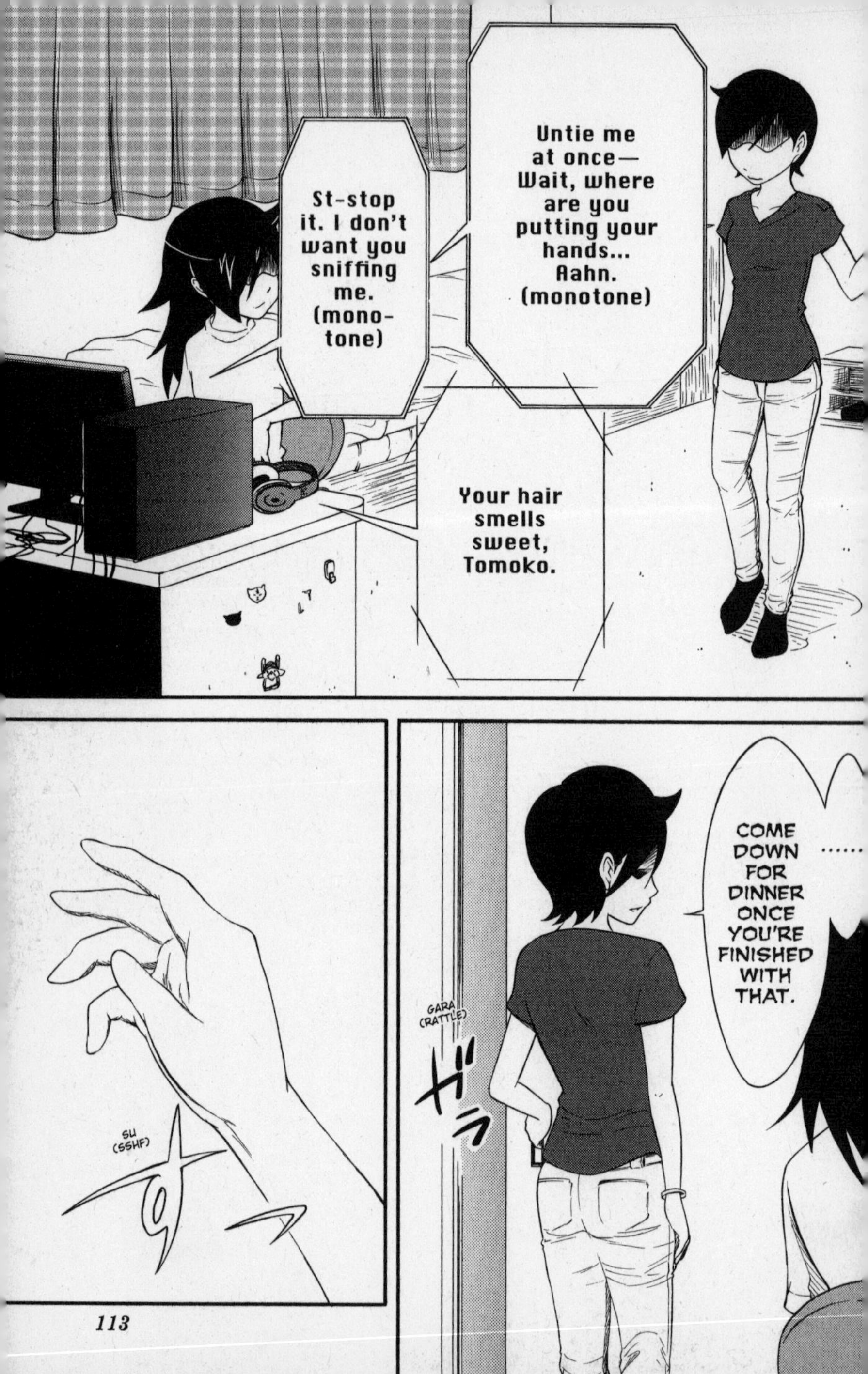
Untie me at once— Wait, where are you putting your hands... Aahn. (monotone)
St-stop it. I don't want you sniffing me. (mono-tone)
Your hair smells sweet, Tomoko.
......
COME DOWN FOR DINNER ONCE YOU'RE FINISHED WITH THAT.
GARA (RATTLE)
SU (SSHF)

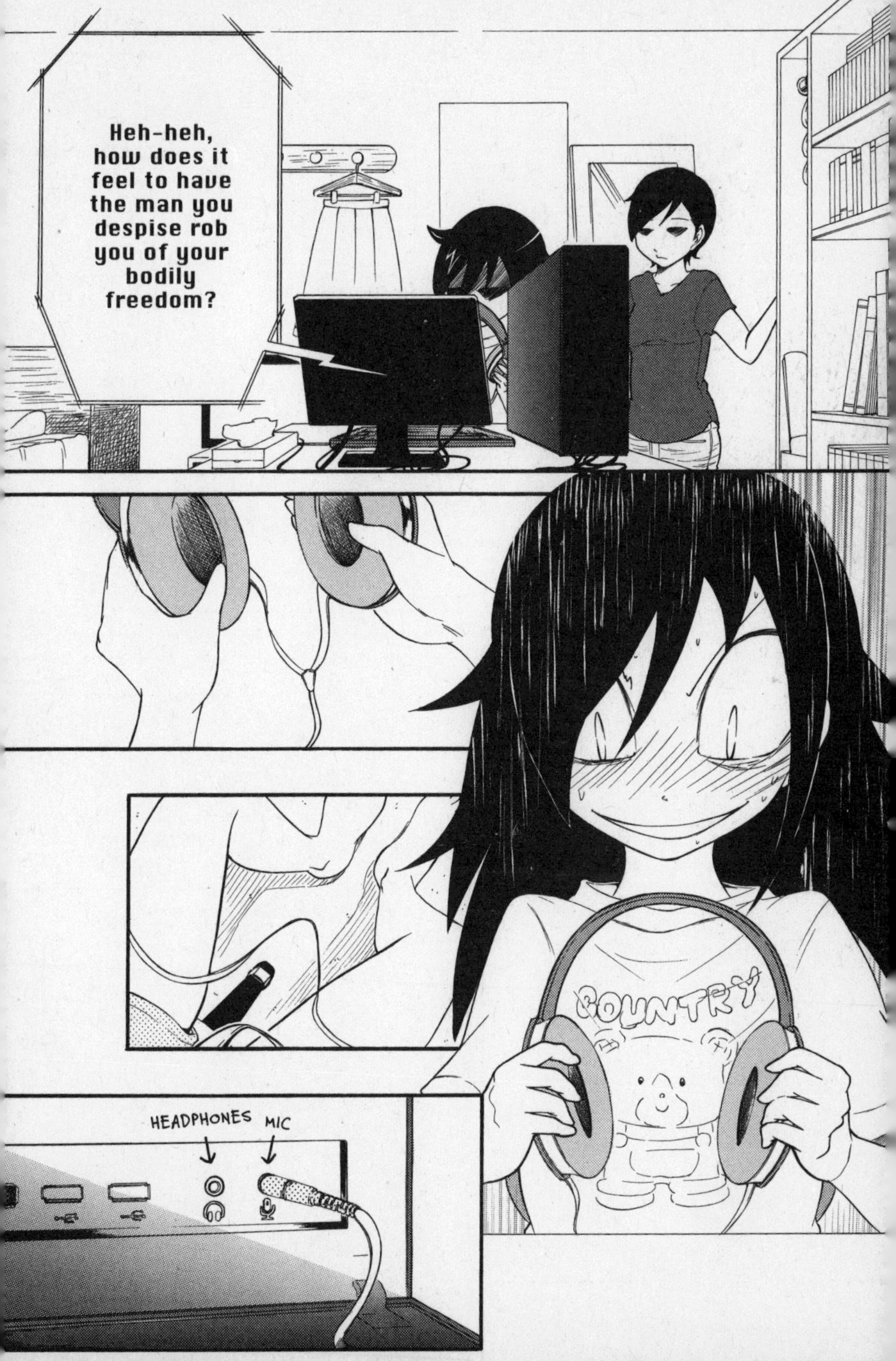
Heh-heh, how does it feel to have the man you despise rob you of your bodily freedom?
COUNTRY
HEADPHONES
MIC

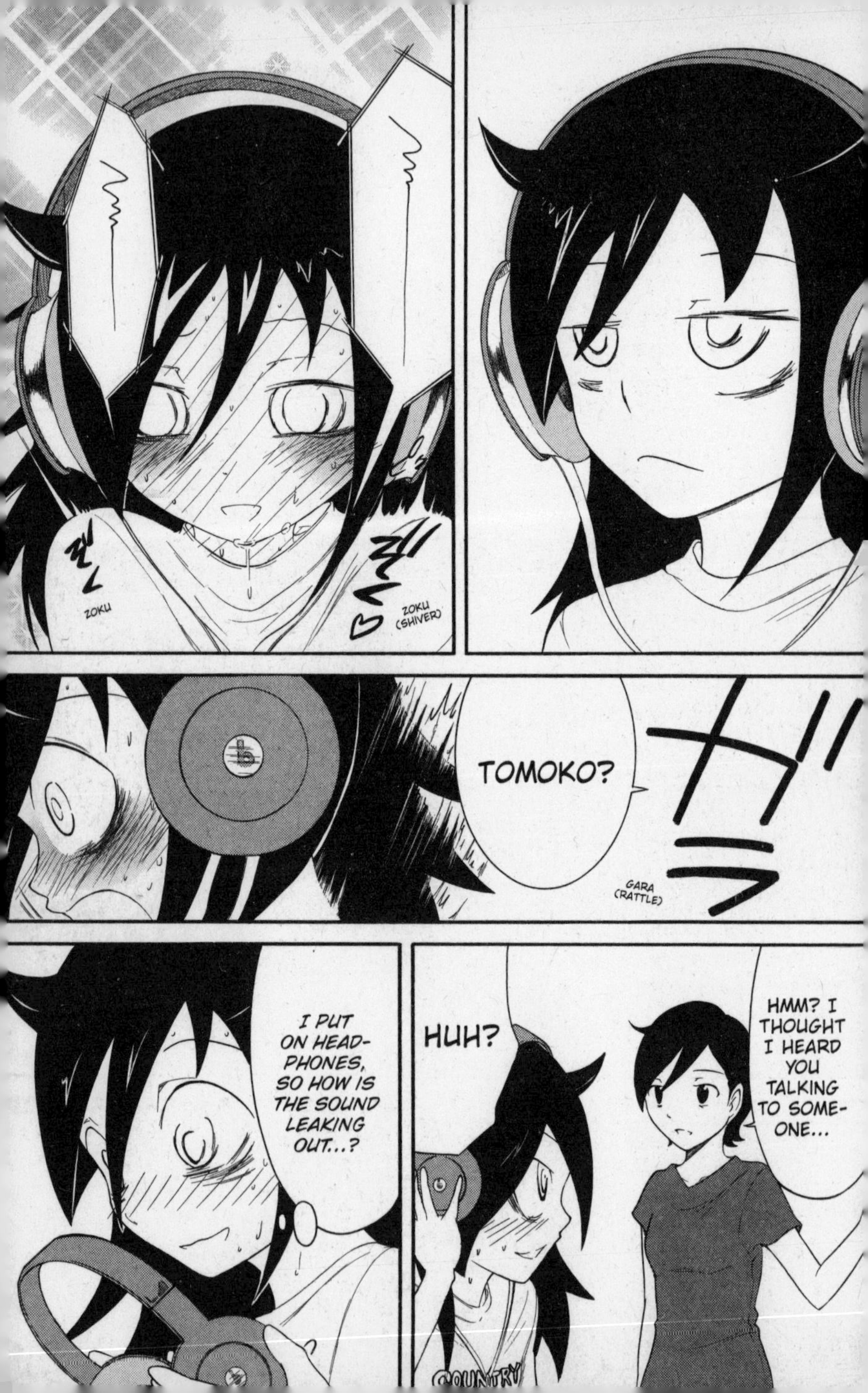
ZOKU (SHIVER)
ZOKU
GARA (RATTLE)
TOMOKO?
HMM? I THOUGHT I HEARD YOU TALKING TO SOME-ONE...
HUH?
COUNTRY
I PUT ON HEAD-PHONES, SO HOW IS THE SOUND LEAKING OUT...?

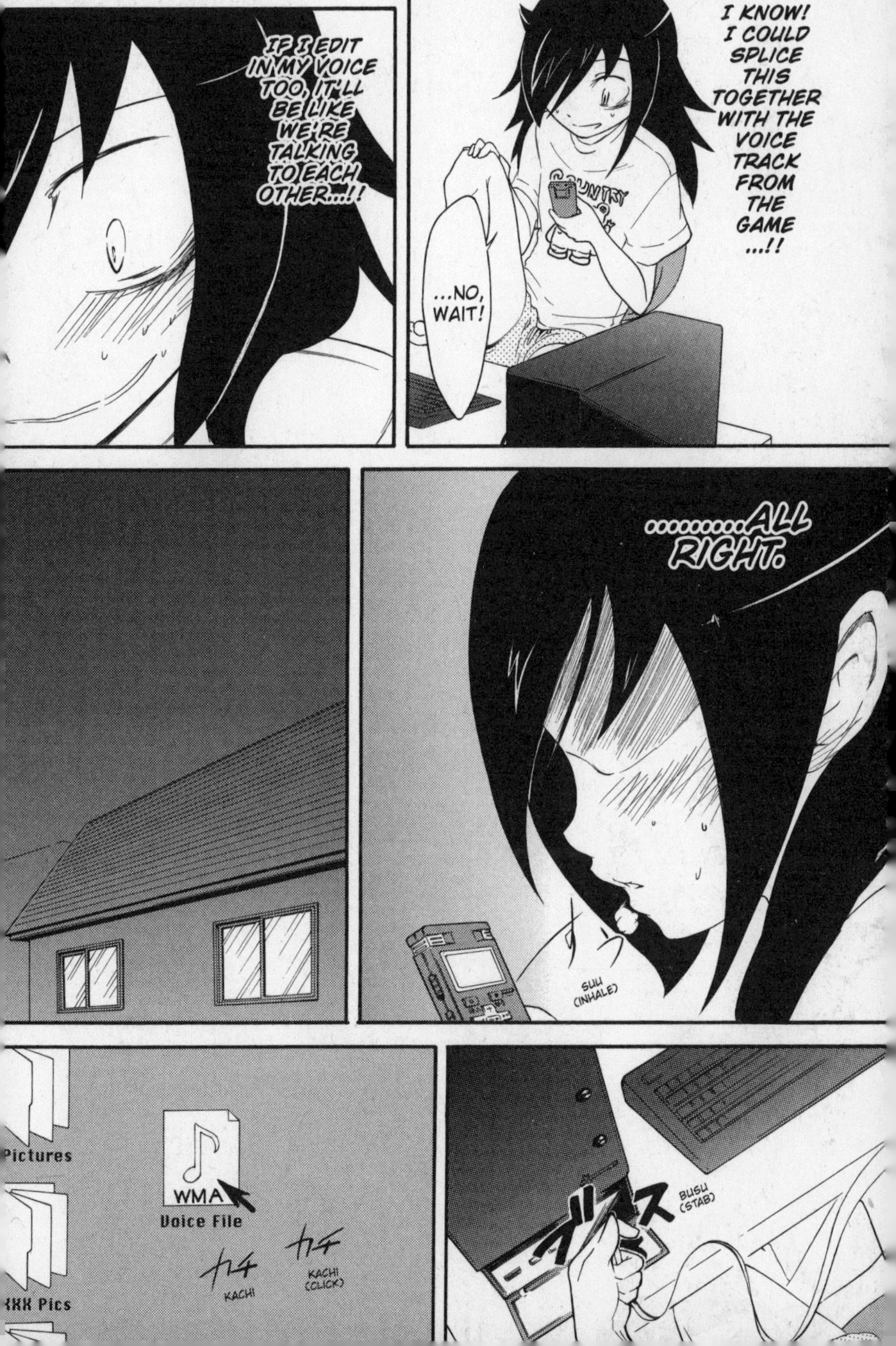
I KNOW! I COULD SPLICE THIS TOGETHER WITH THE VOICE TRACK FROM THE GAME ...!!
...NO, WAIT!
IF I EDIT IN MY VOICE TOO, IT'LL BE LIKE WE'RE TALKING TO EACH OTHER...!!
..........ALL RIGHT.
SUU (INHALE)
BUSU (STAB)
Pictures
WMA
Voice File
KACHI (CLICK)
KACHI

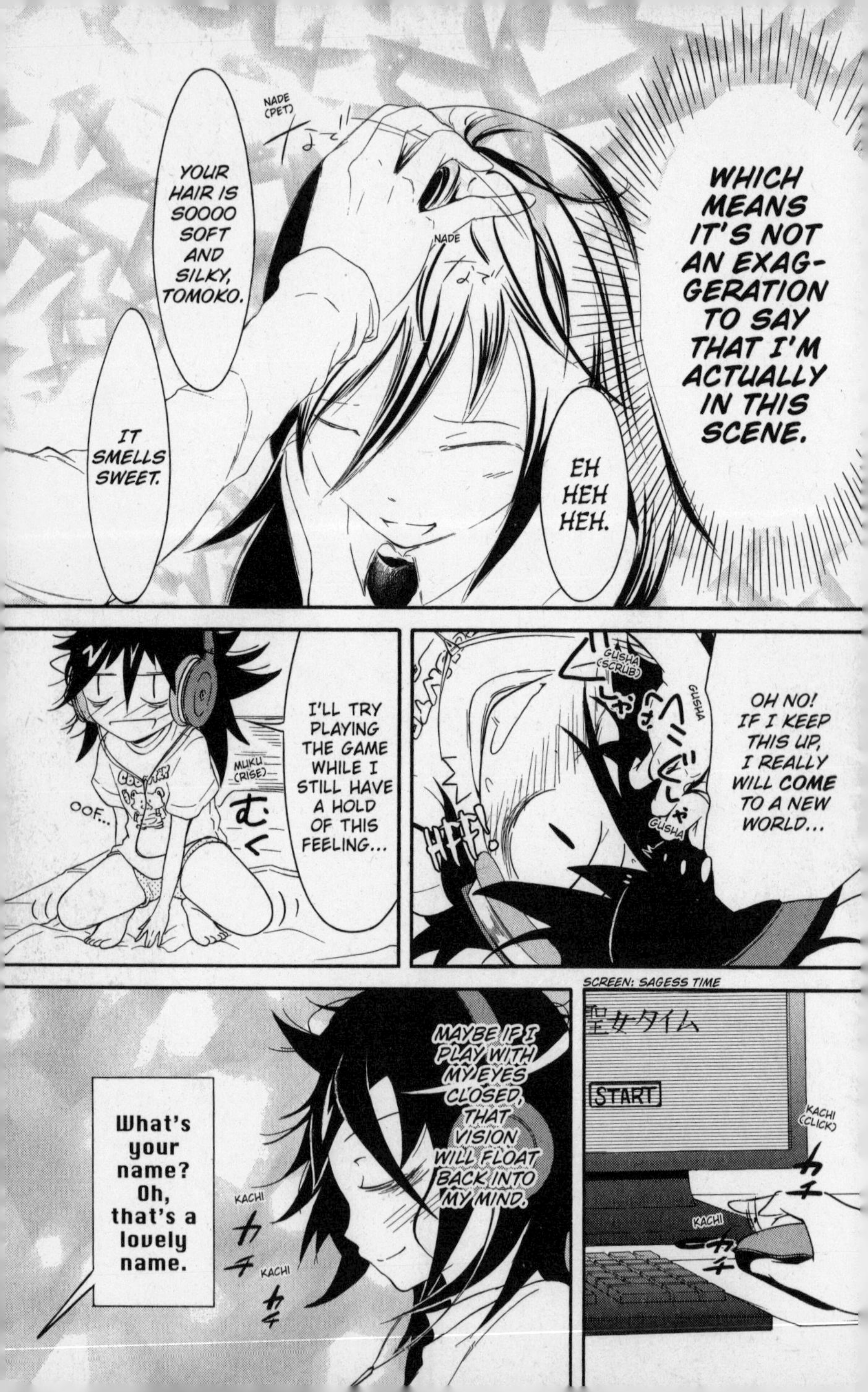
WHICH MEANS IT'S NOT AN EXAGGERATION TO SAY THAT I'M ACTUALLY IN THIS SCENE.
NADE (PET)
YOUR HAIR IS SOOOO SOFT AND SILKY, TOMOKO.
NADE
EH HEH HEH.
IT SMELLS SWEET.
GUSHA (SCRUB)
GUSHA
OH NO! IF I KEEP THIS UP, I REALLY WILL COME TO A NEW WORLD...
GUSHA
HFF!
I'LL TRY PLAYING THE GAME WHILE I STILL HAVE A HOLD OF THIS FEELING...
MUKU (RISE)
OOF...
SCREEN: SAGESS TIME
聖女タイム
START
KACHI (CLICK)
KACHI
MAYBE IF I PLAY WITH MY EYES CLOSED, THAT VISION WILL FLOAT BACK INTO MY MIND.
What's your name? Oh, that's a lovely name.
KACHI
KACHI

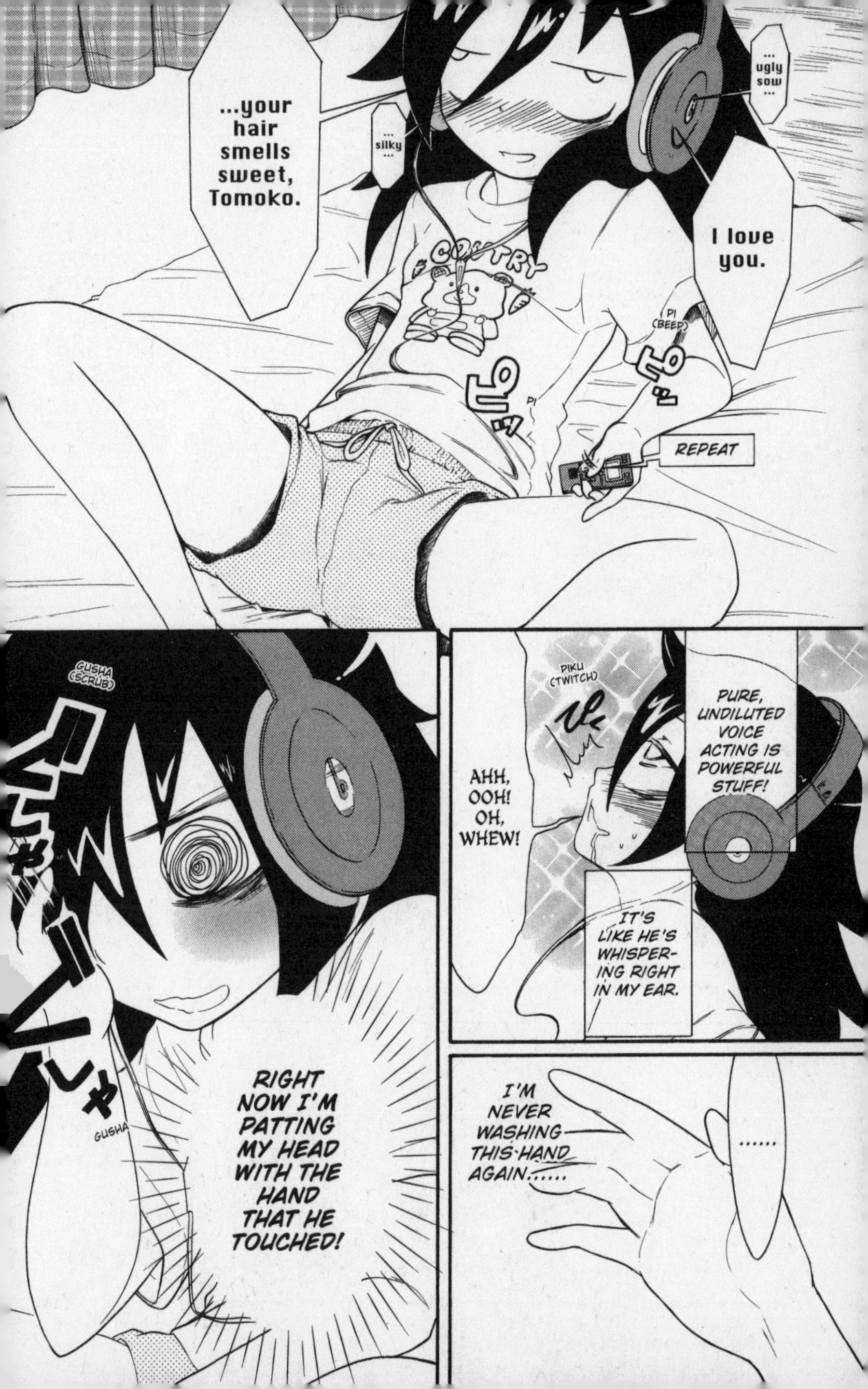
...ugly sow...
I love you.
...silky...
...your hair smells sweet, Tomoko.
PI (BEEP)
PI
REPEAT
PURE, UNDILUTED VOICE ACTING IS POWERFUL STUFF!
PIKU (TWITCH)
AHH, OOH! OH, WHEW!
IT'S LIKE HE'S WHISPERING RIGHT IN MY EAR.
......
I'M NEVER WASHING THIS HAND AGAIN......
GUSHA (SCRUB)
GUSHA
RIGHT NOW I'M PATTING MY HEAD WITH THE HAND THAT HE TOUCHED!

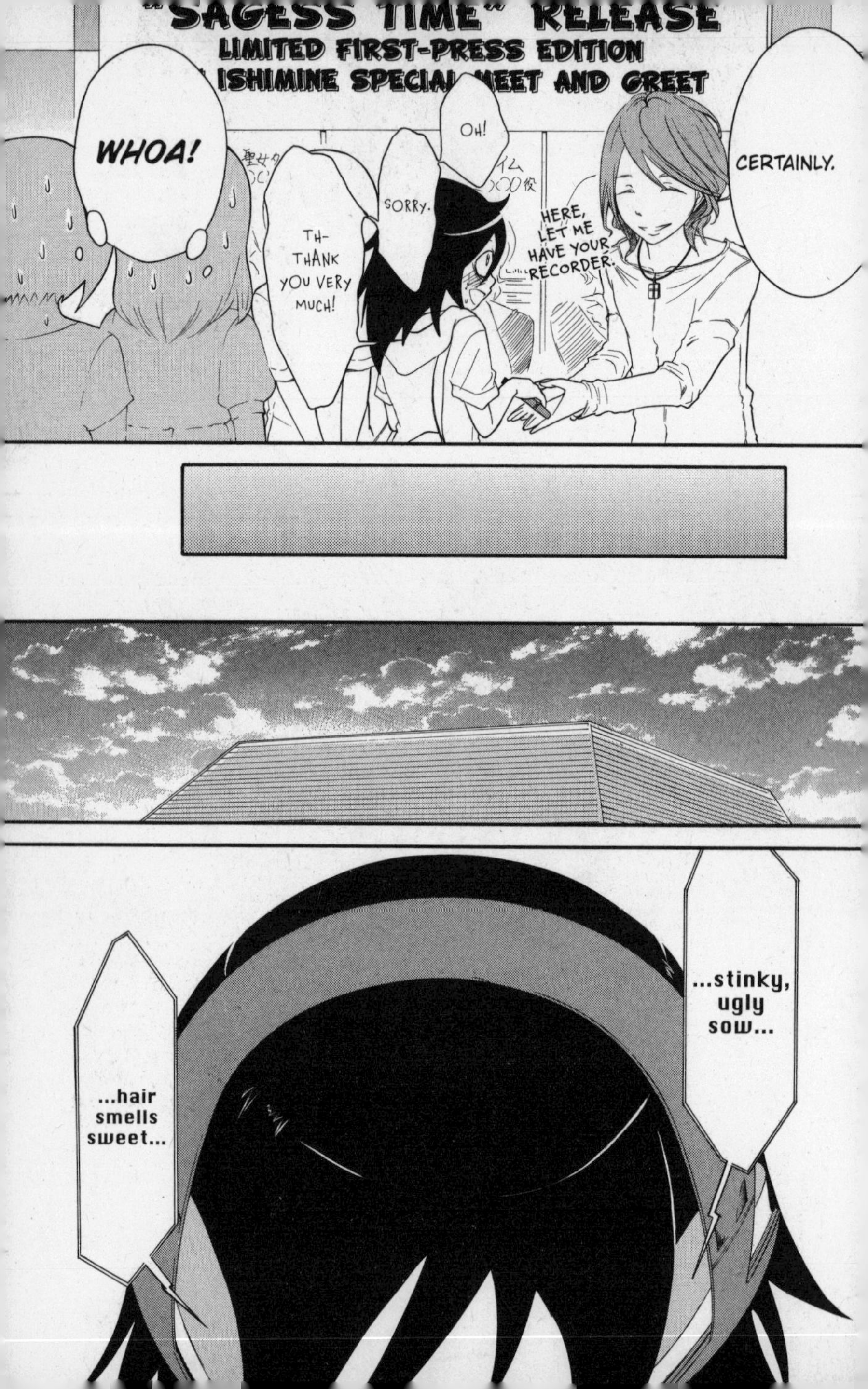
"SAGESS TIME" RELEASE
LIMITED FIRST-PRESS EDITION
ISHIMINE SPECIAL EET AND GREET
CERTAINLY.
HERE, LET ME HAVE YOUR RECORDER.
OH!
SORRY.
TH-THANK YOU VERY MUCH!
WHOA!
...stinky, ugly sow...
...hair smells sweet...

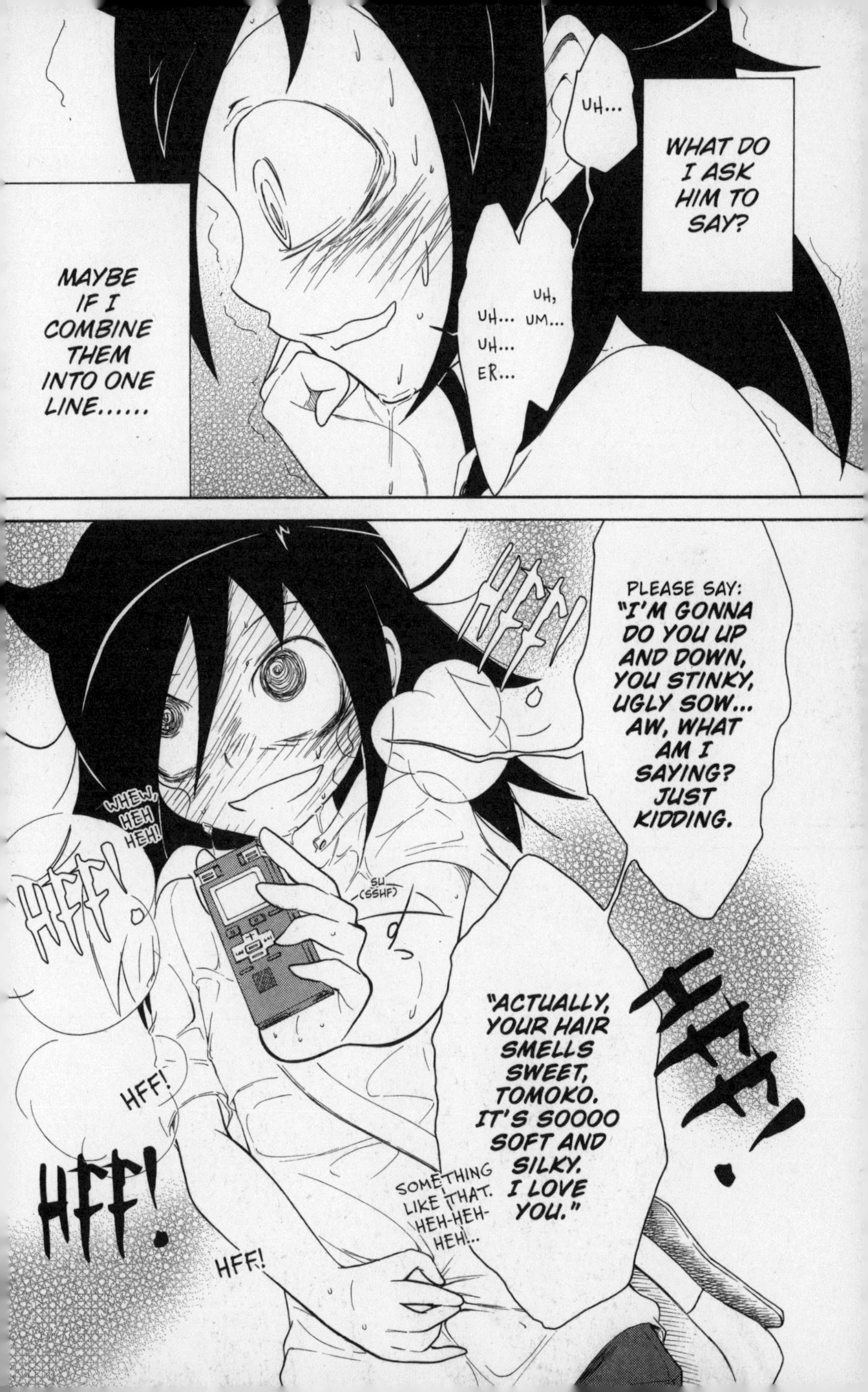
UH...
WHAT DO I ASK HIM TO SAY?
UH, UH... UM... UH... ER...
MAYBE IF I COMBINE THEM INTO ONE LINE......
PLEASE SAY: "I'M GONNA DO YOU UP AND DOWN, YOU STINKY, UGLY SOW... AW, WHAT AM I SAYING? JUST KIDDING.
HFF!
HFF!
"ACTUALLY, YOUR HAIR SMELLS SWEET, TOMOKO. IT'S SOOOO SOFT AND SILKY. I LOVE YOU."
SOMETHING LIKE THAT. HEH-HEH-HEH...
SU (SSHF)
WHEW, HEH HEH!
HFF!
HFF!
HFF!
HFF!

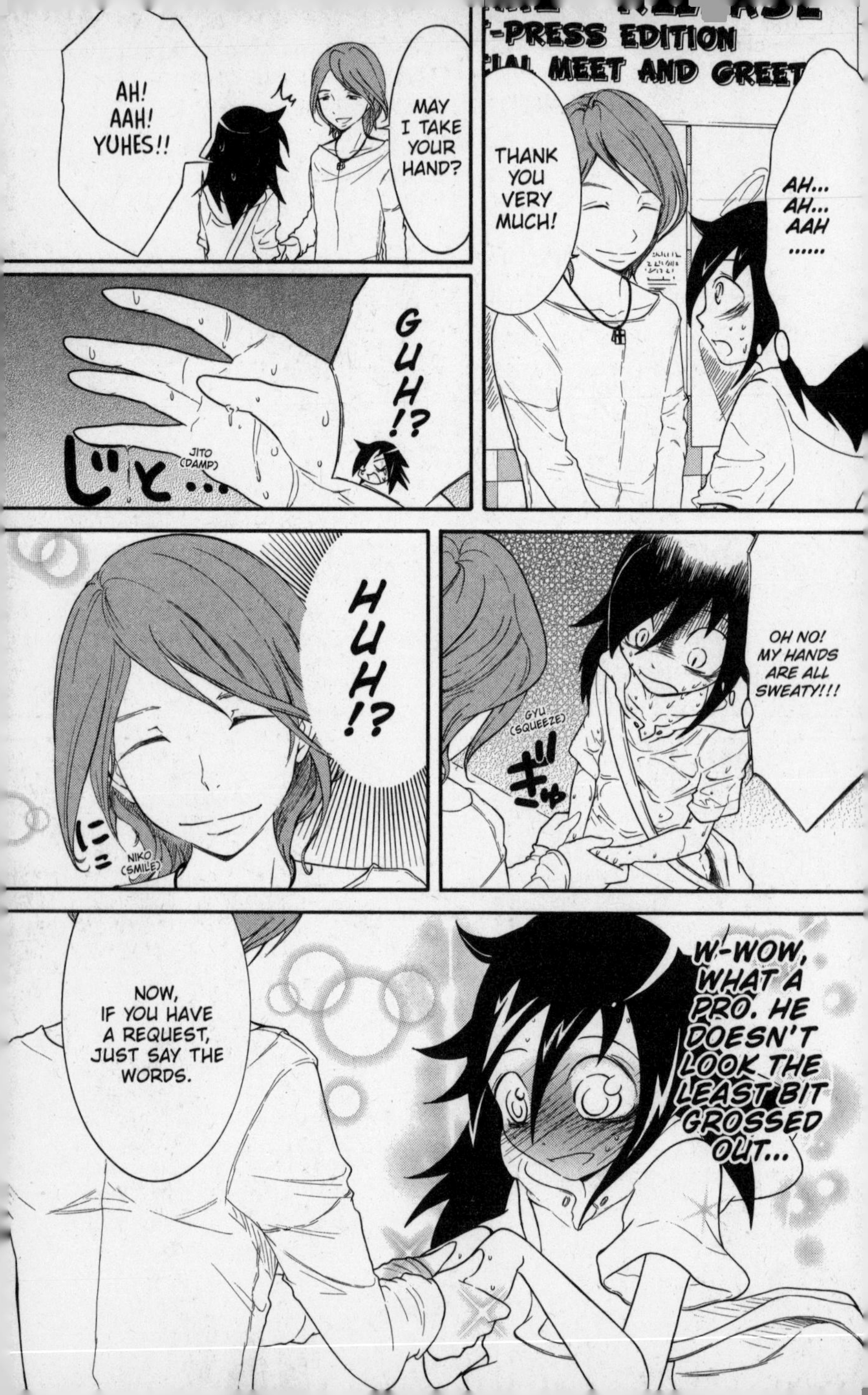
-PRESS EDITION
MEET AND GREET
THANK YOU VERY MUCH!
AH... AH... AAH ......
MAY I TAKE YOUR HAND?
AH! AAH! YUHES!!
GUH!?
じと…
JITO (DAMP)
OH NO! MY HANDS ARE ALL SWEATY!!!
ぎゅ
GYU (SQUEEZE)
HUH!?
にこ
NIKO (SMILE)
W-WOW, WHAT A PRO. HE DOESN'T LOOK THE LEAST BIT GROSSED OUT...
NOW, IF YOU HAVE A REQUEST, JUST SAY THE WORDS.

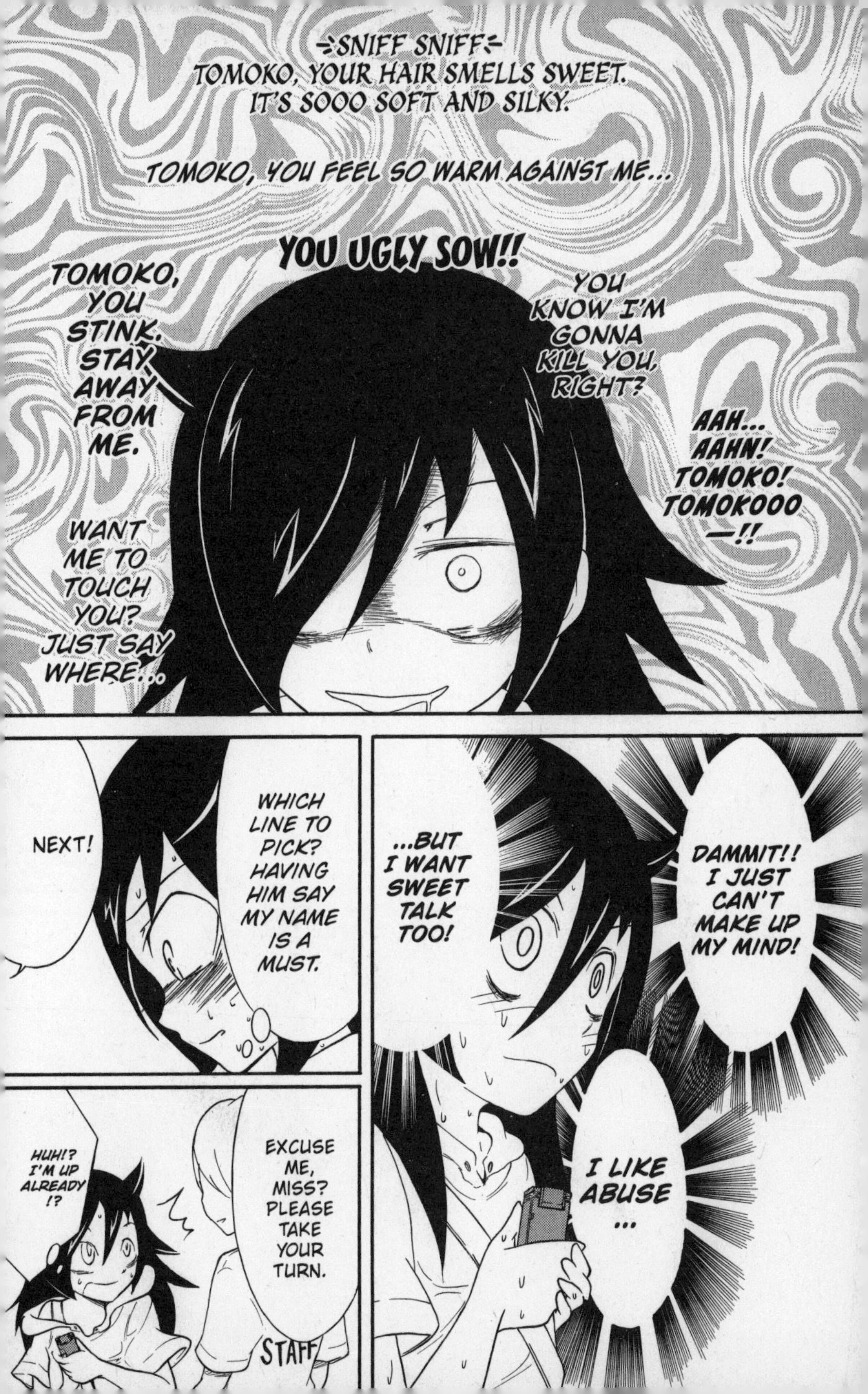

SNIFF SNIFF
TOMOKO, YOUR HAIR SMELLS SWEET. IT'S SOOO SOFT AND SILKY.
TOMOKO, YOU FEEL SO WARM AGAINST ME...
YOU UGLY SOW!!
YOU KNOW I'M GONNA KILL YOU, RIGHT?
AAH... AAHN! TOMOKO! TOMOKOOO—!!
TOMOKO, YOU STINK. STAY AWAY FROM ME.
WANT ME TO TOUCH YOU? JUST SAY WHERE...
DAMMIT!! I JUST CAN'T MAKE UP MY MIND!
...BUT I WANT SWEET TALK TOO!
I LIKE ABUSE ...
WHICH LINE TO PICK? HAVING HIM SAY MY NAME IS A MUST.
NEXT!
EXCUSE ME, MISS? PLEASE TAKE YOUR TURN.
HUH!? I'M UP ALREADY !?
STAFF

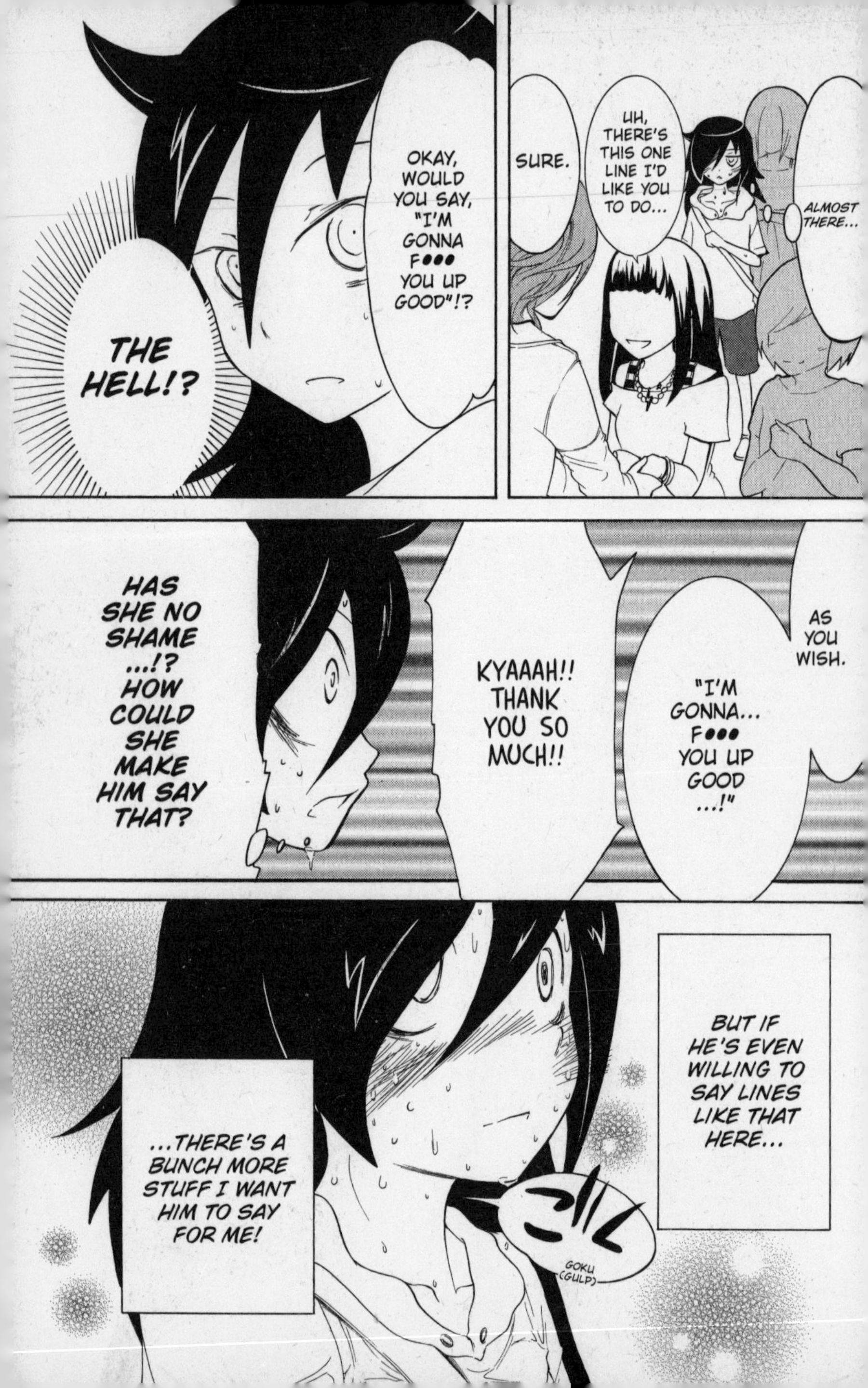
UH, THERE'S THIS ONE LINE I'D LIKE YOU TO DO...
SURE.
ALMOST THERE...
OKAY, WOULD YOU SAY, "I'M GONNA F●●● YOU UP GOOD"!?
THE HELL!?
AS YOU WISH.
"I'M GONNA... F●●● YOU UP GOOD ...!"
KYAAAH!! THANK YOU SO MUCH!!
HAS SHE NO SHAME ...!? HOW COULD SHE MAKE HIM SAY THAT?
BUT IF HE'S EVEN WILLING TO SAY LINES LIKE THAT HERE...
GOKU (GULP)
...THERE'S A BUNCH MORE STUFF I WANT HIM TO SAY FOR ME!

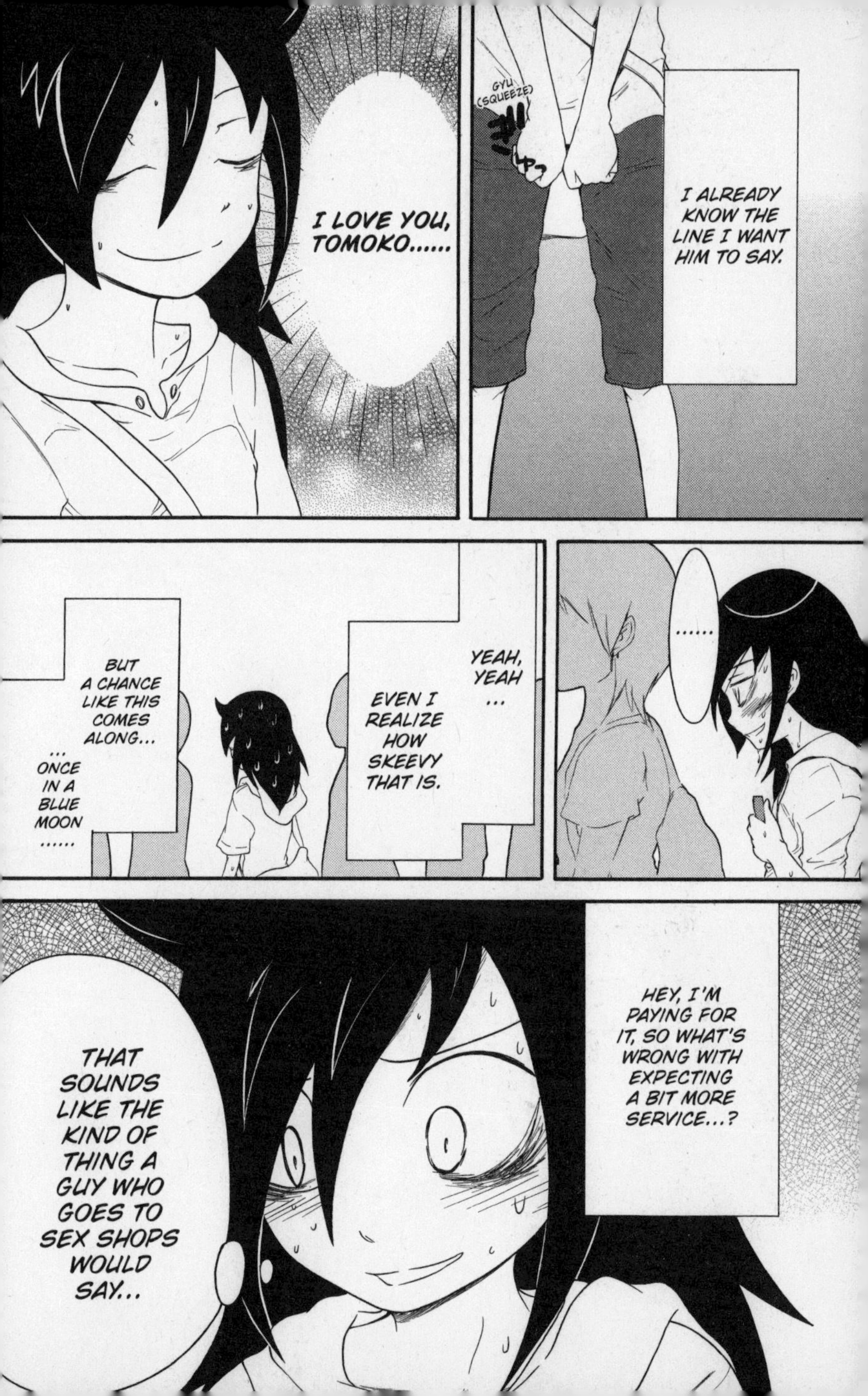
GYU (SQUEEZE)
I ALREADY KNOW THE LINE I WANT HIM TO SAY.
I LOVE YOU, TOMOKO......
......
YEAH, YEAH ...
EVEN I REALIZE HOW SKEEVY THAT IS.
BUT A CHANCE LIKE THIS COMES ALONG...
... ONCE IN A BLUE MOON ......
HEY, I'M PAYING FOR IT, SO WHAT'S WRONG WITH EXPECTING A BIT MORE SERVICE...?
THAT SOUNDS LIKE THE KIND OF THING A GUY WHO GOES TO SEX SHOPS WOULD SAY...

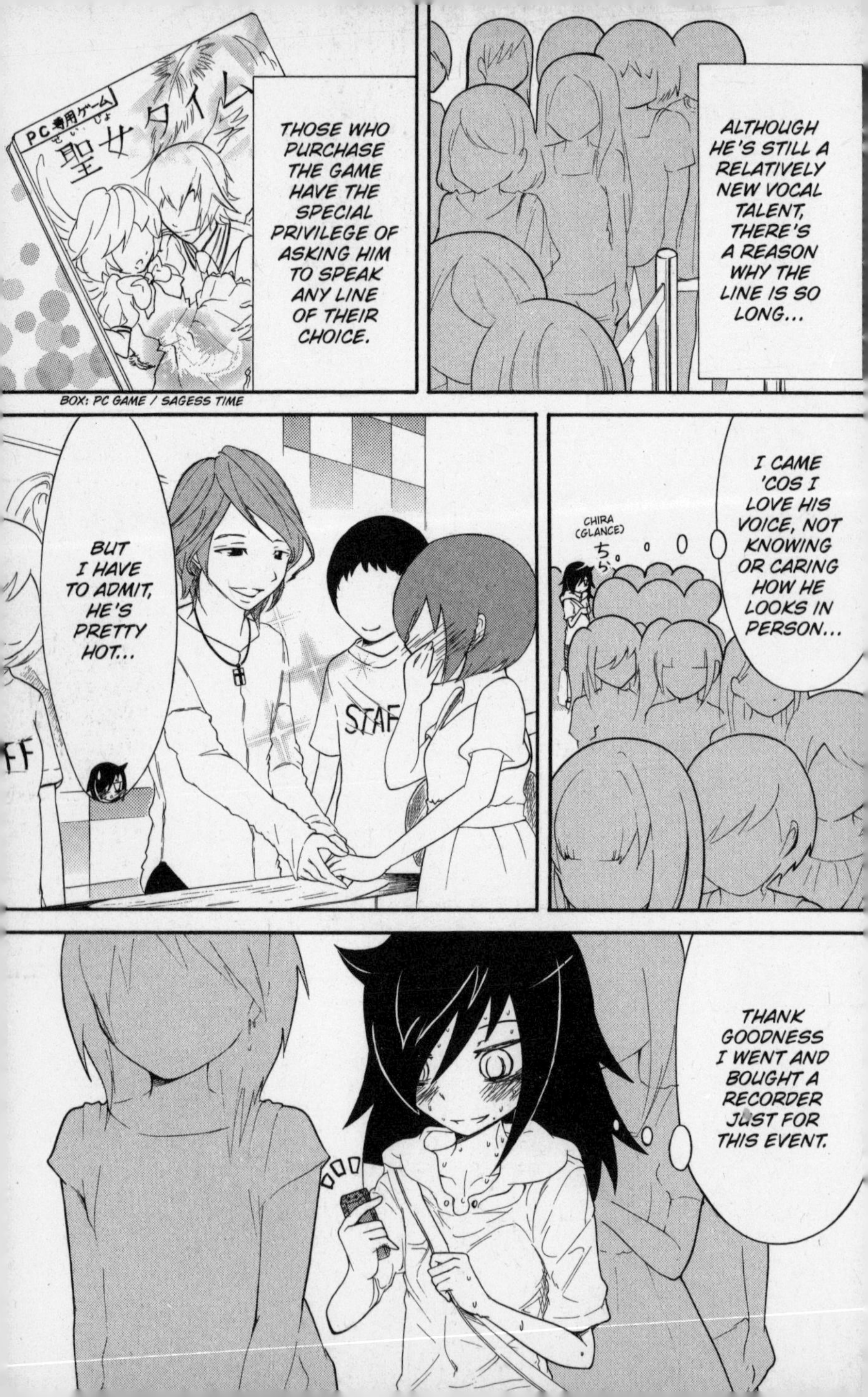

ALTHOUGH HE'S STILL A RELATIVELY NEW VOCAL TALENT, THERE'S A REASON WHY THE LINE IS SO LONG...
THOSE WHO PURCHASE THE GAME HAVE THE SPECIAL PRIVILEGE OF ASKING HIM TO SPEAK ANY LINE OF THEIR CHOICE.
PC専用ゲーム
聖女タイム
BOX: PC GAME / SAGESS TIME
I CAME 'COS I LOVE HIS VOICE, NOT KNOWING OR CARING HOW HE LOOKS IN PERSON...
CHIRA (GLANCE)
ちら
BUT I HAVE TO ADMIT, HE'S PRETTY HOT...
STAF
FF
THANK GOODNESS I WENT AND BOUGHT A RECORDER JUST FOR THIS EVENT.

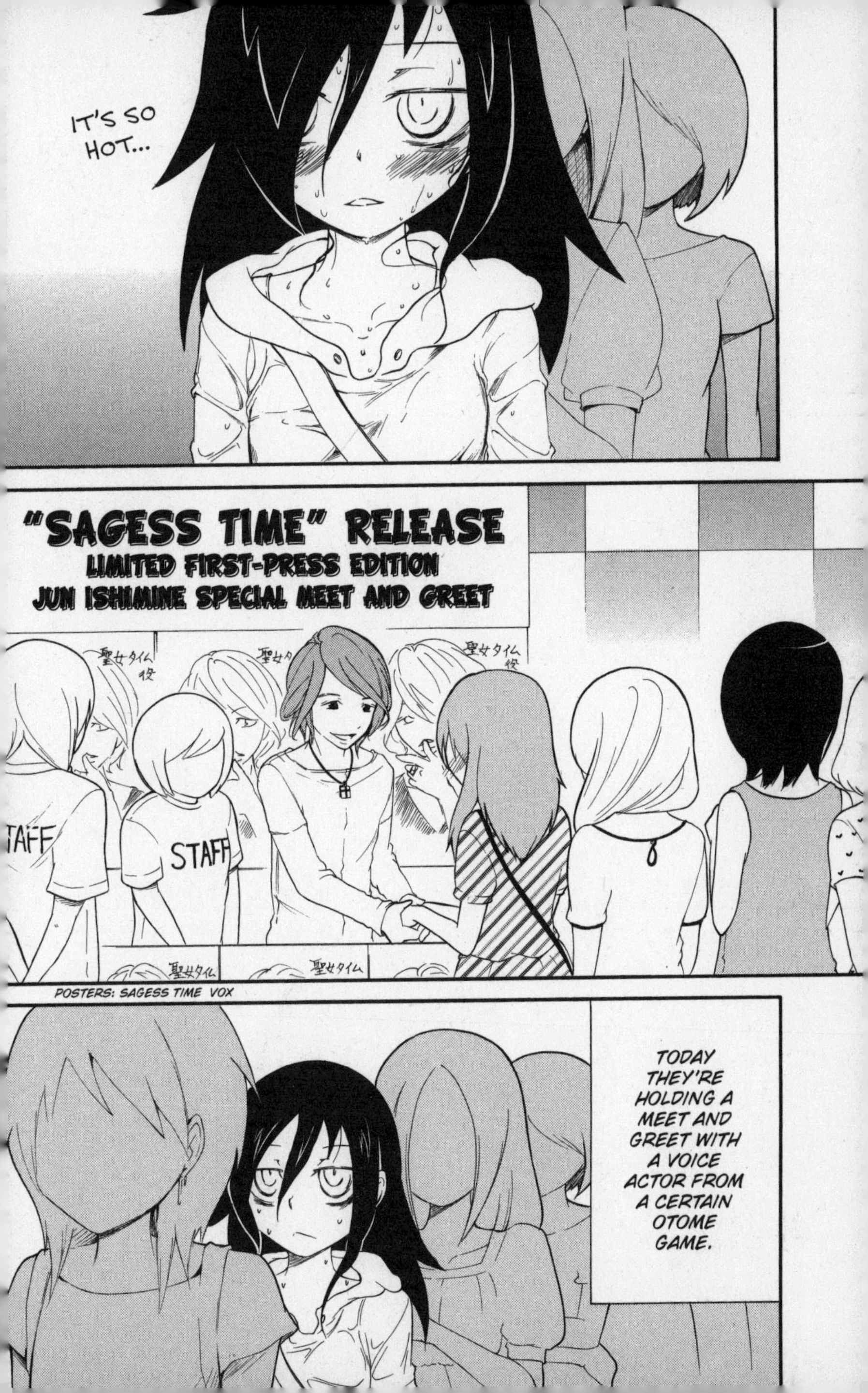
IT'S SO HOT...
"SAGESS TIME" RELEASE
LIMITED FIRST-PRESS EDITION
JUN ISHIMINE SPECIAL MEET AND GREET
聖女タイム
STAFF
STAFF
POSTERS: SAGESS TIME VOX
TODAY THEY'RE HOLDING A MEET AND GREET WITH A VOICE ACTOR FROM A CERTAIN OTOME GAME.

FAIL 17: I'M NOT POPULAR, SO I'LL GO TO A MEET AND GREET.

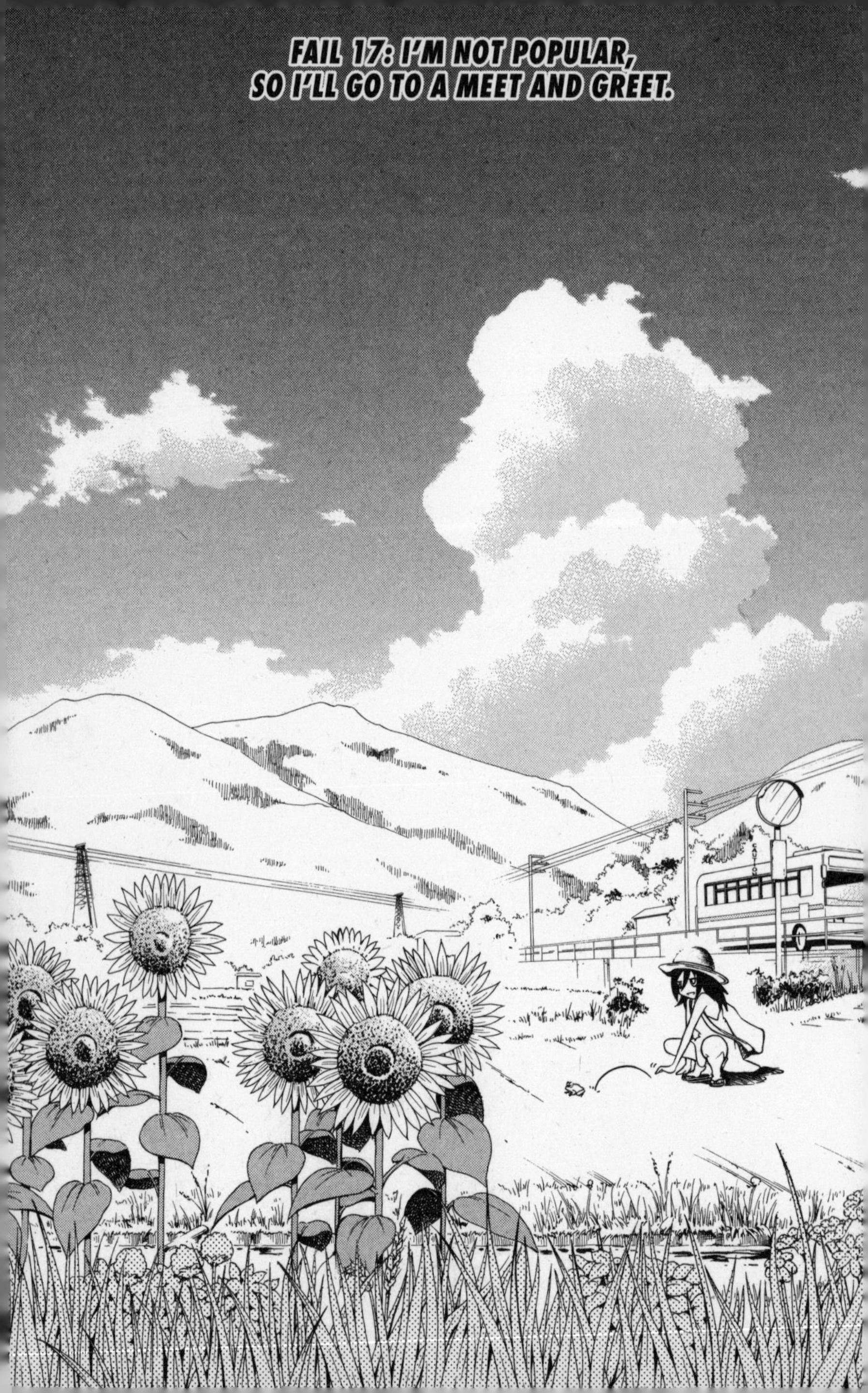

No Matter How I Look at It, It's You Guys' Fault I'm Not Popular!

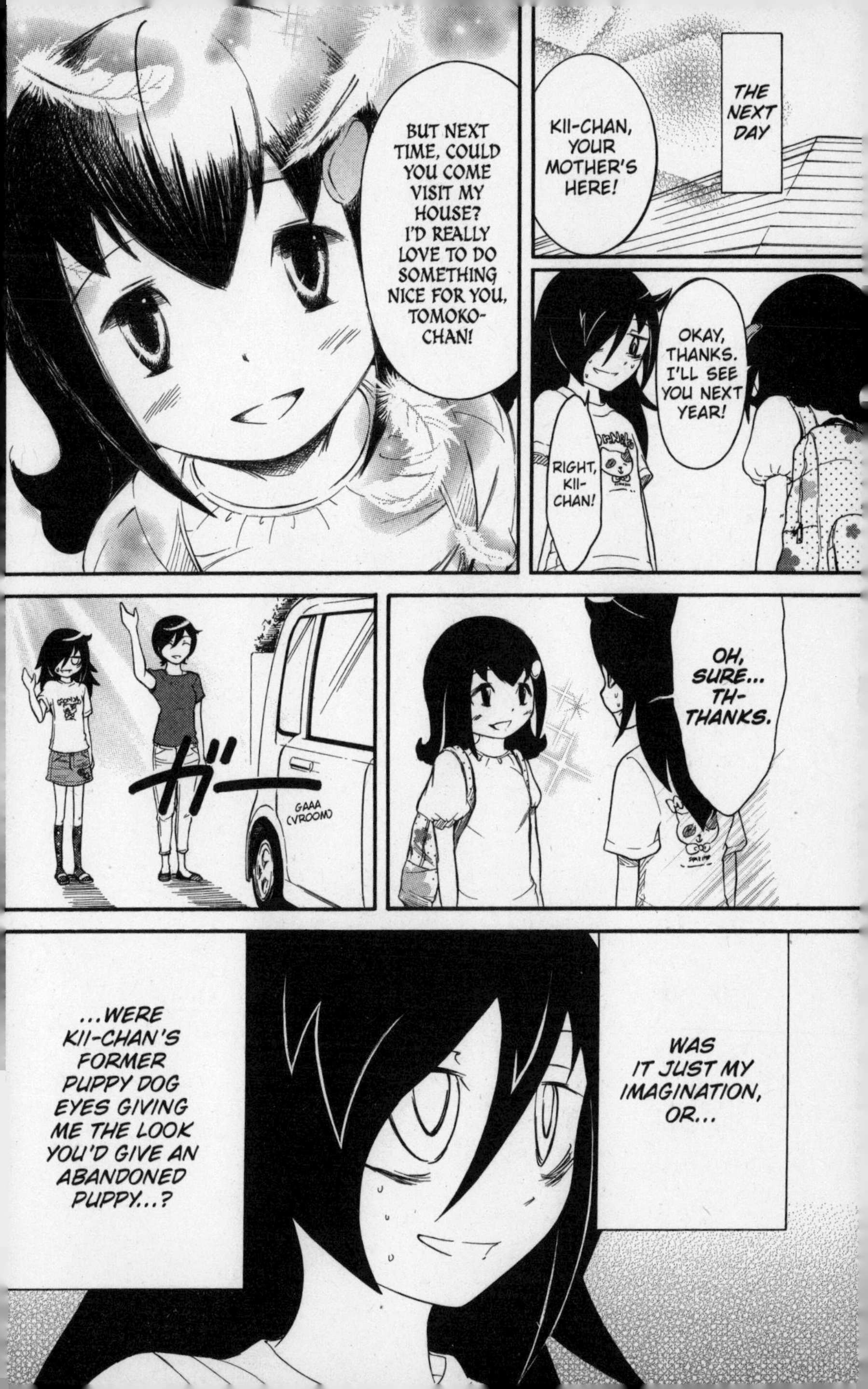
THE NEXT DAY
KII-CHAN, YOUR MOTHER'S HERE!
OKAY, THANKS. I'LL SEE YOU NEXT YEAR!
RIGHT, KII-CHAN!
BUT NEXT TIME, COULD YOU COME VISIT MY HOUSE? I'D REALLY LOVE TO DO SOMETHING NICE FOR YOU, TOMOKO-CHAN!
OH, SURE... TH-THANKS.
ガー
GAAA (VROOM)
WAS IT JUST MY IMAGINATION, OR...
...WERE KII-CHAN'S FORMER PUPPY DOG EYES GIVING ME THE LOOK YOU'D GIVE AN ABANDONED PUPPY...?

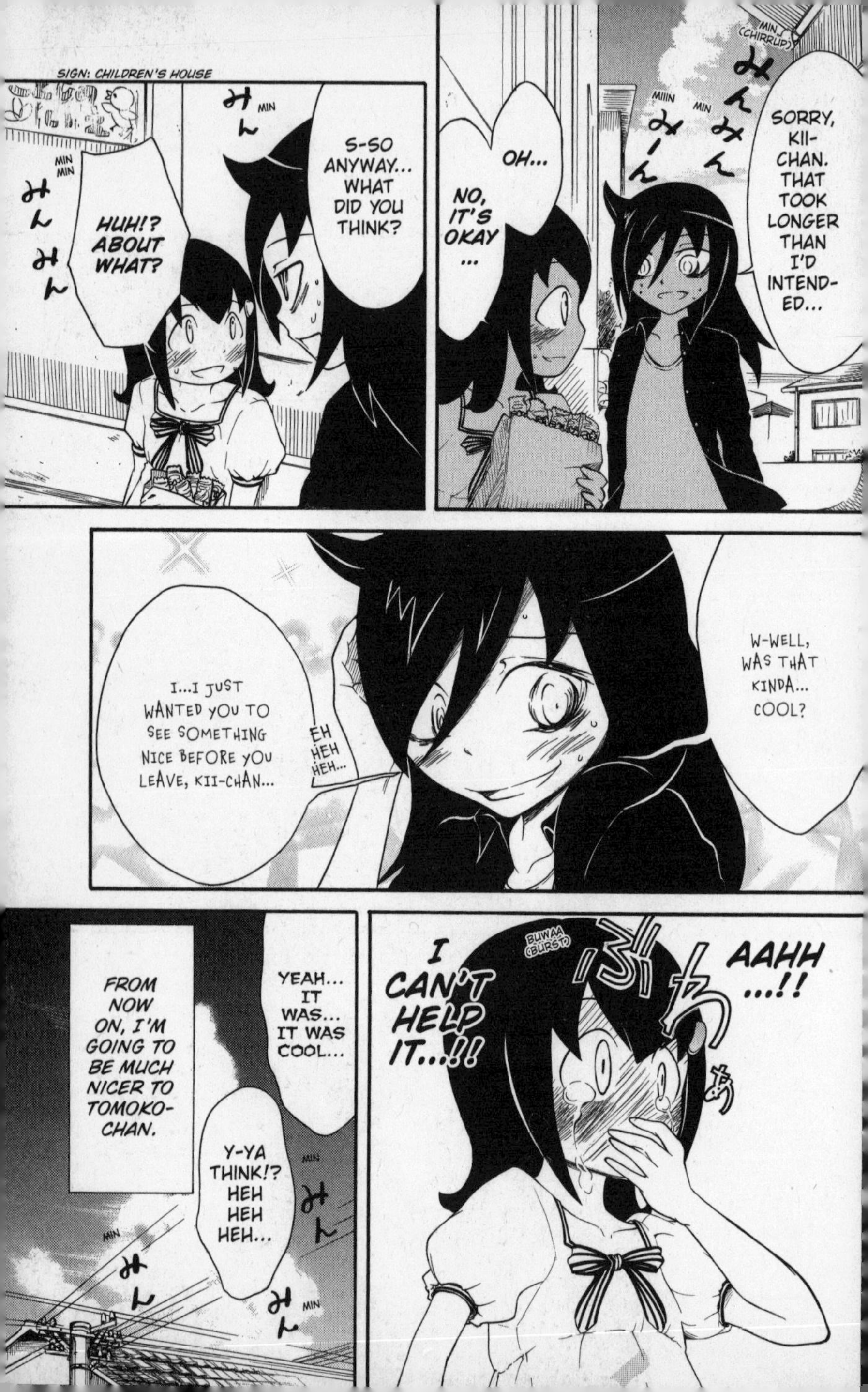
MIN (CHIRRUP)
MIIN MIN
SORRY, KII-CHAN. THAT TOOK LONGER THAN I'D INTENDED...
OH...
NO, IT'S OKAY...
SIGN: CHILDREN'S HOUSE
MIN
S-SO ANYWAY... WHAT DID YOU THINK?
MIN MIN
HUH!? ABOUT WHAT?
W-WELL, WAS THAT KINDA... COOL?
EH HEH HEH...
I...I JUST WANTED YOU TO SEE SOMETHING NICE BEFORE YOU LEAVE, KII-CHAN...
BUWAA (BURST)
AAHH ...!!
I CAN'T HELP IT...!!
YEAH... IT WAS... IT WAS COOL...
Y-YA THINK!? HEH HEH HEH...
MIN
MIN
FROM NOW ON, I'M GOING TO BE MUCH NICER TO TOMOKO-CHAN.
MIN

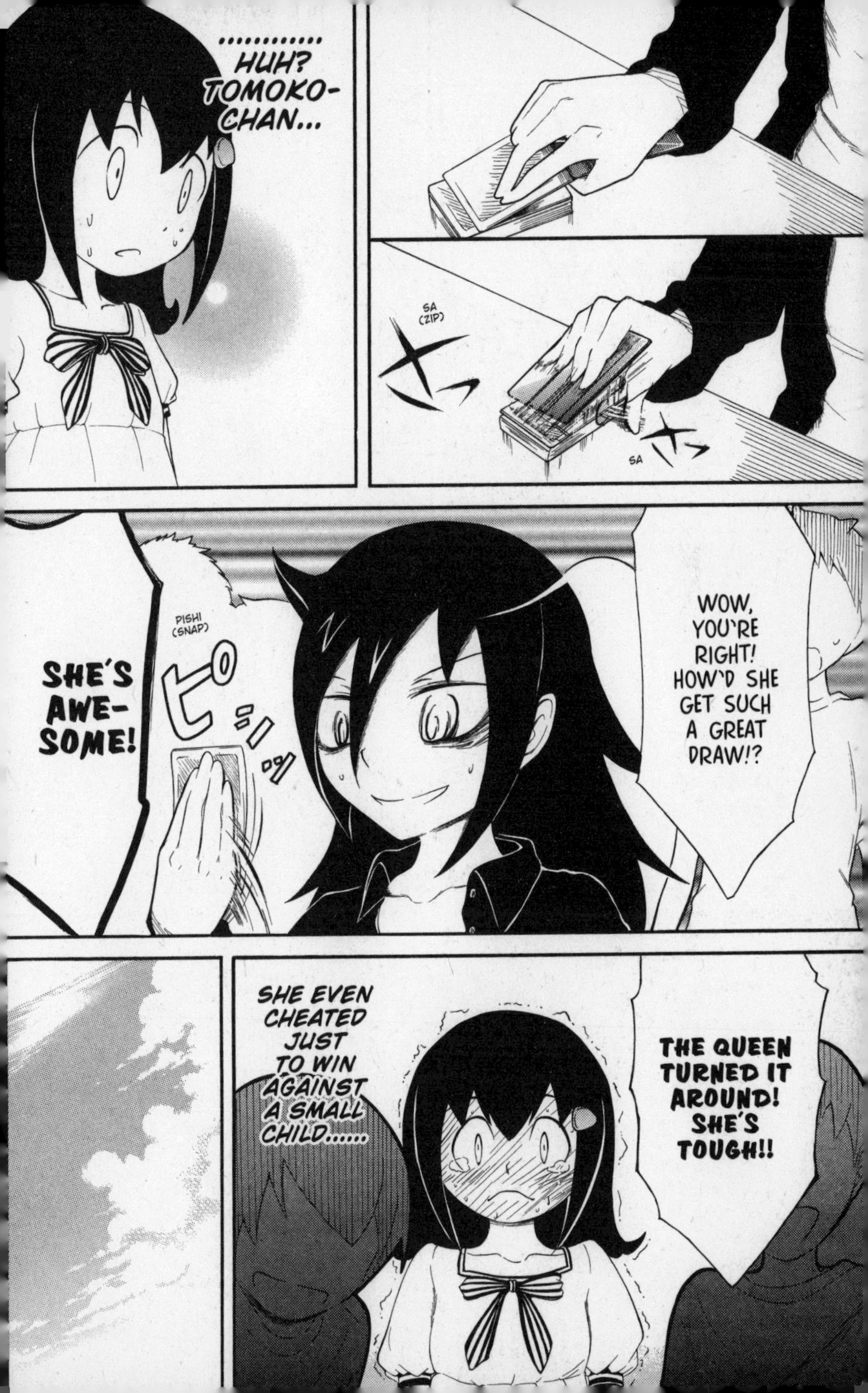
SA (ZIP)
SA
....
HUH? TOMOKO-CHAN...
WOW, YOU'RE RIGHT! HOW'D SHE GET SUCH A GREAT DRAW!?
PISHI (SNAP)
SHE'S AWE-SOME!
THE QUEEN TURNED IT AROUND! SHE'S TOUGH!!
SHE EVEN CHEATED JUST TO WIN AGAINST A SMALL CHILD......

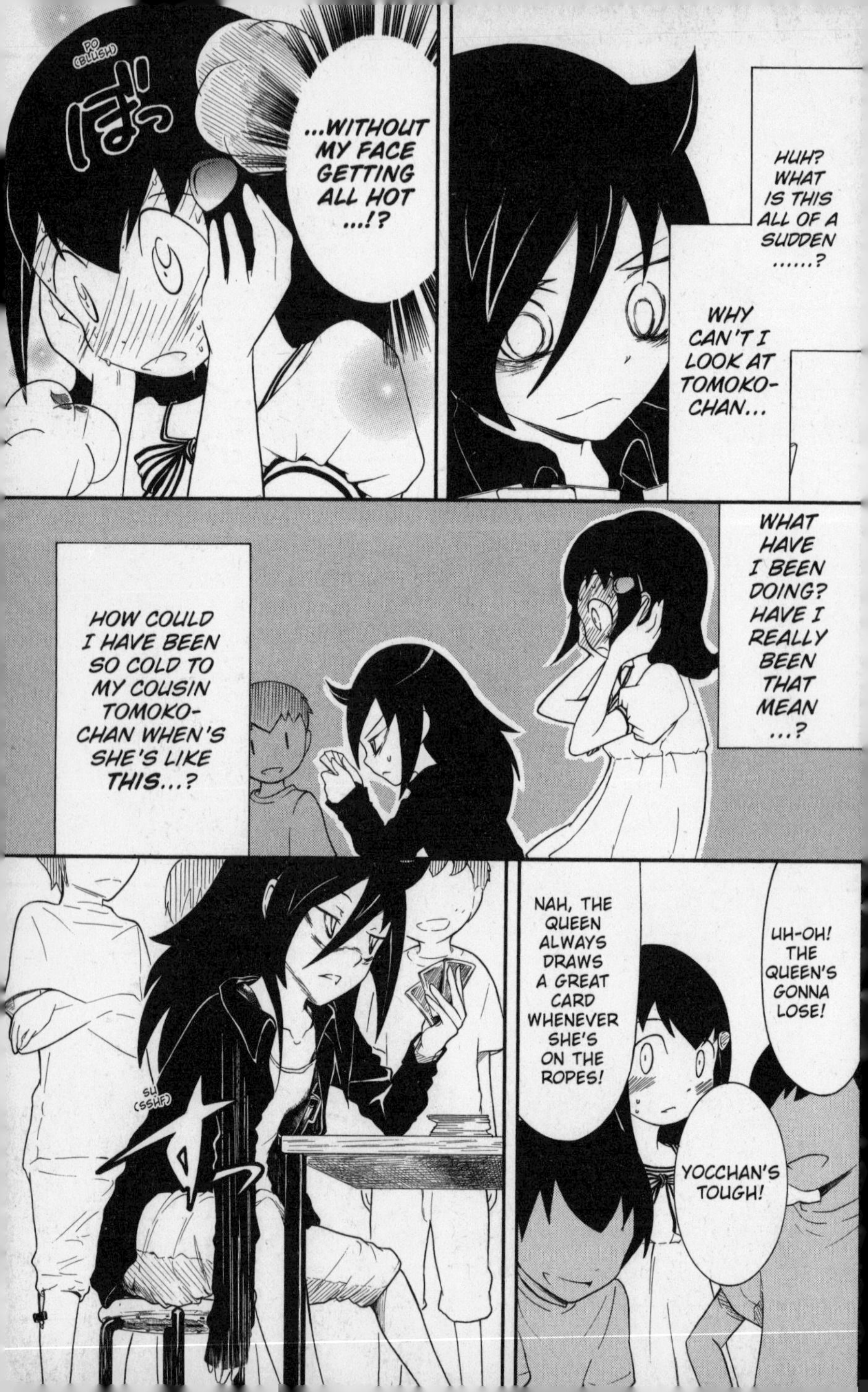
HUH? WHAT IS THIS ALL OF A SUDDEN ......?
WHY CAN'T I LOOK AT TOMOKO-CHAN...
...WITHOUT MY FACE GETTING ALL HOT ...!?
ぼっ
PO (BLUSH)
WHAT HAVE I BEEN DOING? HAVE I REALLY BEEN THAT MEAN ...?
HOW COULD I HAVE BEEN SO COLD TO MY COUSIN TOMOKO-CHAN WHEN'S SHE'S LIKE THIS...?
UH-OH! THE QUEEN'S GONNA LOSE!
NAH, THE QUEEN ALWAYS DRAWS A GREAT CARD WHENEVER SHE'S ON THE ROPES!
YOCCHAN'S TOUGH!
SU (SSHF)

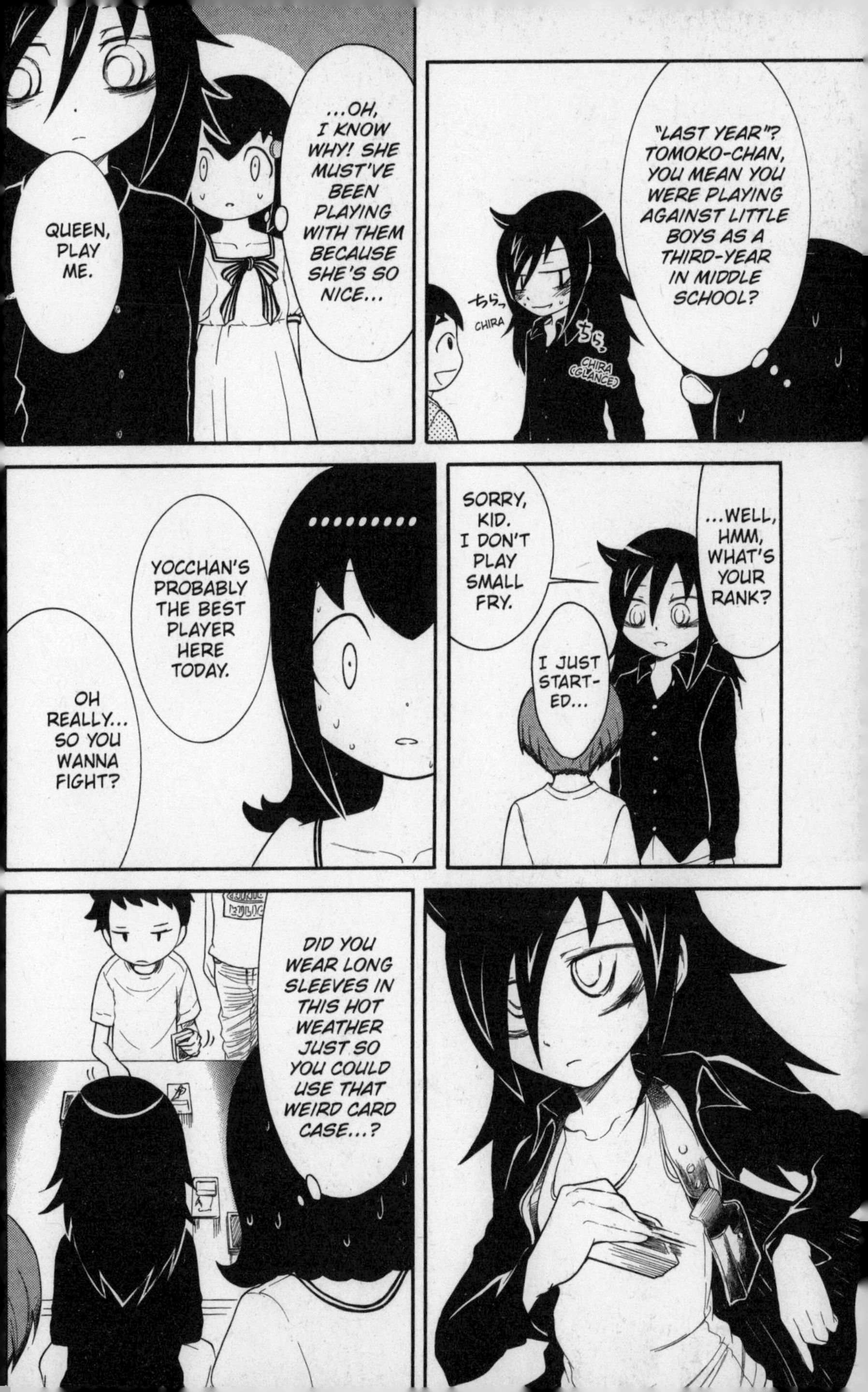
"LAST YEAR"? TOMOKO-CHAN, YOU MEAN YOU WERE PLAYING AGAINST LITTLE BOYS AS A THIRD-YEAR IN MIDDLE SCHOOL?
ちら CHIRA (GLANCE)
ちらっ CHIRA
...OH, I KNOW WHY! SHE MUST'VE BEEN PLAYING WITH THEM BECAUSE SHE'S SO NICE...
QUEEN, PLAY ME.
...WELL, HMM, WHAT'S YOUR RANK?
SORRY, KID. I DON'T PLAY SMALL FRY.
I JUST START-ED...
....
YOCCHAN'S PROBABLY THE BEST PLAYER HERE TODAY.
OH REALLY... SO YOU WANNA FIGHT?
DID YOU WEAR LONG SLEEVES IN THIS HOT WEATHER JUST SO YOU COULD USE THAT WEIRD CARD CASE...?

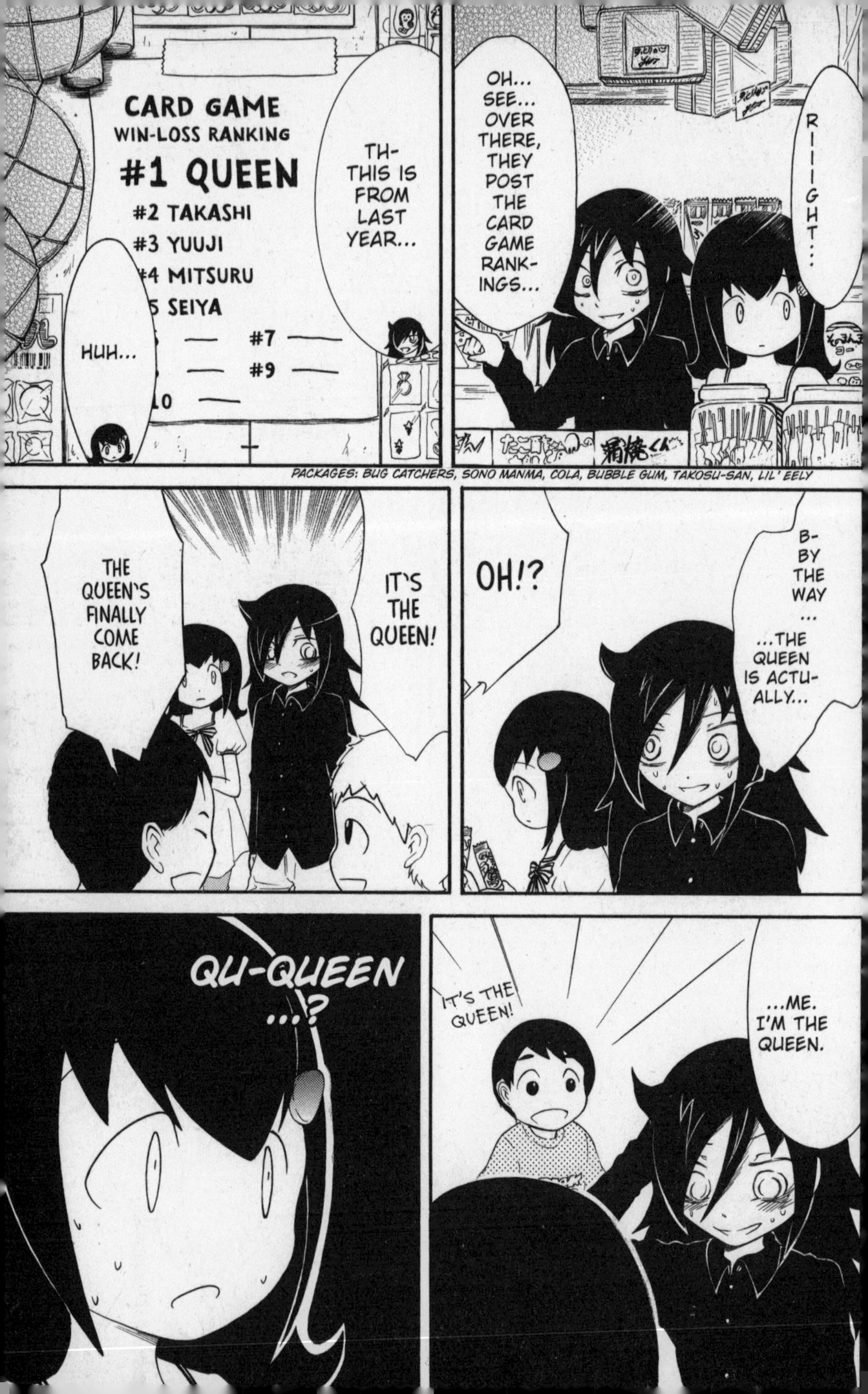

OH... SEE... OVER THERE, THEY POST THE CARD GAME RANKINGS...
RIIIGHT...
TH- THIS IS FROM LAST YEAR...
CARD GAME WIN-LOSS RANKING
#1 QUEEN
#2 TAKASHI
#3 YUUJI
#4 MITSURU
5 SEIYA
#7
#9
10
HUH...
PACKAGES: BUG CATCHERS, SONO MANMA, COLA, BUBBLE GUM, TAKOSU-SAN, LIL' EELY
B- BY THE WAY ... ...THE QUEEN IS ACTUALLY...
OH!?
IT'S THE QUEEN!
THE QUEEN'S FINALLY COME BACK!
...ME. I'M THE QUEEN.
IT'S THE QUEEN!
QU-QUEEN ...?

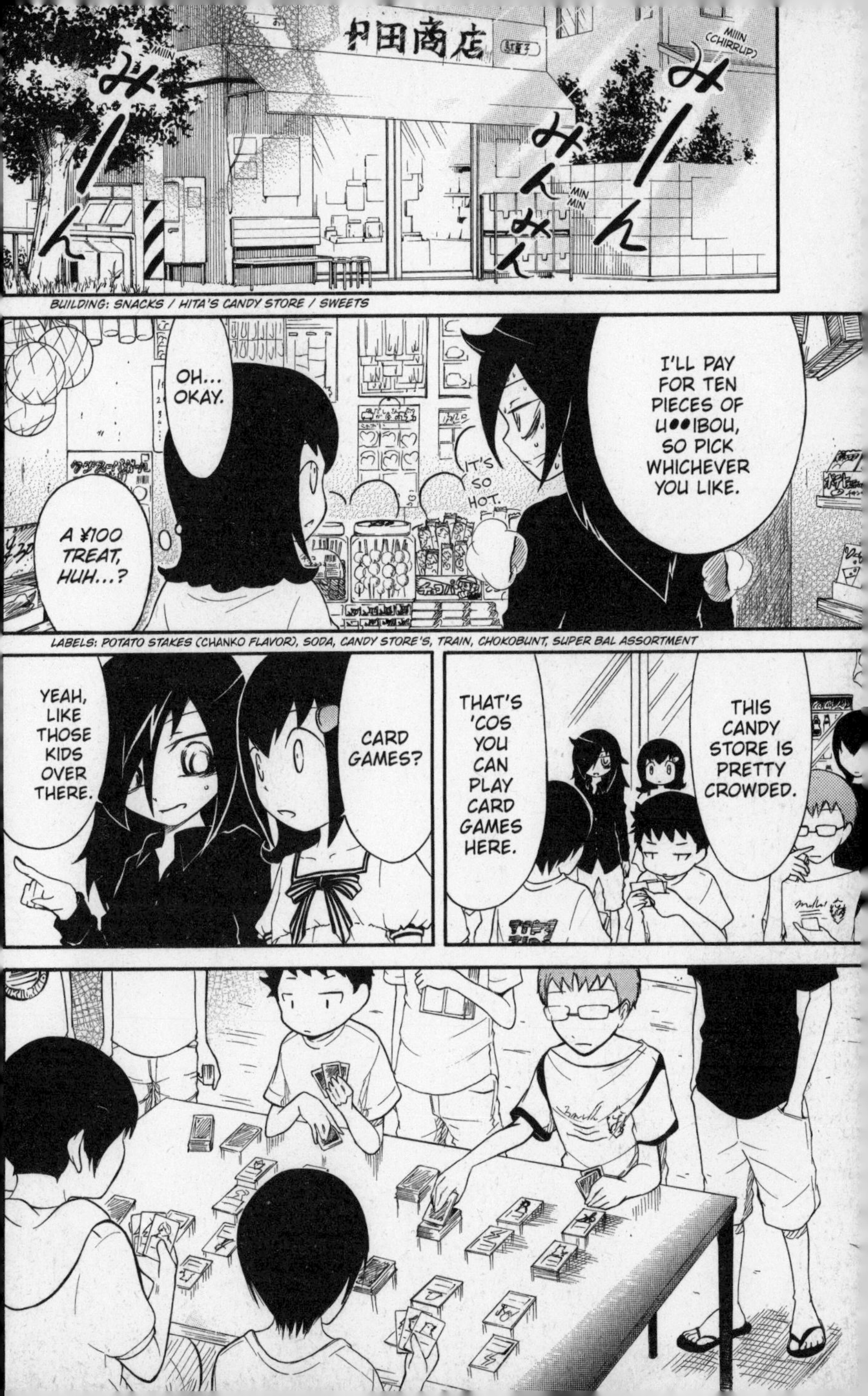
MIIIN (CHIRRUP)
MIN MIN
MIIIN
BUILDING: SNACKS / HITA'S CANDY STORE / SWEETS
I'LL PAY FOR TEN PIECES OF U••IBOU, SO PICK WHICHEVER YOU LIKE.
IT'S SO HOT.
OH... OKAY.
A ¥100 TREAT, HUH...?
LABELS: POTATO STAKES (CHANKO FLAVOR), SODA, CANDY STORE'S, TRAIN, CHOKOBUNT, SUPER BAL ASSORTMENT
THIS CANDY STORE IS PRETTY CROWDED.
THAT'S 'COS YOU CAN PLAY CARD GAMES HERE.
CARD GAMES?
YEAH, LIKE THOSE KIDS OVER THERE.

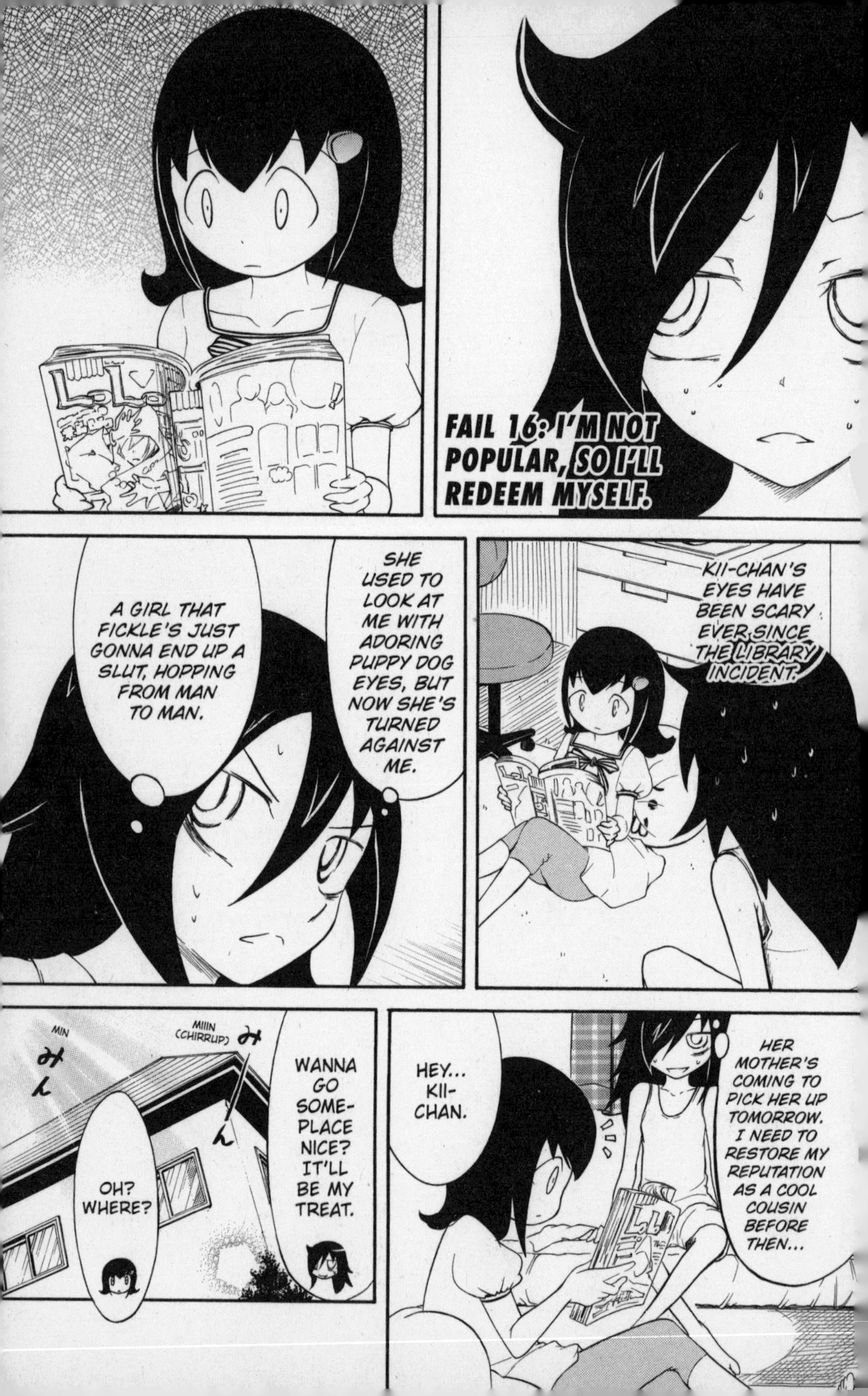
FAIL 16: I'M NOT POPULAR, SO I'LL REDEEM MYSELF.
KII-CHAN'S EYES HAVE BEEN SCARY EVER SINCE THE LIBRARY INCIDENT.
SHE USED TO LOOK AT ME WITH ADORING PUPPY DOG EYES, BUT NOW SHE'S TURNED AGAINST ME.
A GIRL THAT FICKLE'S JUST GONNA END UP A SLUT, HOPPING FROM MAN TO MAN.
HER MOTHER'S COMING TO PICK HER UP TOMORROW. I NEED TO RESTORE MY REPUTATION AS A COOL COUSIN BEFORE THEN...
HEY... KII-CHAN.
みーん
MIIN (CHIRRUP)
WANNA GO SOME-PLACE NICE? IT'LL BE MY TREAT.
みん
MIN
OH? WHERE?

No Matter How I Look at It, It's You Guys' Fault I'm Not Popular!

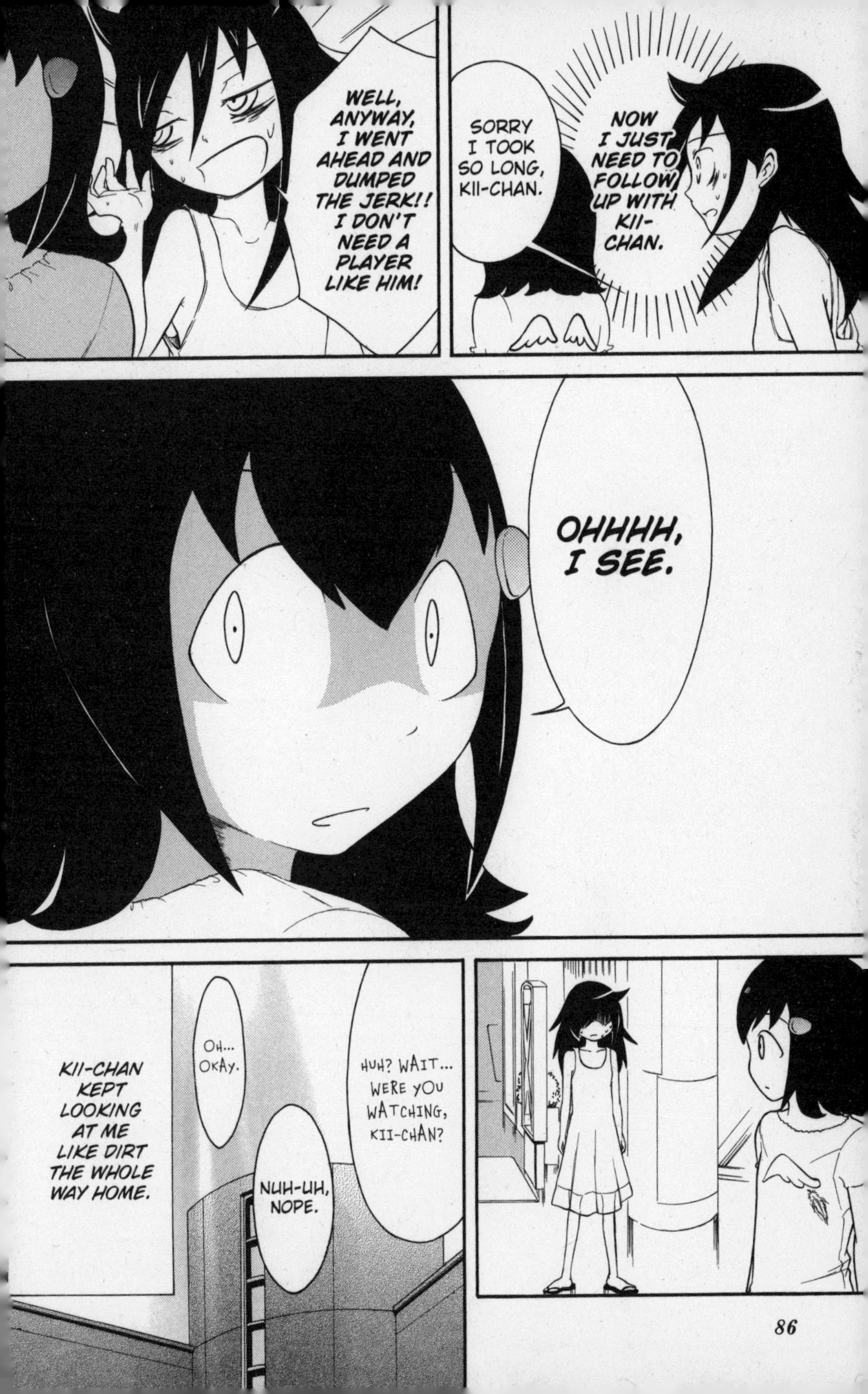
NOW I JUST NEED TO FOLLOW UP WITH KII-CHAN.
SORRY I TOOK SO LONG, KII-CHAN.
WELL, ANYWAY, I WENT AHEAD AND DUMPED THE JERK!! I DON'T NEED A PLAYER LIKE HIM!
OHHHH, I SEE.
HUH? WAIT... WERE YOU WATCHING, KII-CHAN?
NUH-UH, NOPE.
OH... OKAY.
KII-CHAN KEPT LOOKING AT ME LIKE DIRT THE WHOLE WAY HOME.

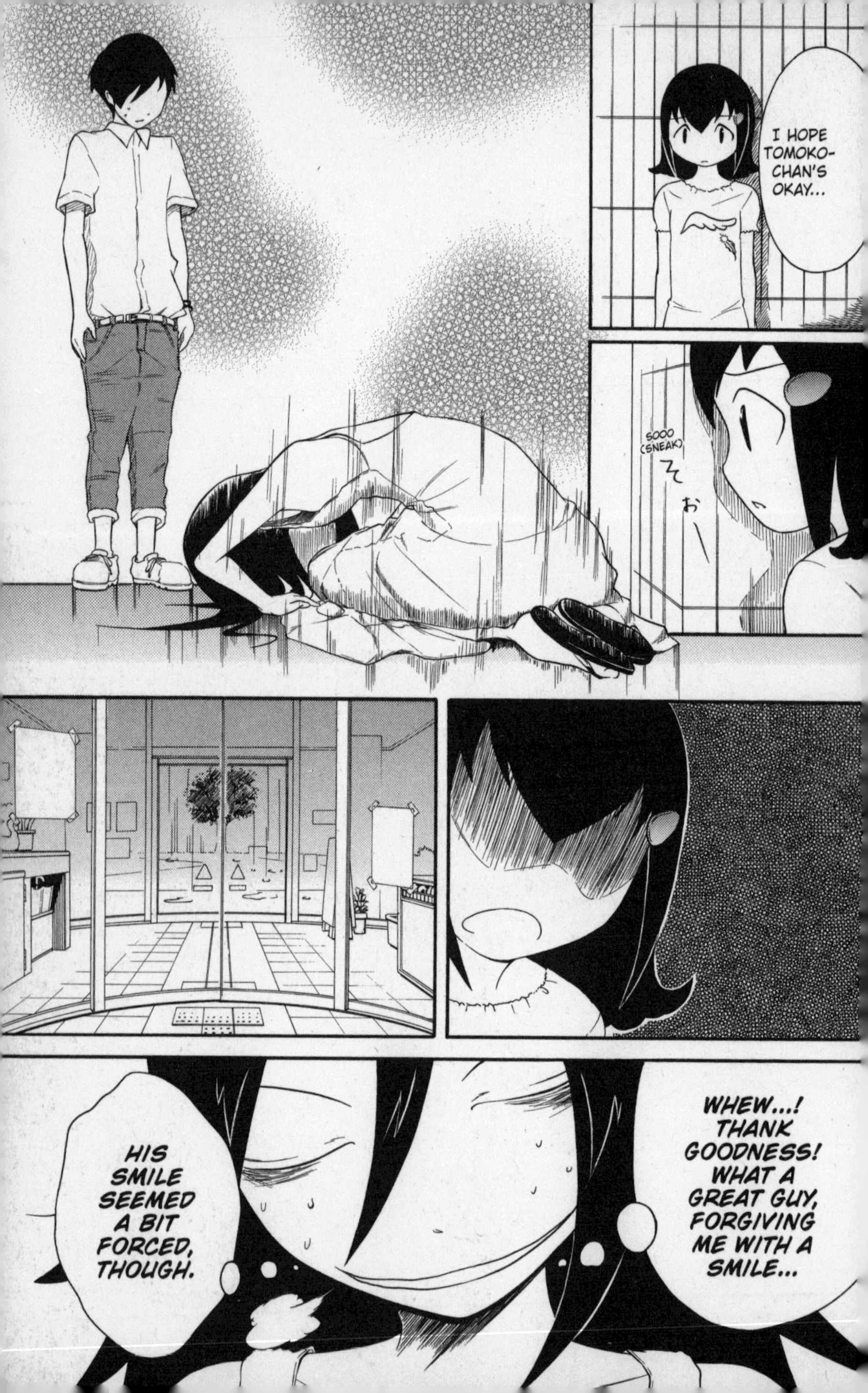
I HOPE TOMOKO-CHAN'S OKAY...
SOOO (SNEAK)
WHEW...! THANK GOODNESS! WHAT A GREAT GUY, FORGIVING ME WITH A SMILE...
HIS SMILE SEEMED A BIT FORCED, THOUGH.

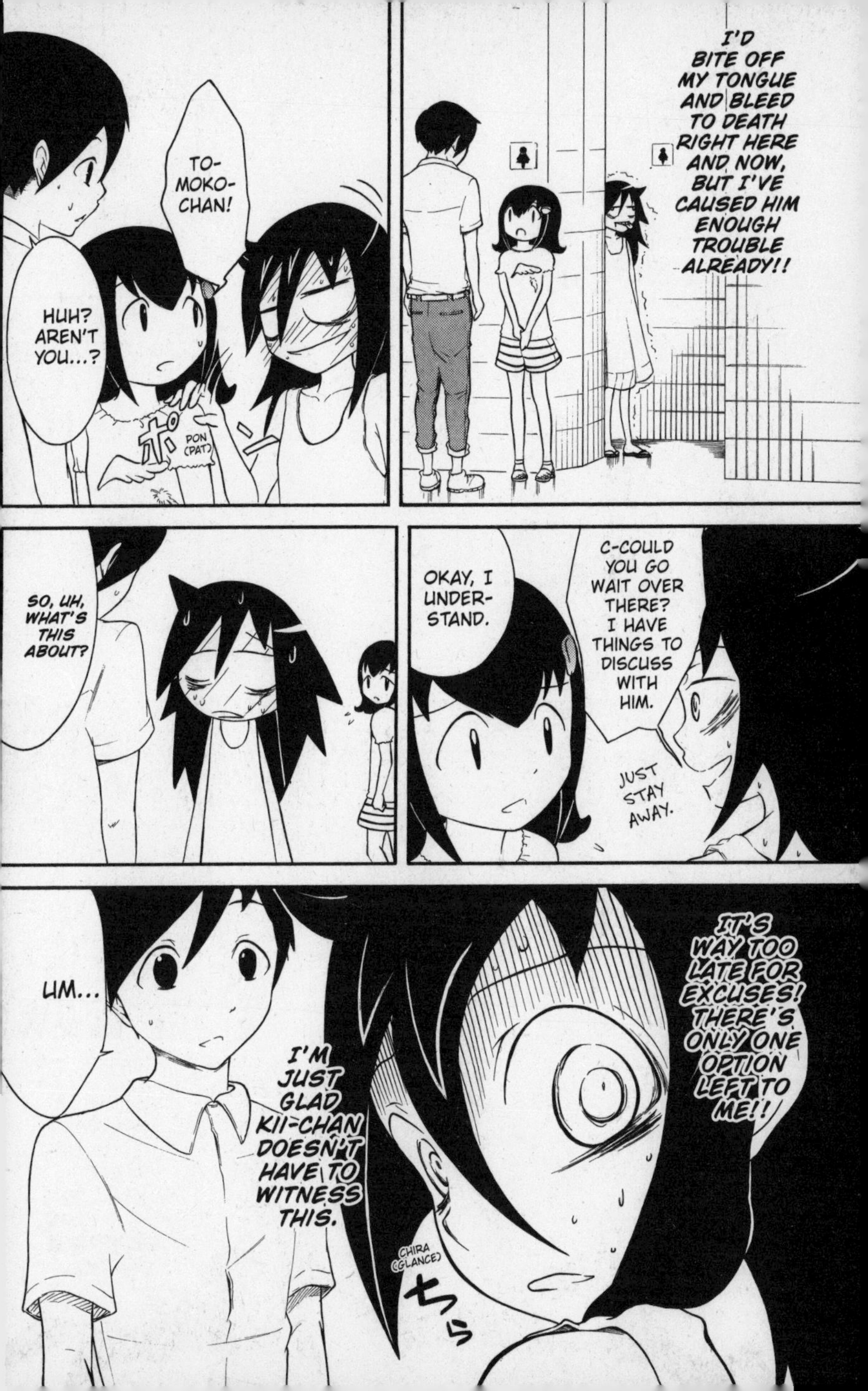
I'D BITE OFF MY TONGUE AND BLEED TO DEATH RIGHT HERE AND NOW, BUT I'VE CAUSED HIM ENOUGH TROUBLE ALREADY!!
TO-MOKO-CHAN!
PON (PAT)
HUH? AREN'T YOU...?
C-COULD YOU GO WAIT OVER THERE? I HAVE THINGS TO DISCUSS WITH HIM.
OKAY, I UNDER-STAND.
JUST STAY AWAY.
SO, UH, WHAT'S THIS ABOUT?
IT'S WAY TOO LATE FOR EXCUSES! THERE'S ONLY ONE OPTION LEFT TO ME!!
I'M JUST GLAD KII-CHAN DOESN'T HAVE TO WITNESS THIS.
UM...
CHIRA (GLANCE)

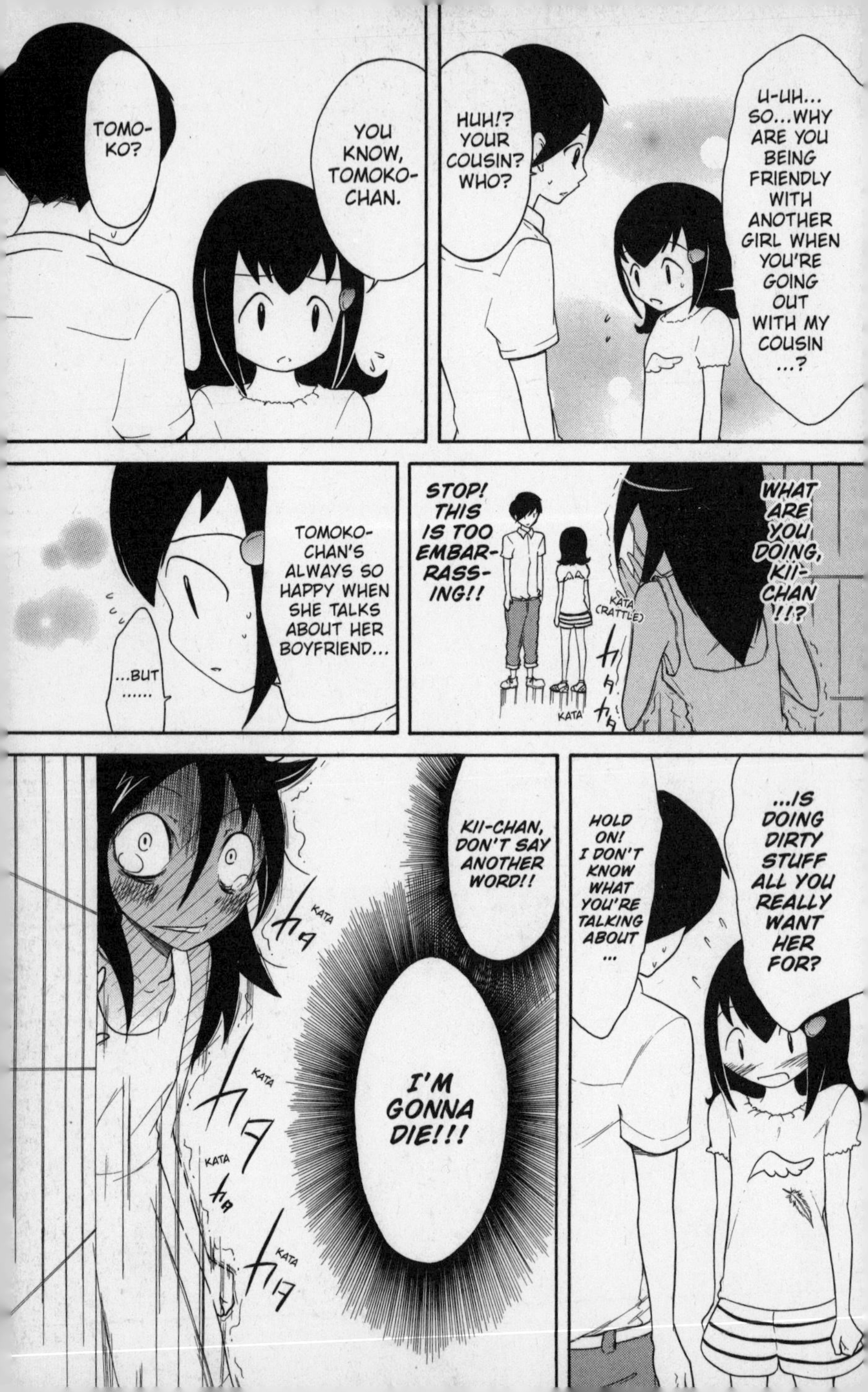
U-UH... SO...WHY ARE YOU BEING FRIENDLY WITH ANOTHER GIRL WHEN YOU'RE GOING OUT WITH MY COUSIN ...?
HUH!? YOUR COUSIN? WHO?
YOU KNOW, TOMOKO-CHAN.
TOMOKO?
WHAT ARE YOU DOING, KII-CHAN!!?
STOP! THIS IS TOO EMBARRASSING!!
KATA (RATTLE)
KATA
TOMOKO-CHAN'S ALWAYS SO HAPPY WHEN SHE TALKS ABOUT HER BOYFRIEND...
...BUT ......
...IS DOING DIRTY STUFF ALL YOU REALLY WANT HER FOR?
HOLD ON! I DON'T KNOW WHAT YOU'RE TALKING ABOUT ...
KII-CHAN, DON'T SAY ANOTHER WORD!!
KATA
I'M GONNA DIE!!!
KATA
KATA
KATA

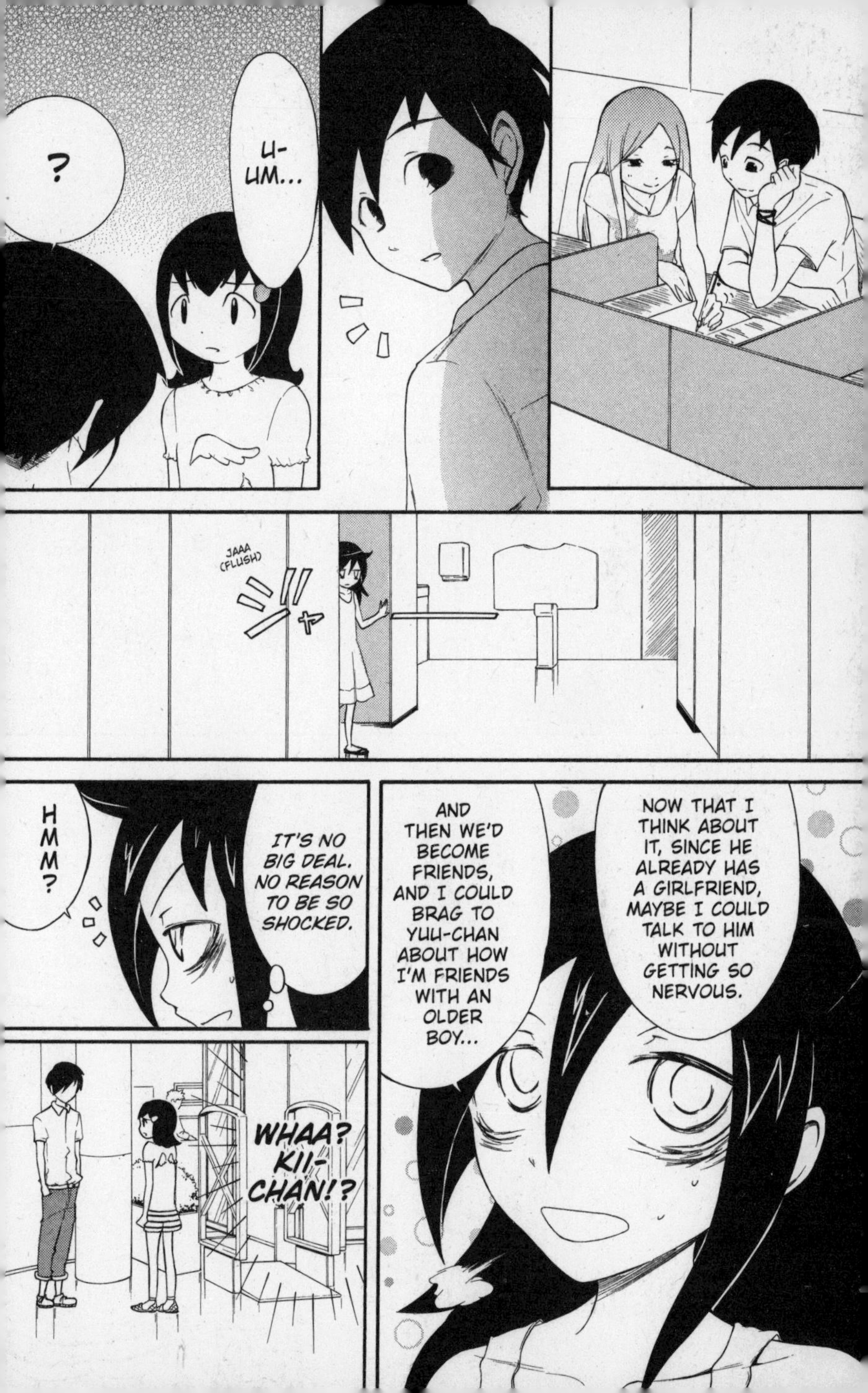
U-UM...
?
JAAA (FLUSH)
NOW THAT I THINK ABOUT IT, SINCE HE ALREADY HAS A GIRLFRIEND, MAYBE I COULD TALK TO HIM WITHOUT GETTING SO NERVOUS.
AND THEN WE'D BECOME FRIENDS, AND I COULD BRAG TO YUU-CHAN ABOUT HOW I'M FRIENDS WITH AN OLDER BOY...
IT'S NO BIG DEAL. NO REASON TO BE SO SHOCKED.
HMMM?
WHAA? KII-CHAN!?

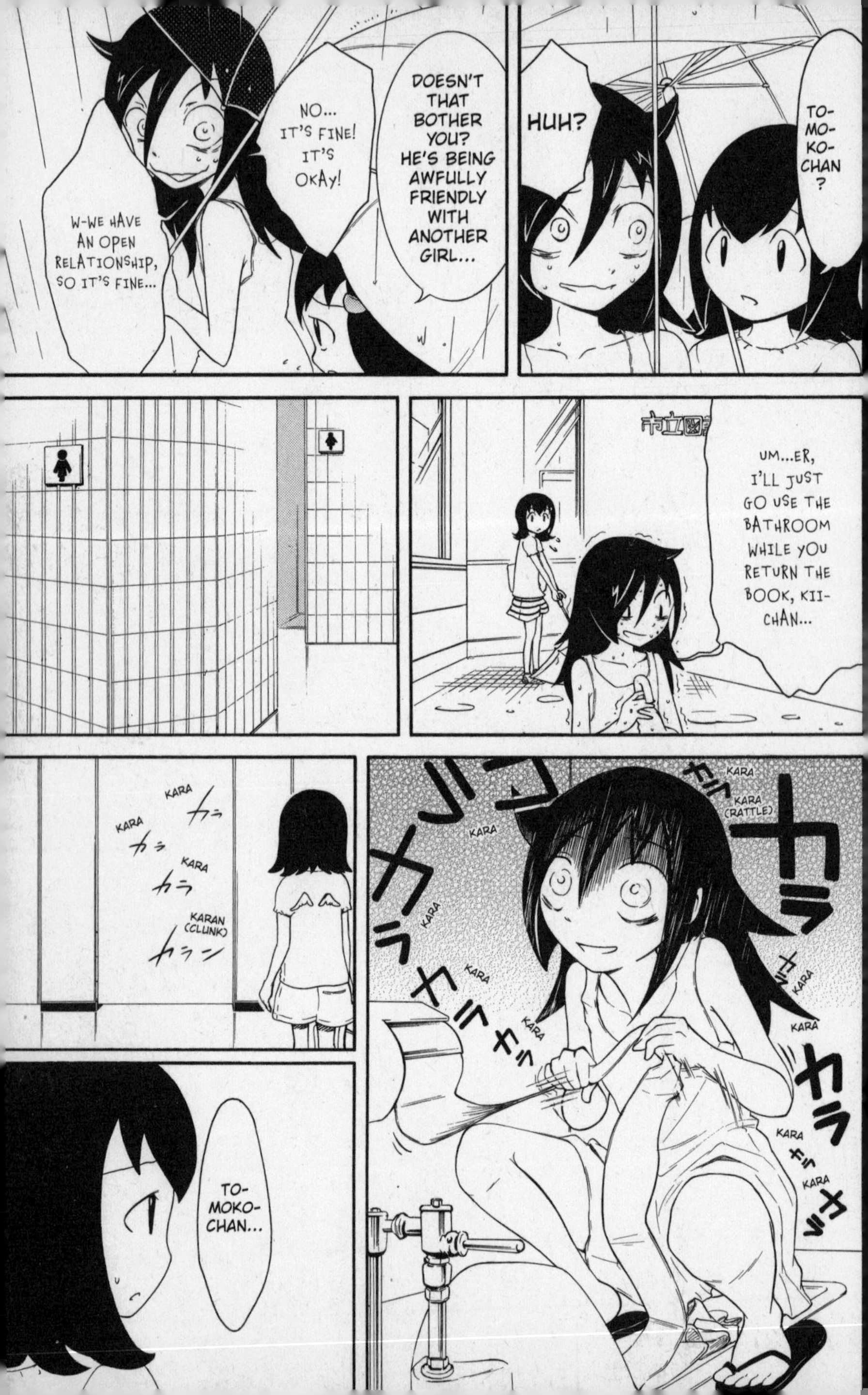
TO-MO-KO-CHAN?
HUH?
DOESN'T THAT BOTHER YOU? HE'S BEING AWFULLY FRIENDLY WITH ANOTHER GIRL...
NO... IT'S FINE! IT'S OKAY!
W-WE HAVE AN OPEN RELATIONSHIP, SO IT'S FINE...
UM...ER, I'LL JUST GO USE THE BATHROOM WHILE YOU RETURN THE BOOK, KII-CHAN...
KARA
KARA (RATTLE)
KARA
KARA
KARA
KARA
KARA
KARA
KARA
KARA
KARA
KARA
KARA
KARAN (CLUNK)
TO-MOKO-CHAN...

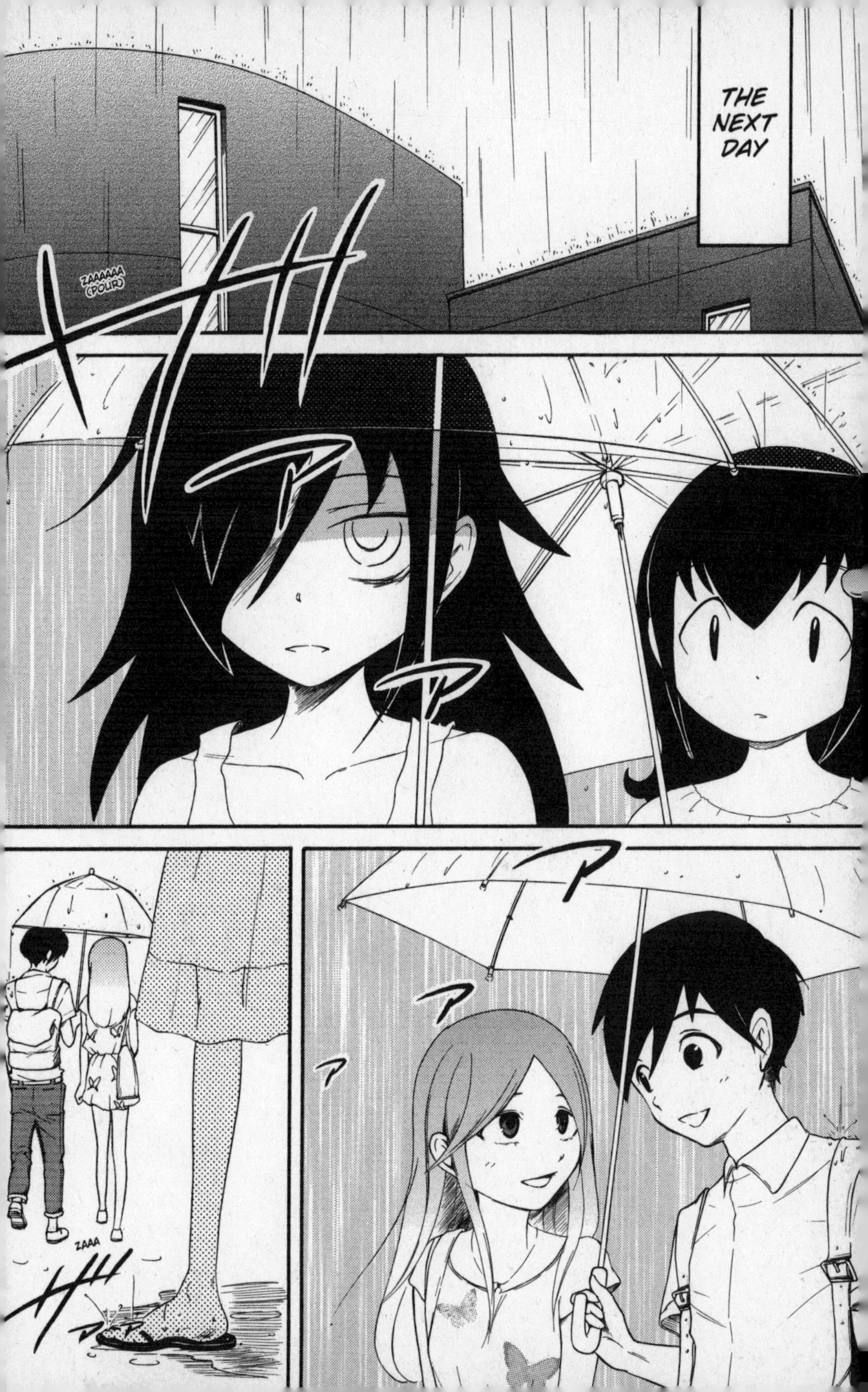
THE NEXT DAY
ZAAAAAA (POUR)
ZAAA

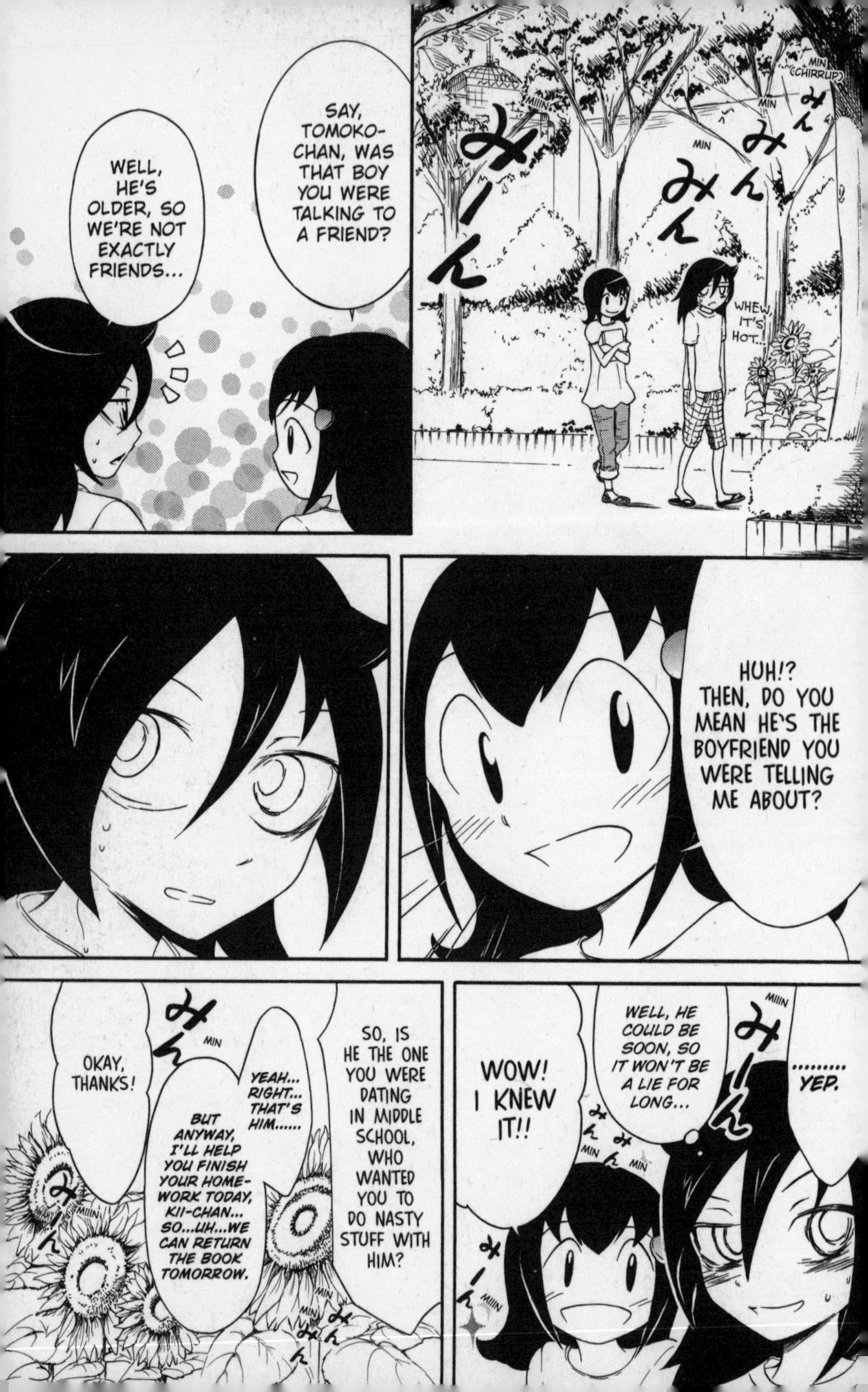
MIN (CHIRRUP)
みん
MIN
みん
MIN
みん
MIIN
みーん
WHEW, IT'S HOT...
SAY, TOMOKO-CHAN, WAS THAT BOY YOU WERE TALKING TO A FRIEND?
WELL, HE'S OLDER, SO WE'RE NOT EXACTLY FRIENDS...
HUH!? THEN, DO YOU MEAN HE'S THE BOYFRIEND YOU WERE TELLING ME ABOUT?
MIIN
みーん
........YEP.
WELL, HE COULD BE SOON, SO IT WON'T BE A LIE FOR LONG...
WOW! I KNEW IT!!
MIN
MIN
MIIN
SO, IS HE THE ONE YOU WERE DATING IN MIDDLE SCHOOL, WHO WANTED YOU TO DO NASTY STUFF WITH HIM?
YEAH... RIGHT... THAT'S HIM......
MIN
みん
BUT ANYWAY, I'LL HELP YOU FINISH YOUR HOME-WORK TODAY, KII-CHAN... SO...UH...WE CAN RETURN THE BOOK TOMORROW.
OKAY, THANKS!
MIIN
MIN
MIN

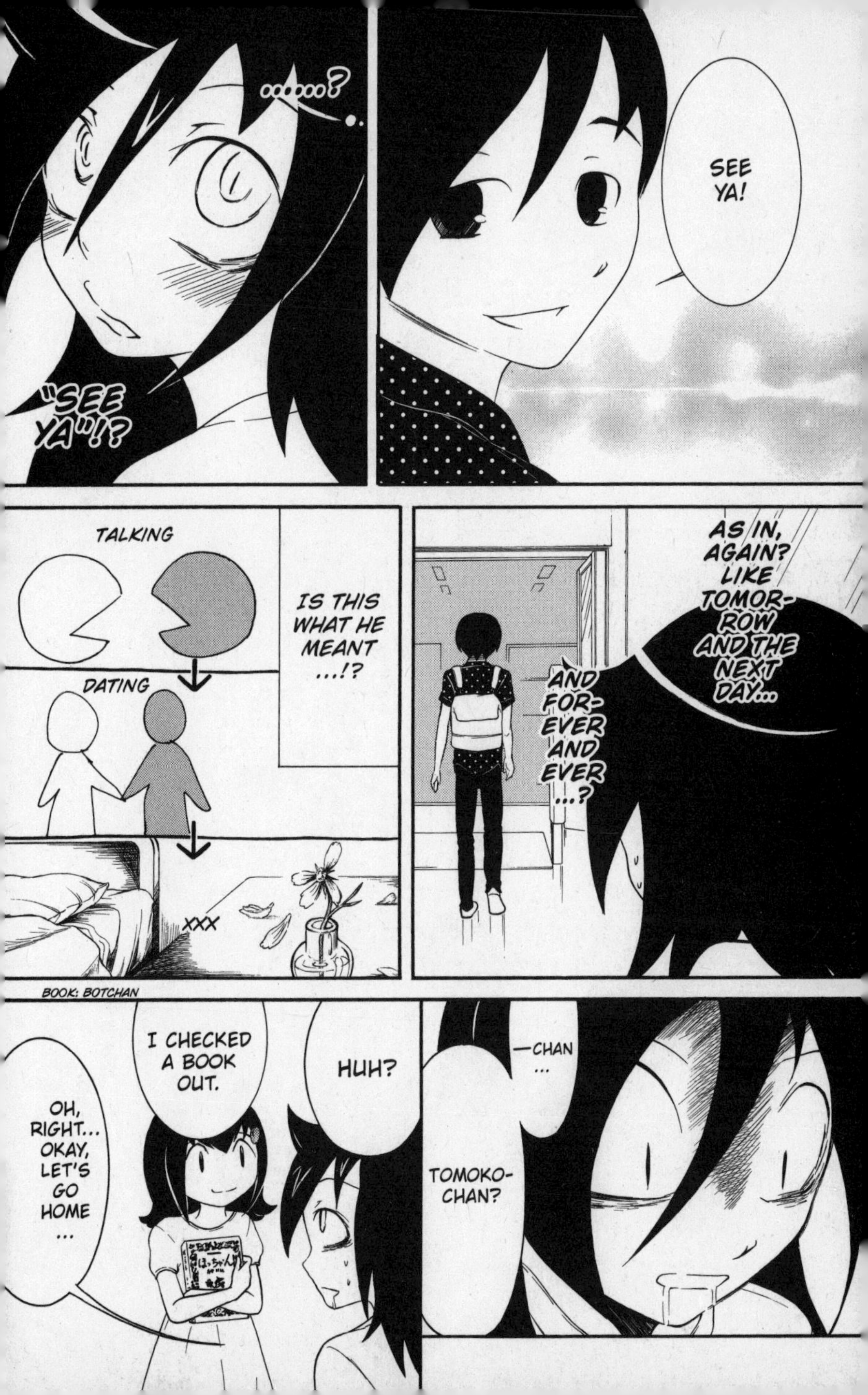
SEE YA!
......?
"SEE YA"!?
AS IN, AGAIN? LIKE TOMORROW AND THE NEXT DAY...
AND FOREVER AND EVER...?
IS THIS WHAT HE MEANT...!?
TALKING
DATING
XXX
BOOK: BOTCHAN
—CHAN...
TOMOKO-CHAN?
HUH?
I CHECKED A BOOK OUT.
OH, RIGHT... OKAY, LET'S GO HOME...

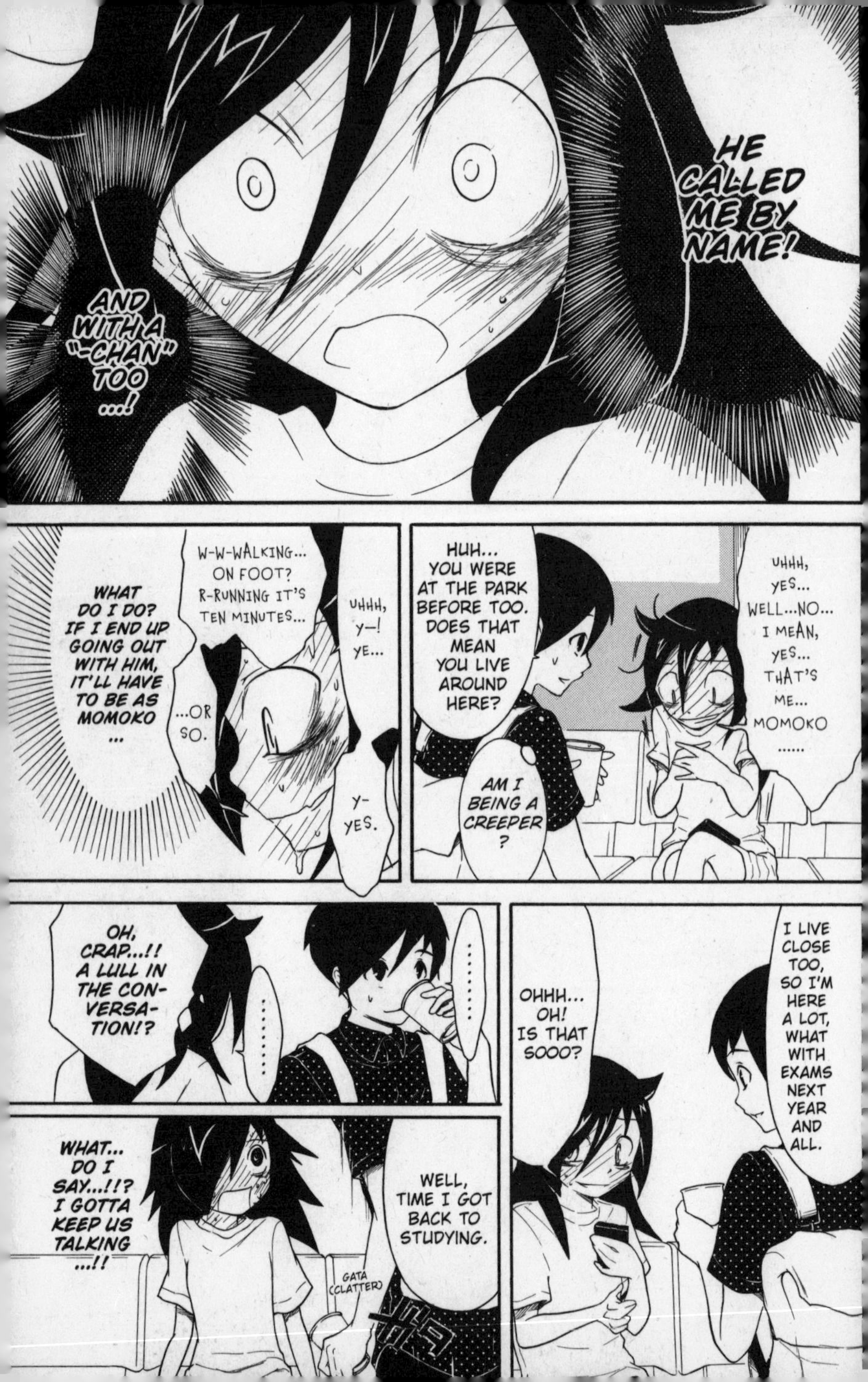
HE CALLED ME BY NAME!
AND WITH A "-CHAN" TOO ...!
UHHH, YES... WELL...NO... I MEAN, YES... THAT'S ME... MOMOKO ......
HUH... YOU WERE AT THE PARK BEFORE TOO. DOES THAT MEAN YOU LIVE AROUND HERE?
AM I BEING A CREEPER?
UHHH, Y—! YE...
Y- YES.
W-W-WALKING... ON FOOT? R-RUNNING IT'S TEN MINUTES...
...OR SO.
WHAT DO I DO? IF I END UP GOING OUT WITH HIM, IT'LL HAVE TO BE AS MOMOKO ...
I LIVE CLOSE TOO, SO I'M HERE A LOT, WHAT WITH EXAMS NEXT YEAR AND ALL.
OHHH... OH! IS THAT SOOO?
......
......
OH, CRAP...!! A LULL IN THE CONVERSATION!?
WELL, TIME I GOT BACK TO STUDYING.
GATA (CLATTER)
WHAT... DO I SAY...!!? I GOTTA KEEP US TALKING ...!!

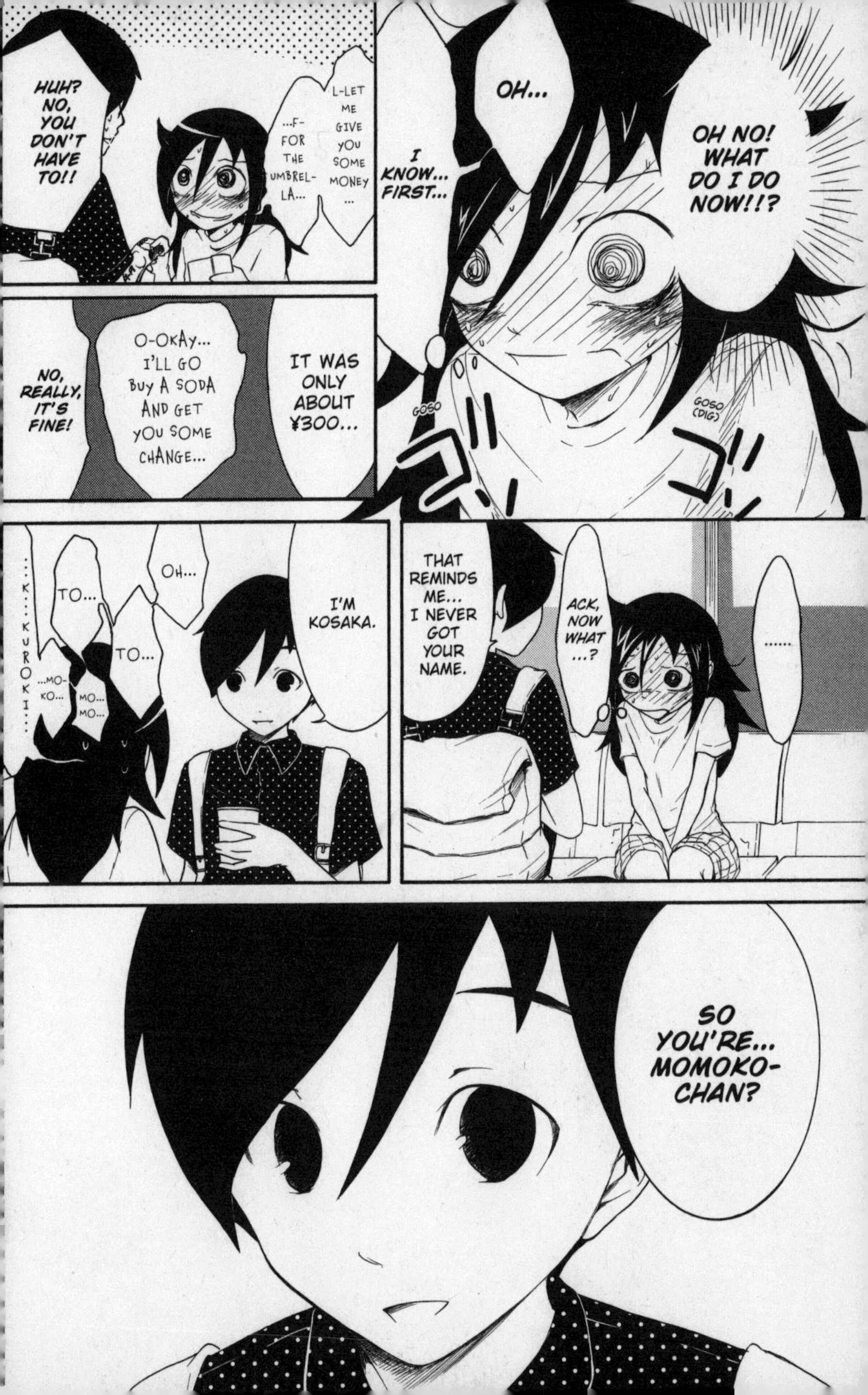
OH...
OH NO! WHAT DO I DO NOW!!?
I KNOW... FIRST...
GOSO (DIG)
GOSO
L-LET ME GIVE YOU SOME MONEY...
...F-FOR THE UMBREL-LA...
HUH? NO, YOU DON'T HAVE TO!!
IT WAS ONLY ABOUT ¥300...
O-OKAY... I'LL GO BUY A SODA AND GET YOU SOME CHANGE...
NO, REALLY, IT'S FINE!
......
ACK, NOW WHAT...?
THAT REMINDS ME... I NEVER GOT YOUR NAME.
I'M KOSAKA.
OH...
TO...
TO...
...K...KUROKI...
...MO-KO...
MO... MO...
SO YOU'RE... MOMOKO-CHAN?

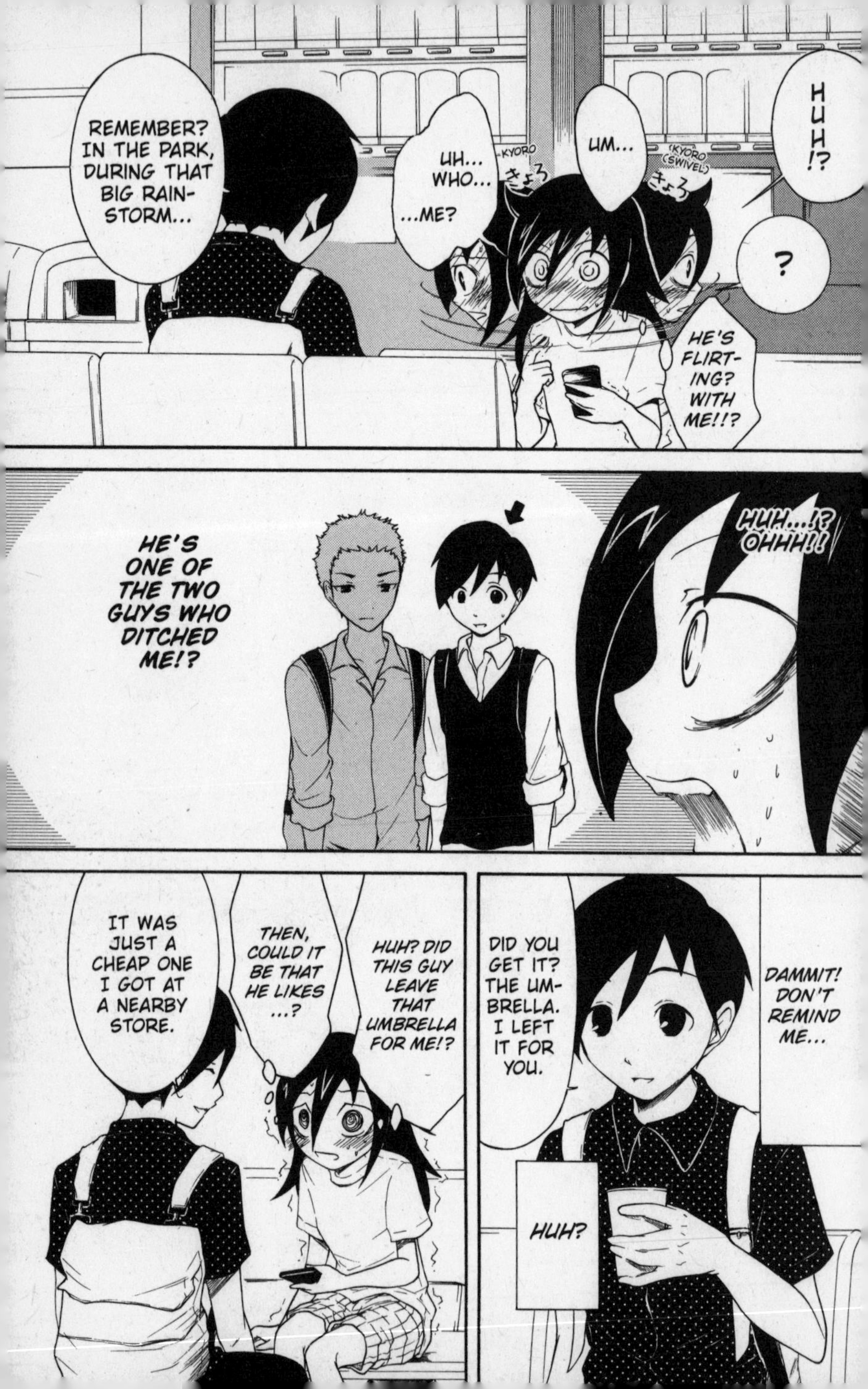
HUH!?
?
UM...
きょろ (KYORO (SWIVEL))
UH... WHO... ...ME?
きょろ KYORO
HE'S FLIRTING? WITH ME!!?
REMEMBER? IN THE PARK, DURING THAT BIG RAINSTORM...
HUH...!? OHHH!!
HE'S ONE OF THE TWO GUYS WHO DITCHED ME!?
DAMMIT! DON'T REMIND ME...
DID YOU GET IT? THE UMBRELLA. I LEFT IT FOR YOU.
HUH?
HUH? DID THIS GUY LEAVE THAT UMBRELLA FOR ME!?
THEN, COULD IT BE THAT HE LIKES ...?
IT WAS JUST A CHEAP ONE I GOT AT A NEARBY STORE.

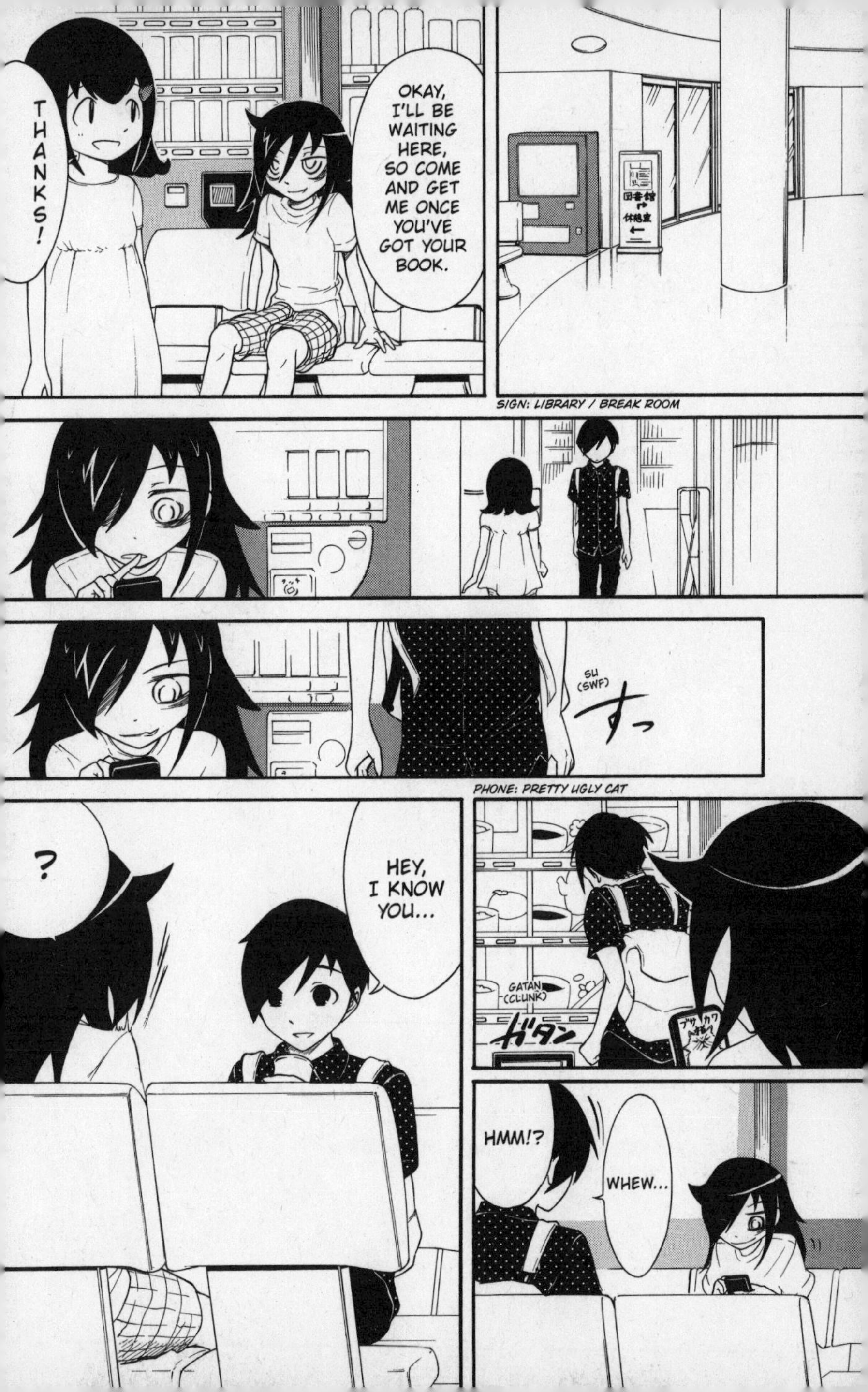
図書館
休憩室
SIGN: LIBRARY / BREAK ROOM
OKAY, I'LL BE WAITING HERE, SO COME AND GET ME ONCE YOU'VE GOT YOUR BOOK.
THANKS!
SU (SWF)
すっ
PHONE: PRETTY UGLY CAT
GATAN (CLUNK)
ガタン
WHEW...
HMM!?
HEY, I KNOW YOU...
?

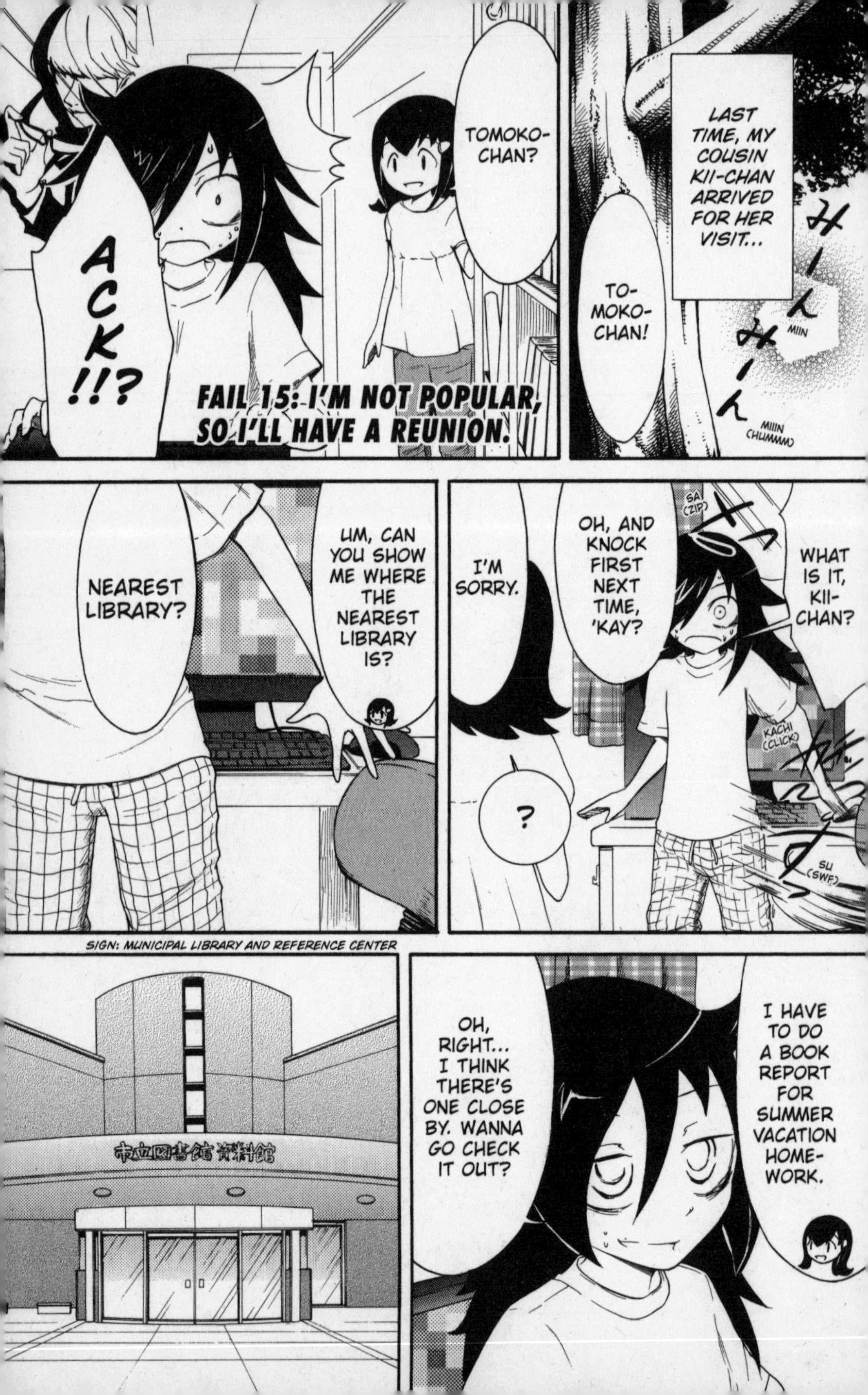
LAST TIME, MY COUSIN KII-CHAN ARRIVED FOR HER VISIT...
TO-MOKO-CHAN!
ミーン ミーン
MIIN MIIN (HUMMM)
TOMOKO-CHAN?
FAIL 15: I'M NOT POPULAR, SO I'LL HAVE A REUNION.
ACK!!?
WHAT IS IT, KII-CHAN?
SA (ZIP)
KACHI (CLICK)
SU (SWF)
OH, AND KNOCK FIRST NEXT TIME, 'KAY?
I'M SORRY.
?
UM, CAN YOU SHOW ME WHERE THE NEAREST LIBRARY IS?
NEAREST LIBRARY?
I HAVE TO DO A BOOK REPORT FOR SUMMER VACATION HOME-WORK.
OH, RIGHT... I THINK THERE'S ONE CLOSE BY. WANNA GO CHECK IT OUT?
SIGN: MUNICIPAL LIBRARY AND REFERENCE CENTER
市立図書館 資料館

No Matter How I Look at It, It's You Guys' Fault I'm Not Popular!

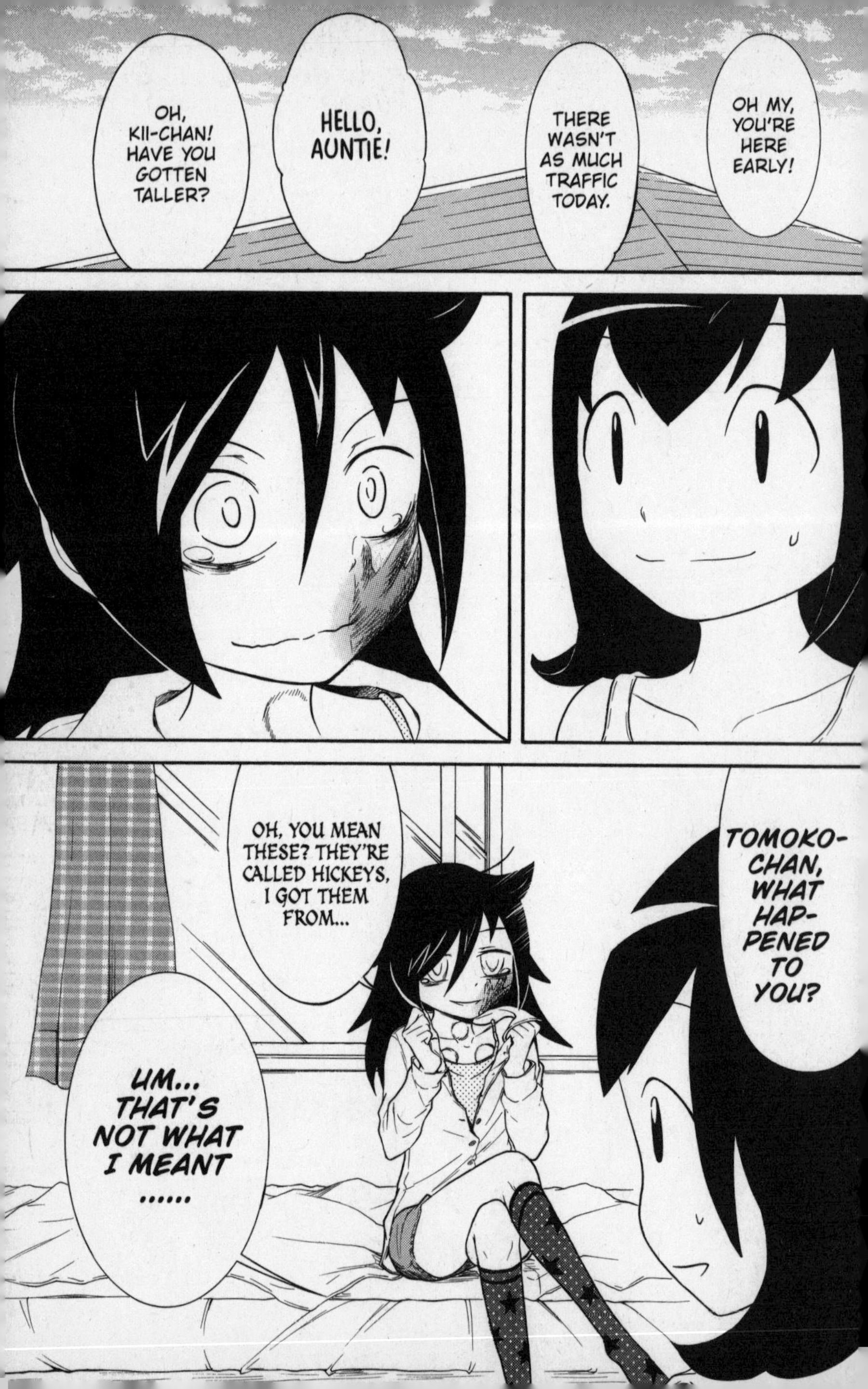
OH MY, YOU'RE HERE EARLY!
THERE WASN'T AS MUCH TRAFFIC TODAY.
HELLO, AUNTIE!
OH, KII-CHAN! HAVE YOU GOTTEN TALLER?
TOMOKO-CHAN, WHAT HAP-PENED TO YOU?
OH, YOU MEAN THESE? THEY'RE CALLED HICKEYS, I GOT THEM FROM...
UM... THAT'S NOT WHAT I MEANT ......

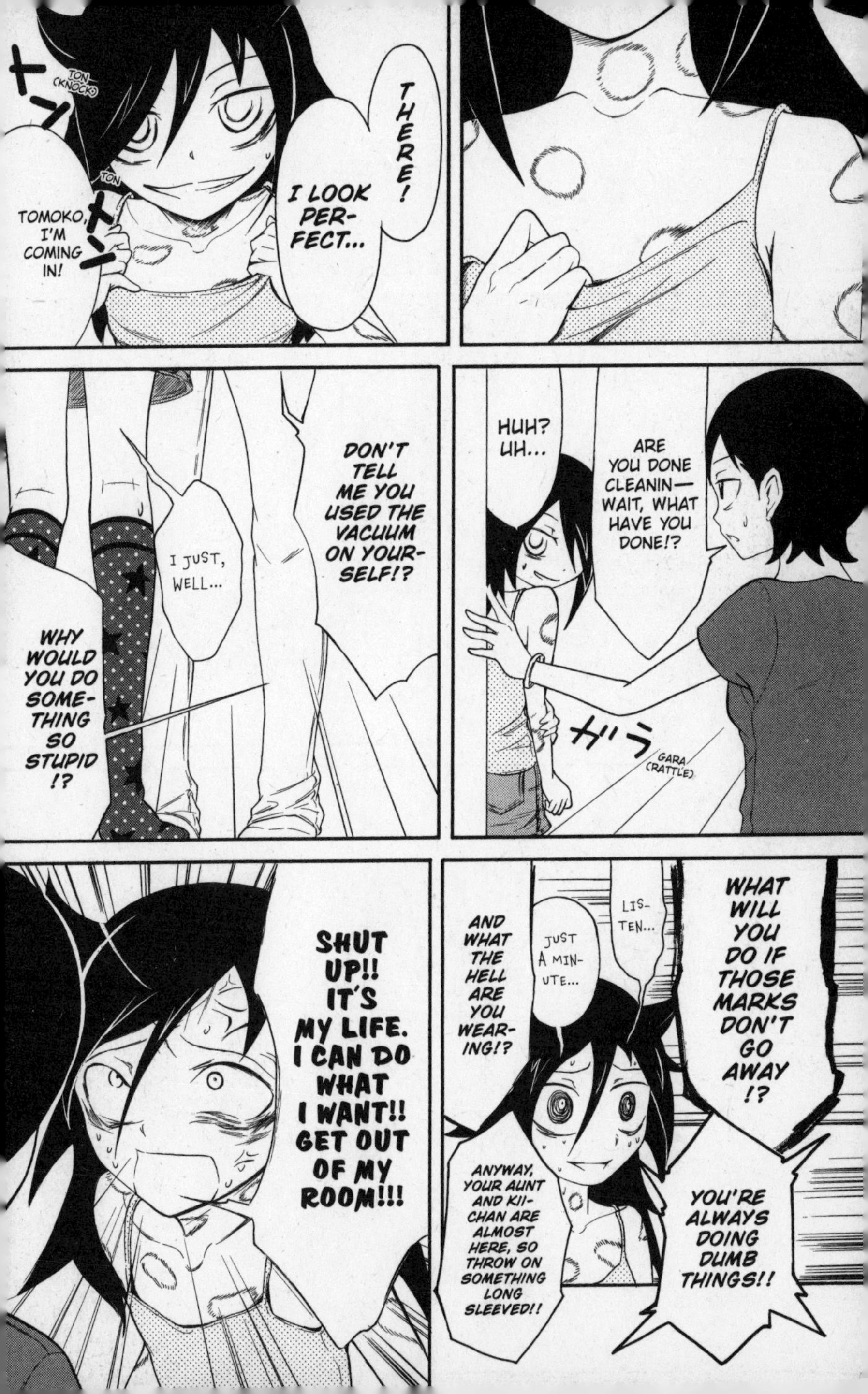
THERE!
I LOOK PER-FECT...
トン
TON (KNOCK)
トン
TON
TOMOKO, I'M COMING IN!
ARE YOU DONE CLEANIN— WAIT, WHAT HAVE YOU DONE!?
HUH? UH...
ガラ
GARA (RATTLE)
DON'T TELL ME YOU USED THE VACUUM ON YOUR-SELF!?
I JUST, WELL...
WHY WOULD YOU DO SOME-THING SO STUPID !?
WHAT WILL YOU DO IF THOSE MARKS DON'T GO AWAY !?
LIS-TEN...
AND WHAT THE HELL ARE YOU WEAR-ING!?
JUST A MIN-UTE...
YOU'RE ALWAYS DOING DUMB THINGS!!
ANYWAY, YOUR AUNT AND KII-CHAN ARE ALMOST HERE, SO THROW ON SOMETHING LONG SLEEVED!!
SHUT UP!! IT'S MY LIFE. I CAN DO WHAT I WANT!! GET OUT OF MY ROOM!!!

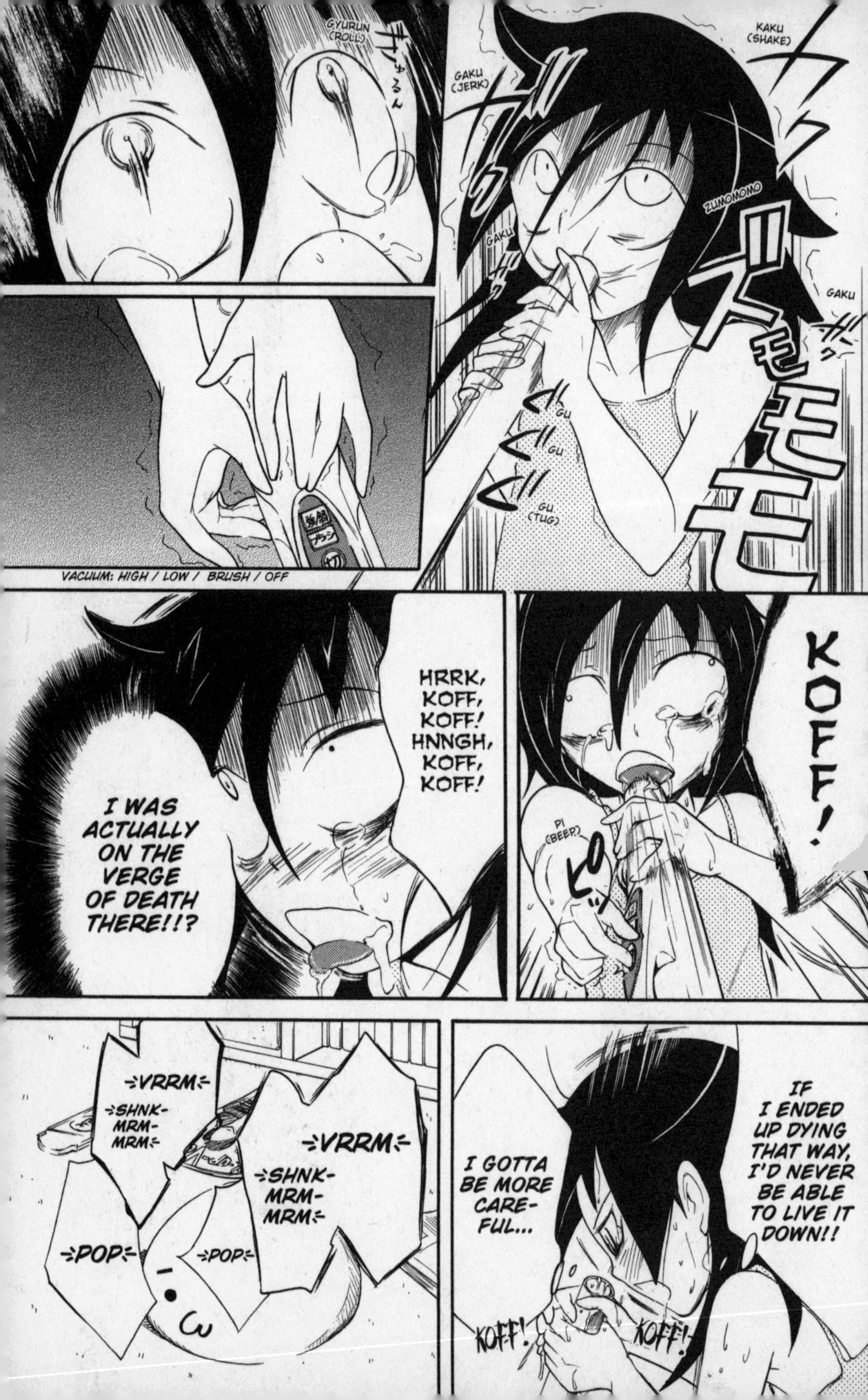
KAKU (SHAKE)
GAKU (JERK)
ZUMOMOMO
GAKU
GAKU
GU
GU
GU (TUG)
GYURUN (ROLL)
VACUUM: HIGH / LOW / BRUSH / OFF
KOFF!
PI (BEEP)
HRRK, KOFF, KOFF! HNNGH, KOFF, KOFF!
I WAS ACTUALLY ON THE VERGE OF DEATH THERE!!?
IF I ENDED UP DYING THAT WAY, I'D NEVER BE ABLE TO LIVE IT DOWN!!
I GOTTA BE MORE CARE-FUL...
KOFF!
KOFF!
VRRM
SHNK-MRM-MRM
POP
VRRM
SHNK-MRM-MRM
POP

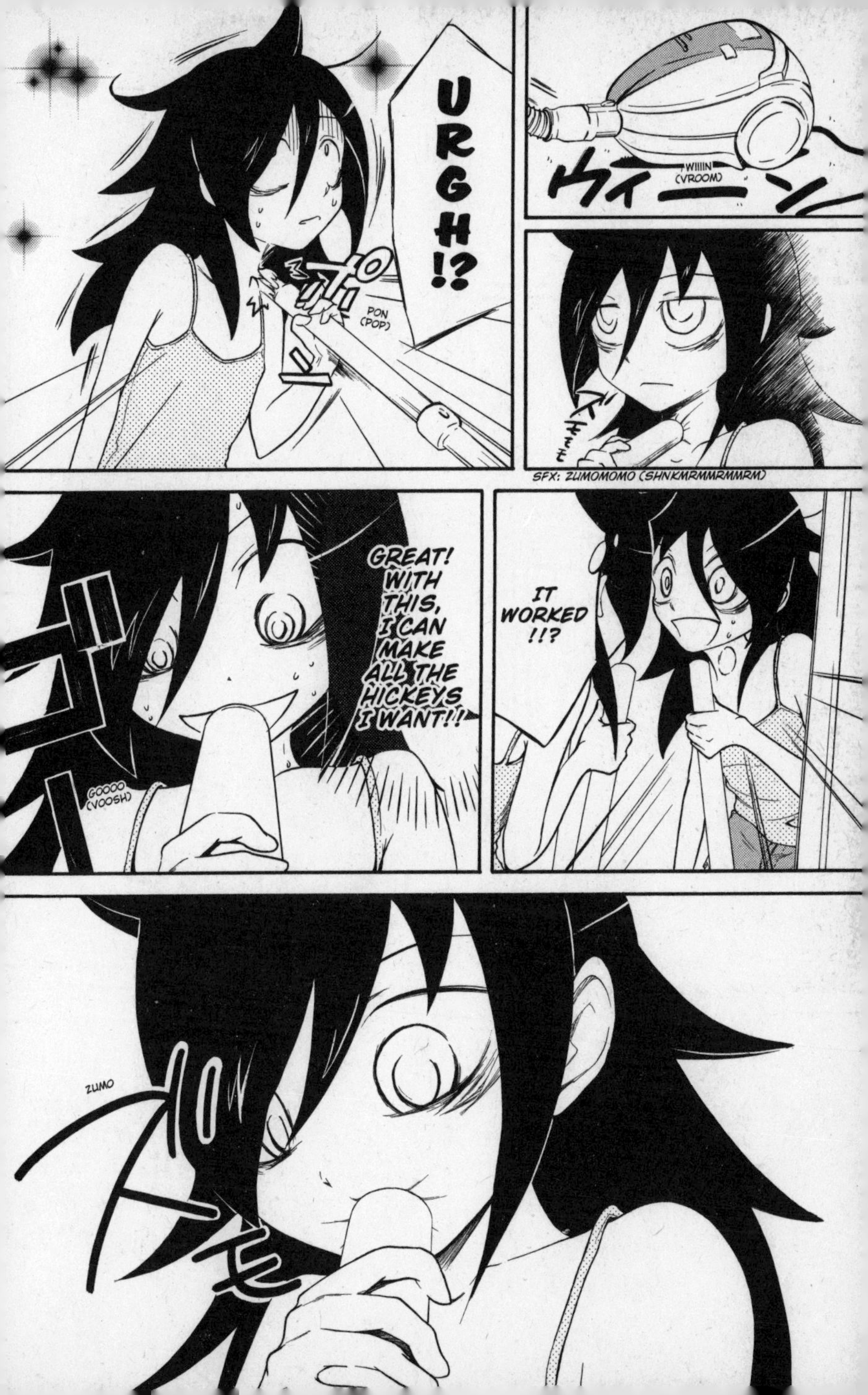
WIIIIN
(VROOM)
SFX: ZUMOMOMO (SHNKMRMMRMMRM)
URGH!?
PON
(POP)
IT WORKED!!?
GREAT! WITH THIS, I CAN MAKE ALL THE HICKEYS I WANT!!
GOOOO
(VOOSH)
ZUMO

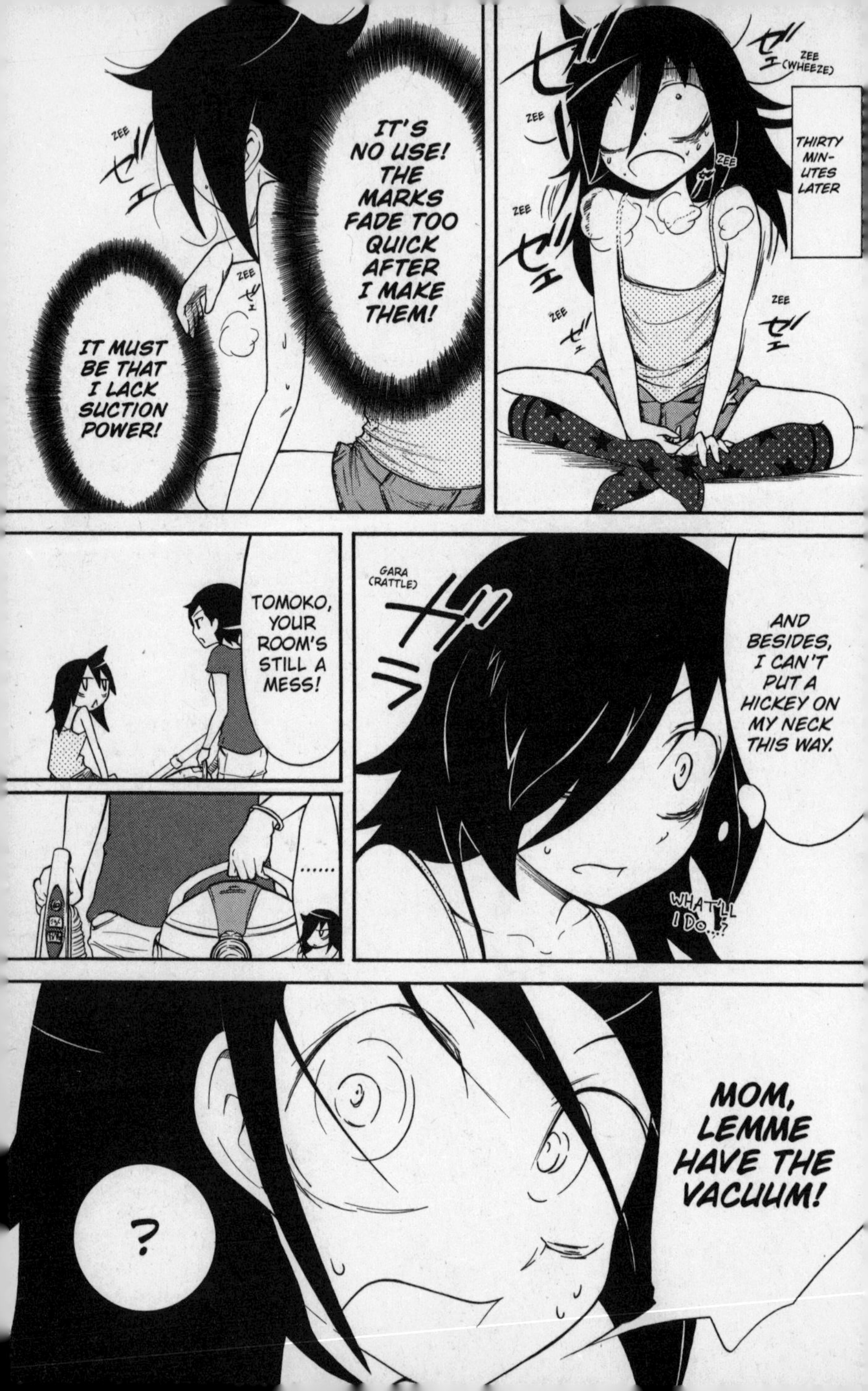
ZEE (WHEEZE)
THIRTY MINUTES LATER
ZEE
ZEE
ZEE
ZEE
ZEE
ZEE
IT'S NO USE! THE MARKS FADE TOO QUICK AFTER I MAKE THEM!
ZEE
IT MUST BE THAT I LACK SUCTION POWER!
GARA (RATTLE)
AND BESIDES, I CAN'T PUT A HICKEY ON MY NECK THIS WAY.
WHAT'LL I DO...?
TOMOKO, YOUR ROOM'S STILL A MESS!
......
MOM, LEMME HAVE THE VACUUM!
?

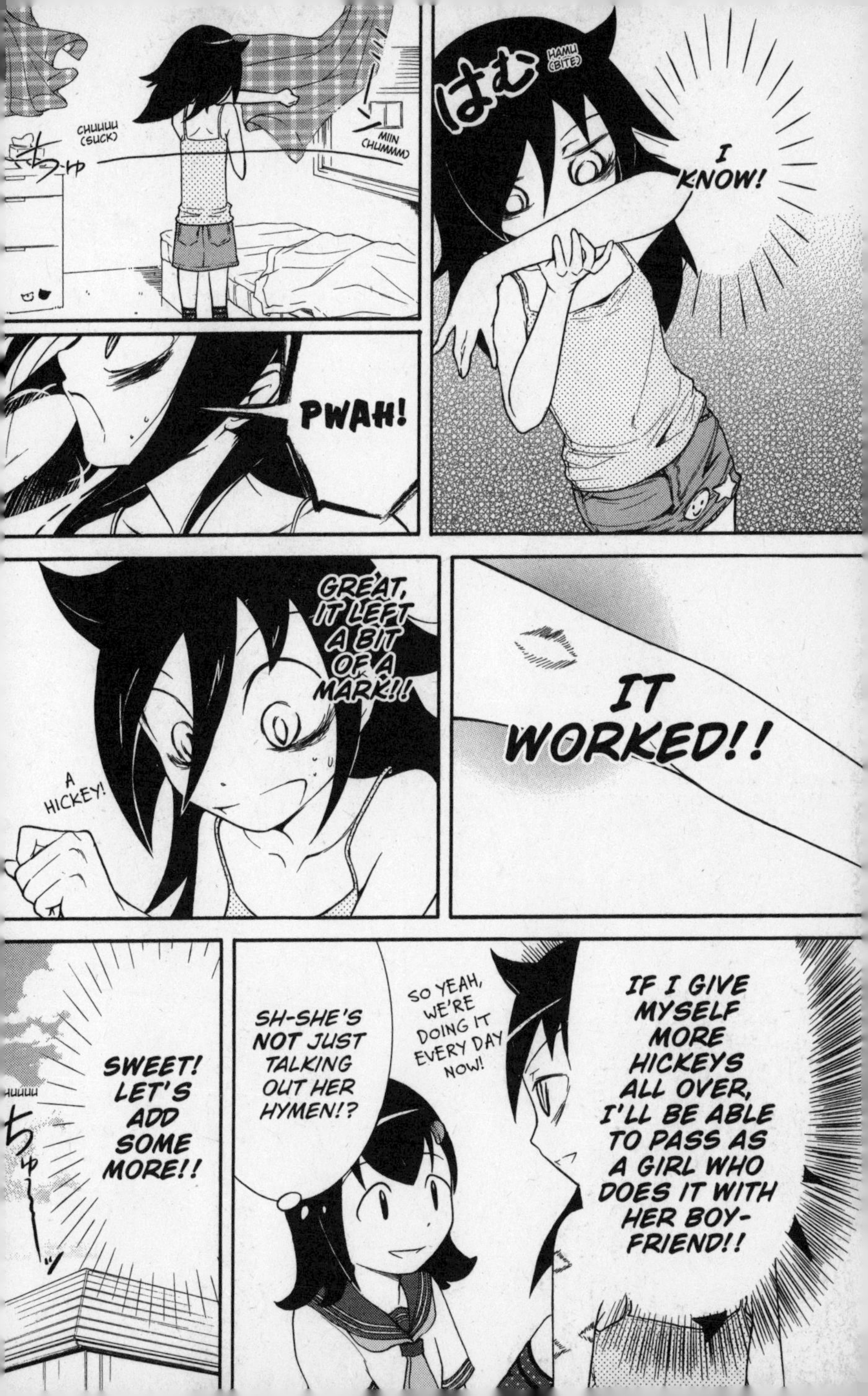
はむ
HAMU (BITE)
I KNOW!
MIIN (CHUMMM)
CHUUUU (SUCK)
PWAH!
IT WORKED!!
GREAT, IT LEFT A BIT OF A MARK!!
A HICKEY!
IF I GIVE MYSELF MORE HICKEYS ALL OVER, I'LL BE ABLE TO PASS AS A GIRL WHO DOES IT WITH HER BOY-FRIEND!!
SO YEAH, WE'RE DOING IT EVERY DAY NOW!
SH-SHE'S NOT JUST TALKING OUT HER HYMEN!?
SWEET! LET'S ADD SOME MORE!!

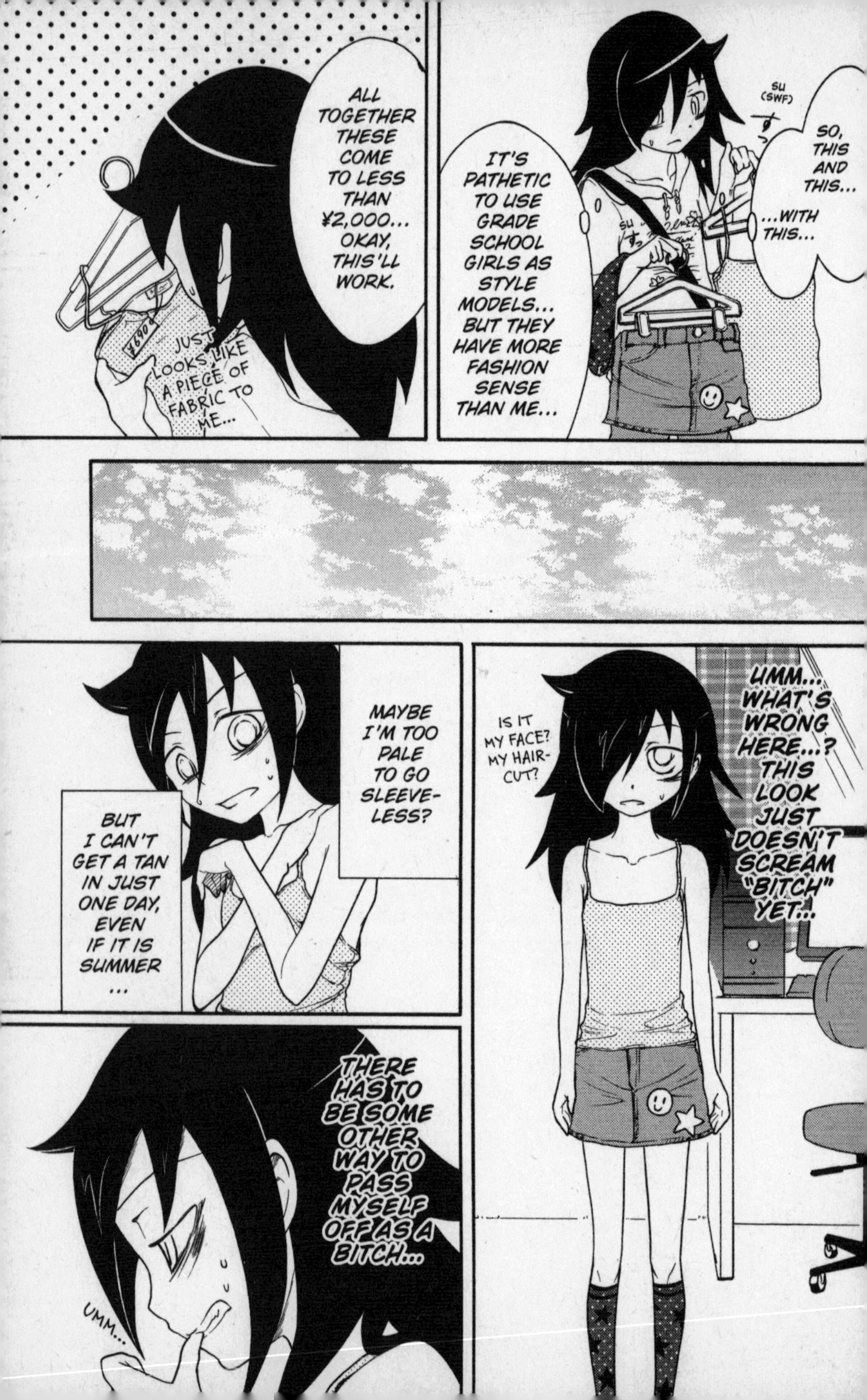
SU (SWF)
SO, THIS AND THIS... ...WITH THIS...
SU
IT'S PATHETIC TO USE GRADE SCHOOL GIRLS AS STYLE MODELS... BUT THEY HAVE MORE FASHION SENSE THAN ME...
ALL TOGETHER THESE COME TO LESS THAN ¥2,000... OKAY, THIS'LL WORK.
JUST LOOKS LIKE A PIECE OF FABRIC TO ME...
UMM... WHAT'S WRONG HERE...? THIS LOOK JUST DOESN'T SCREAM "BITCH" YET...
IS IT MY FACE? MY HAIRCUT?
MAYBE I'M TOO PALE TO GO SLEEVELESS?
BUT I CAN'T GET A TAN IN JUST ONE DAY, EVEN IF IT IS SUMMER...
THERE HAS TO BE SOME OTHER WAY TO PASS MYSELF OFF AS A BITCH...
UMM...

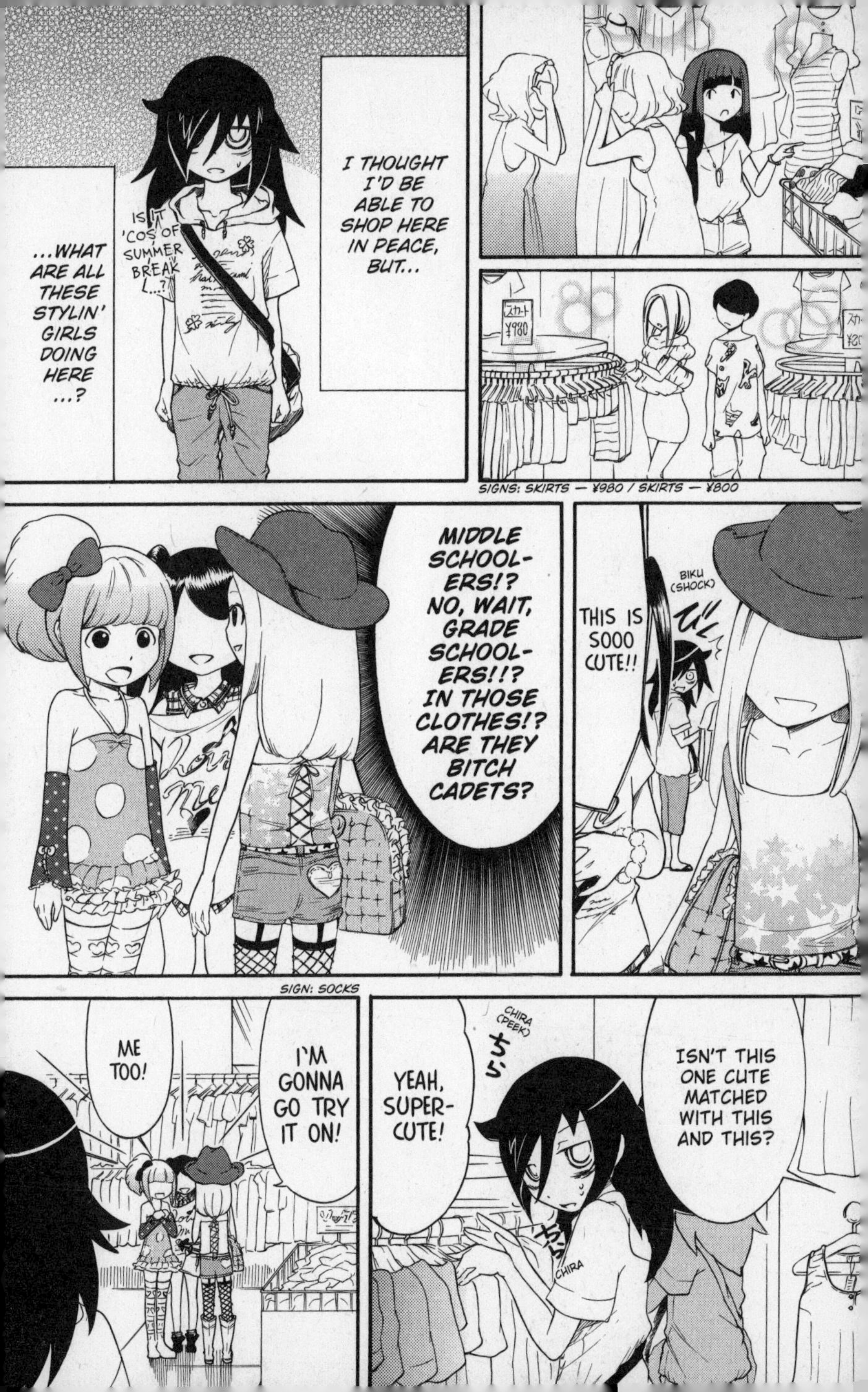
I THOUGHT I'D BE ABLE TO SHOP HERE IN PEACE, BUT...
IS IT 'COS OF SUMMER BREAK ...?
...WHAT ARE ALL THESE STYLIN' GIRLS DOING HERE ...?
SIGNS: SKIRTS — ¥980 / SKIRTS — ¥800
THIS IS SOOO CUTE!!
BIKU (SHOCK)
MIDDLE SCHOOLERS!? NO, WAIT, GRADE SCHOOLERS!!? IN THOSE CLOTHES!? ARE THEY BITCH CADETS?
SIGN: SOCKS
ISN'T THIS ONE CUTE MATCHED WITH THIS AND THIS?
CHIRA (PEEK)
YEAH, SUPER-CUTE!
CHIRA
I'M GONNA GO TRY IT ON!
ME TOO!

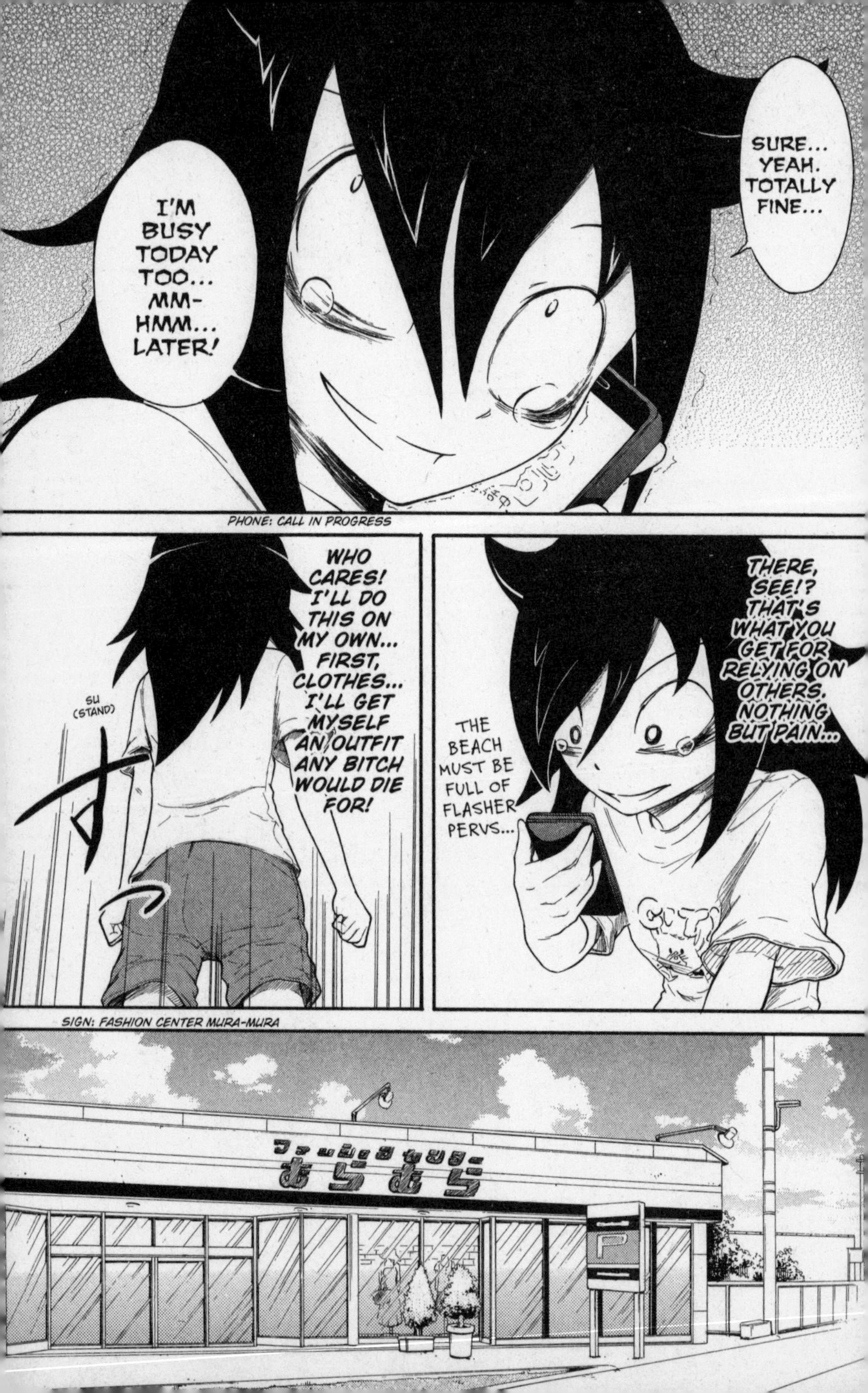
SURE... YEAH. TOTALLY FINE...
I'M BUSY TODAY TOO... MM-HMM... LATER!
PHONE: CALL IN PROGRESS
THERE, SEE!? THAT'S WHAT YOU GET FOR RELYING ON OTHERS. NOTHING BUT PAIN...
THE BEACH MUST BE FULL OF FLASHER PERVS...
WHO CARES! I'LL DO THIS ON MY OWN... FIRST, CLOTHES... I'LL GET MYSELF AN OUTFIT ANY BITCH WOULD DIE FOR!
SU (STAND)
SIGN: FASHION CENTER MURA-MURA

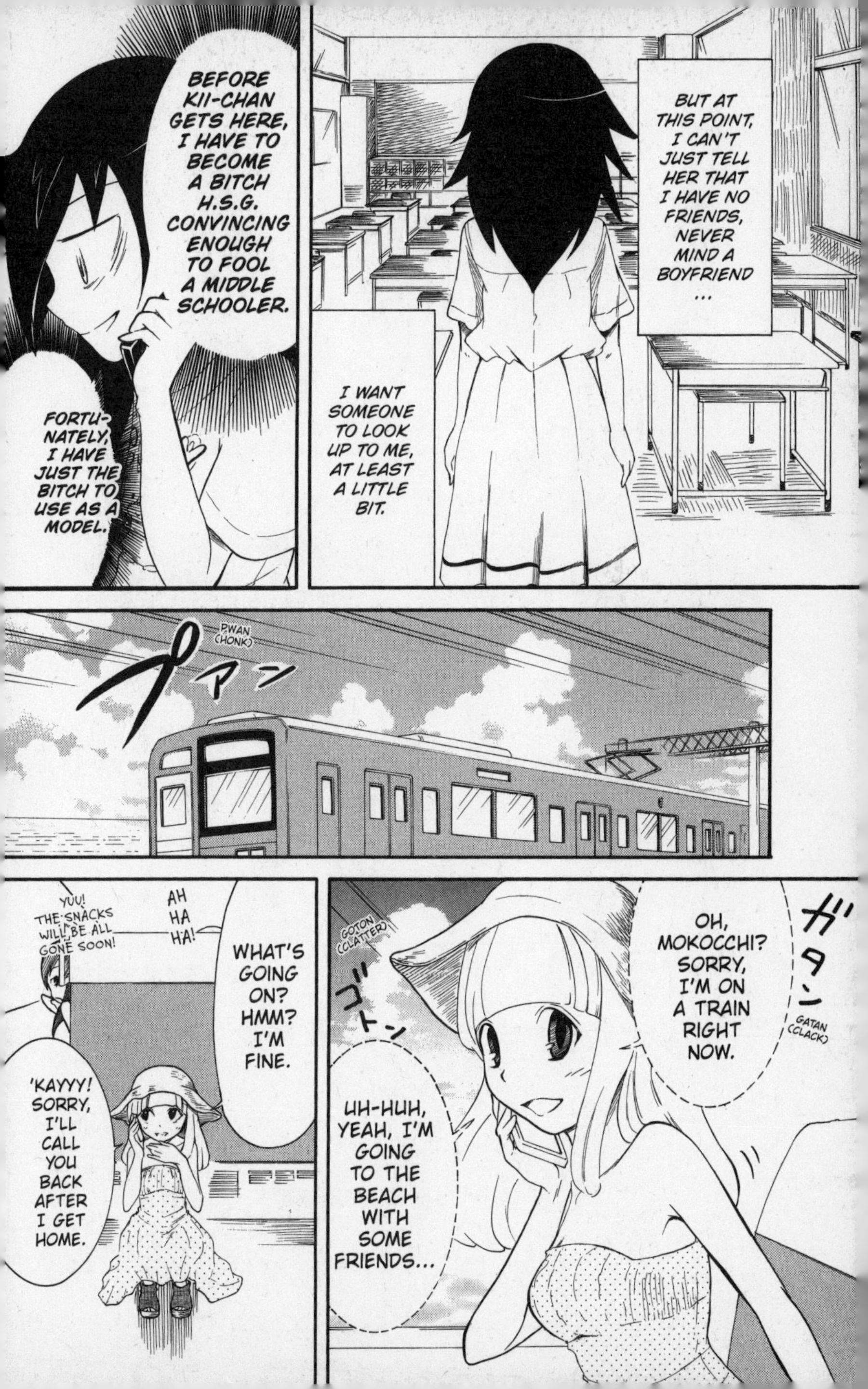
BUT AT THIS POINT, I CAN'T JUST TELL HER THAT I HAVE NO FRIENDS, NEVER MIND A BOYFRIEND...
I WANT SOMEONE TO LOOK UP TO ME, AT LEAST A LITTLE BIT.
BEFORE KII-CHAN GETS HERE, I HAVE TO BECOME A BITCH H.S.G. CONVINCING ENOUGH TO FOOL A MIDDLE SCHOOLER.
FORTU-NATELY, I HAVE JUST THE BITCH TO USE AS A MODEL.
PWAN (HONK)
GATAN (CLACK)
OH, MOKOCCHI? SORRY, I'M ON A TRAIN RIGHT NOW.
GOTON (CLATTER)
UH-HUH, YEAH, I'M GOING TO THE BEACH WITH SOME FRIENDS...
AH HA HA!
WHAT'S GOING ON? HMM? I'M FINE.
YUU! THE SNACKS WILL BE ALL GONE SOON!
'KAYYY! SORRY, I'LL CALL YOU BACK AFTER I GET HOME.

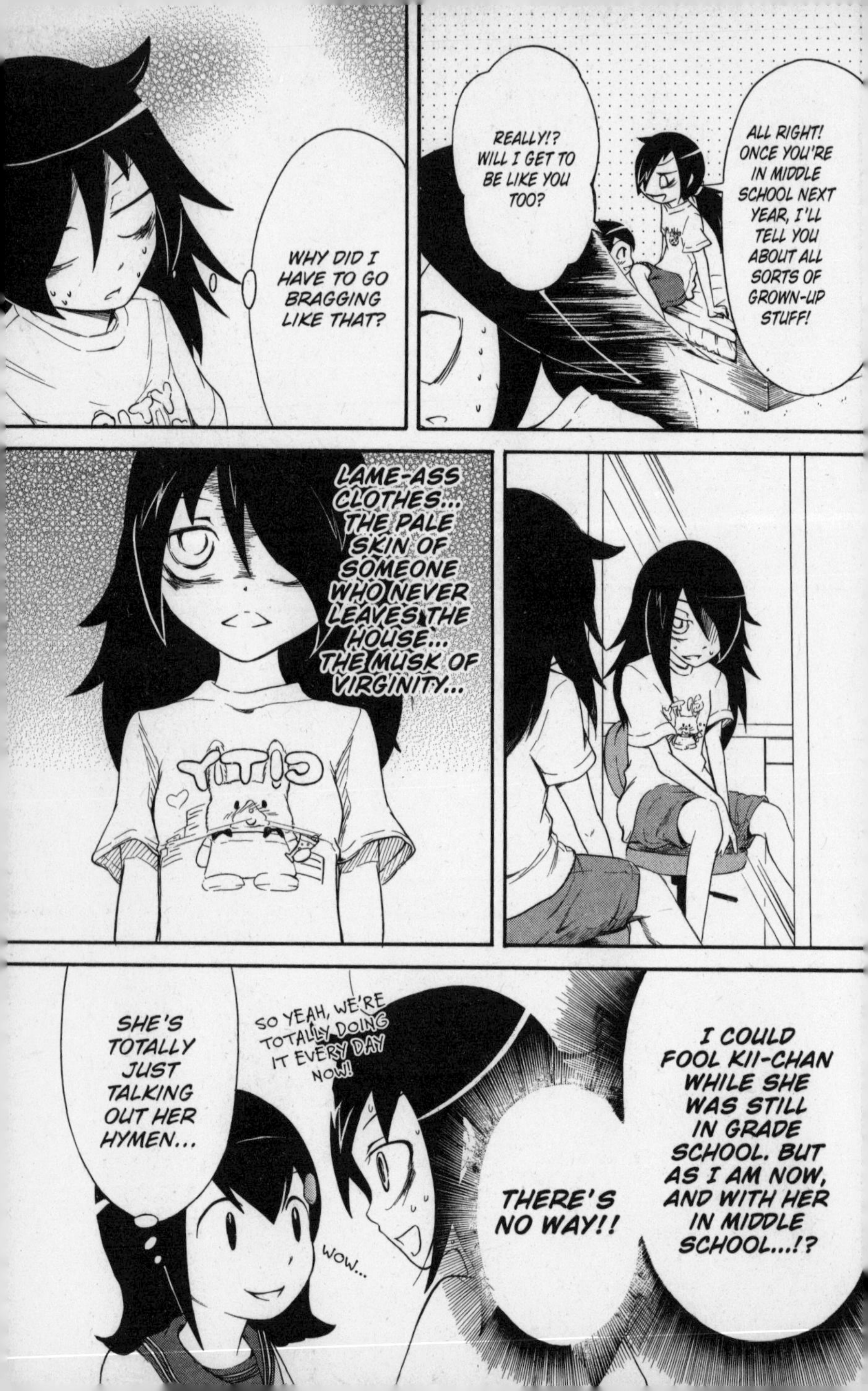
ALL RIGHT! ONCE YOU'RE IN MIDDLE SCHOOL NEXT YEAR, I'LL TELL YOU ABOUT ALL SORTS OF GROWN-UP STUFF!
REALLY!? WILL I GET TO BE LIKE YOU TOO?
WHY DID I HAVE TO GO BRAGGING LIKE THAT?
LAME-ASS CLOTHES... THE PALE SKIN OF SOMEONE WHO NEVER LEAVES THE HOUSE... THE MUSK OF VIRGINITY...
I COULD FOOL KII-CHAN WHILE SHE WAS STILL IN GRADE SCHOOL. BUT AS I AM NOW, AND WITH HER IN MIDDLE SCHOOL...!?
THERE'S NO WAY!!
SO YEAH, WE'RE TOTALLY DOING IT EVERY DAY NOW!
SHE'S TOTALLY JUST TALKING OUT HER HYMEN...
WOW...

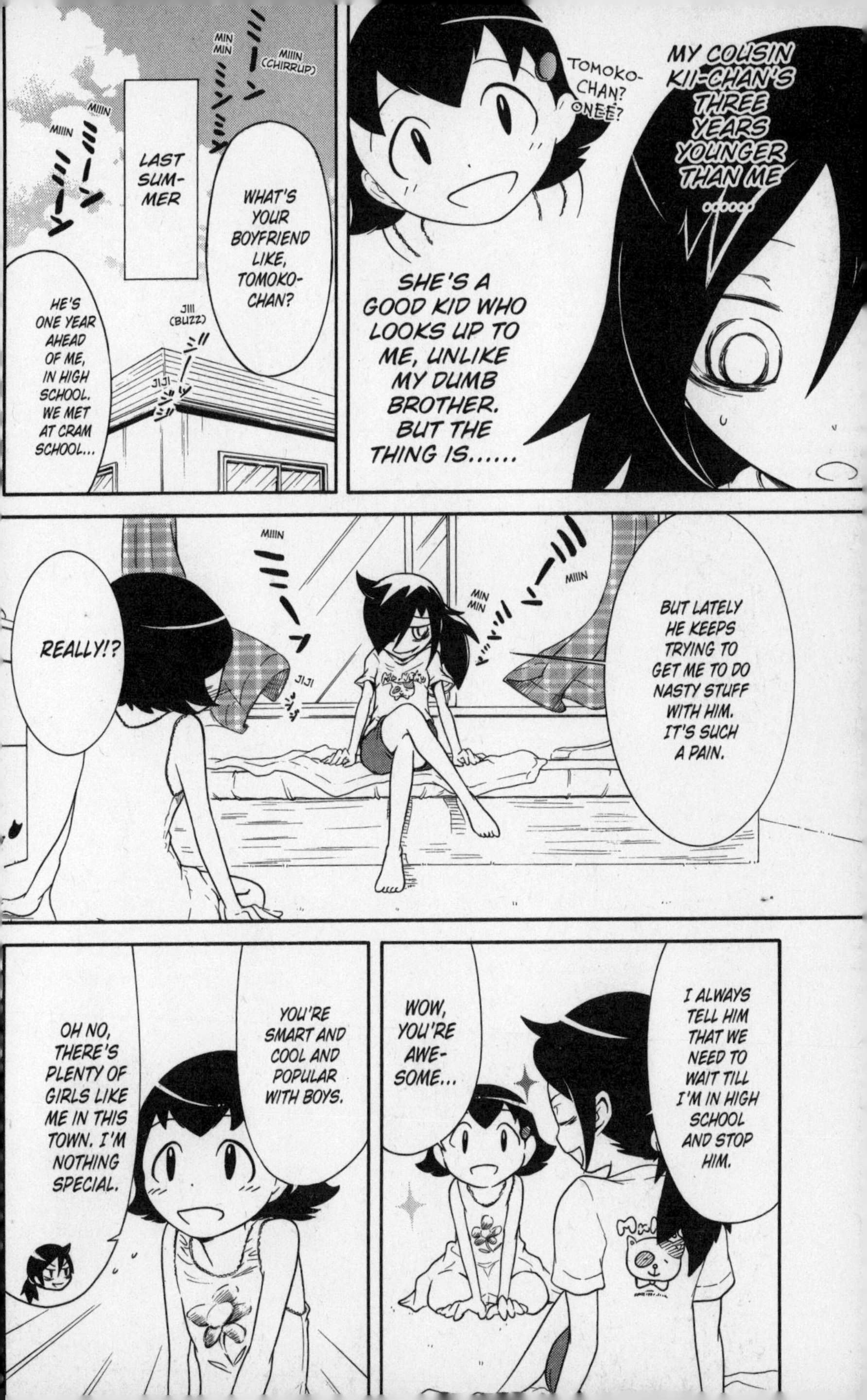
MY COUSIN KII-CHAN'S THREE YEARS YOUNGER THAN ME ......
TOMOKO-CHAN? ONEE?
SHE'S A GOOD KID WHO LOOKS UP TO ME, UNLIKE MY DUMB BROTHER. BUT THE THING IS......
MIN MIN
MIIIN (CHIRRUP)
MIIIN
MIIIN
LAST SUMMER
WHAT'S YOUR BOYFRIEND LIKE, TOMOKO-CHAN?
JIII (BUZZ)
JIJI
HE'S ONE YEAR AHEAD OF ME, IN HIGH SCHOOL. WE MET AT CRAM SCHOOL...
MIIIN
BUT LATELY HE KEEPS TRYING TO GET ME TO DO NASTY STUFF WITH HIM. IT'S SUCH A PAIN.
MIN MIN
MIIIN
JIJI
REALLY!?
I ALWAYS TELL HIM THAT WE NEED TO WAIT TILL I'M IN HIGH SCHOOL AND STOP HIM.
WOW, YOU'RE AWESOME...
YOU'RE SMART AND COOL AND POPULAR WITH BOYS.
OH NO, THERE'S PLENTY OF GIRLS LIKE ME IN THIS TOWN. I'M NOTHING SPECIAL.

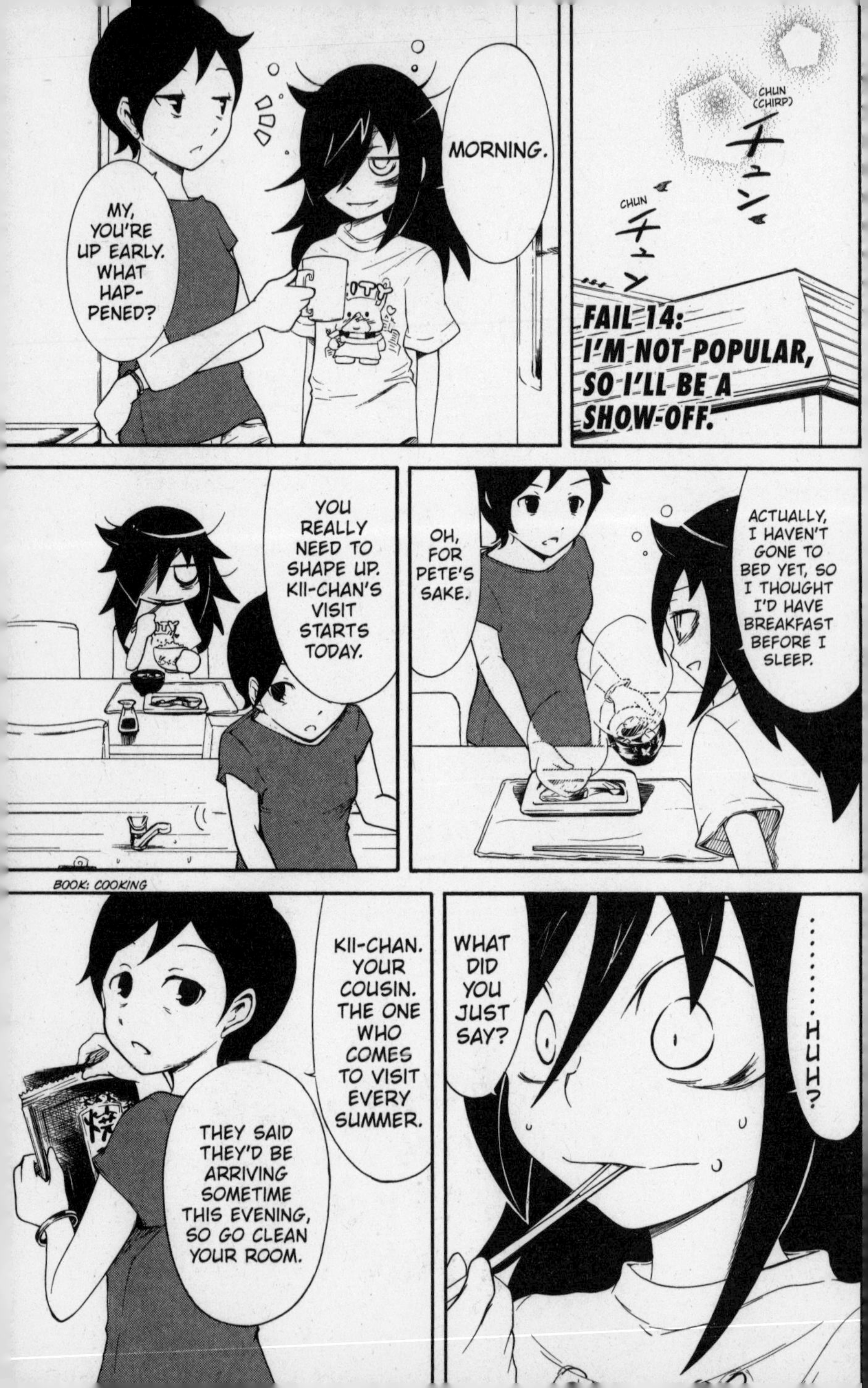

CHUN (CHIRP)
チュン
CHUN
チュン
FAIL 14: I'M NOT POPULAR, SO I'LL BE A SHOW-OFF.
MORNING.
MY, YOU'RE UP EARLY. WHAT HAPPENED?
ACTUALLY, I HAVEN'T GONE TO BED YET, SO I THOUGHT I'D HAVE BREAKFAST BEFORE I SLEEP.
OH, FOR PETE'S SAKE.
YOU REALLY NEED TO SHAPE UP. KII-CHAN'S VISIT STARTS TODAY.
......HUH?
WHAT DID YOU JUST SAY?
KII-CHAN. YOUR COUSIN. THE ONE WHO COMES TO VISIT EVERY SUMMER.
THEY SAID THEY'D BE ARRIVING SOMETIME THIS EVENING, SO GO CLEAN YOUR ROOM.
BOOK: COOKING

No Matter How I Look at It, It's You Guys' Fault I'm Not Popular!

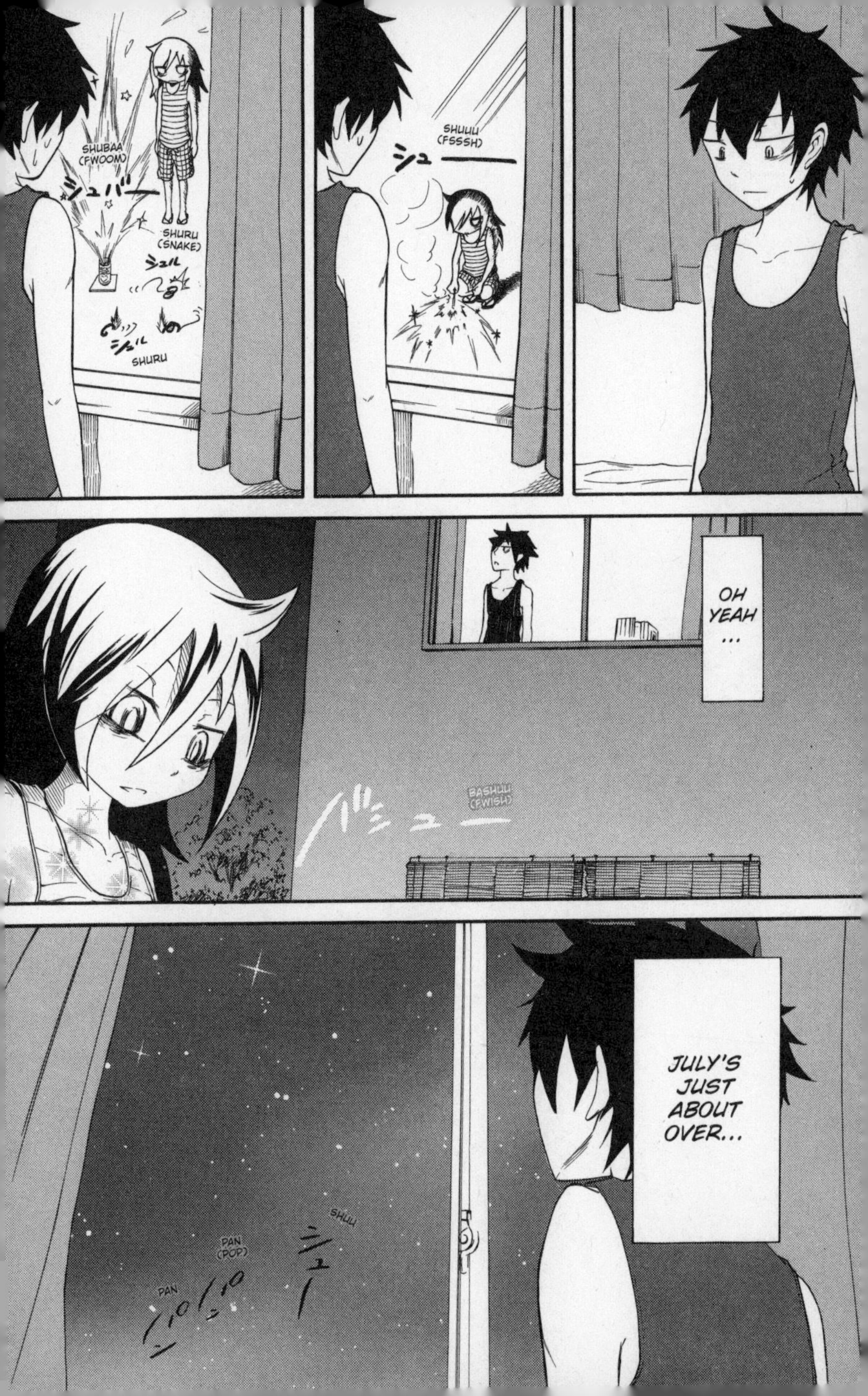
SHUUU (FSSSH)
シュー
SHUBAA (FWOOM)
シュバー
SHURU (SNAKE)
シュル
シュル
SHURU
OH YEAH ...
BASHUU (FWISH)
バシュー
JULY'S JUST ABOUT OVER...
SHUU
シュー
PAN (POP)
PAN

SEVENTH DAY

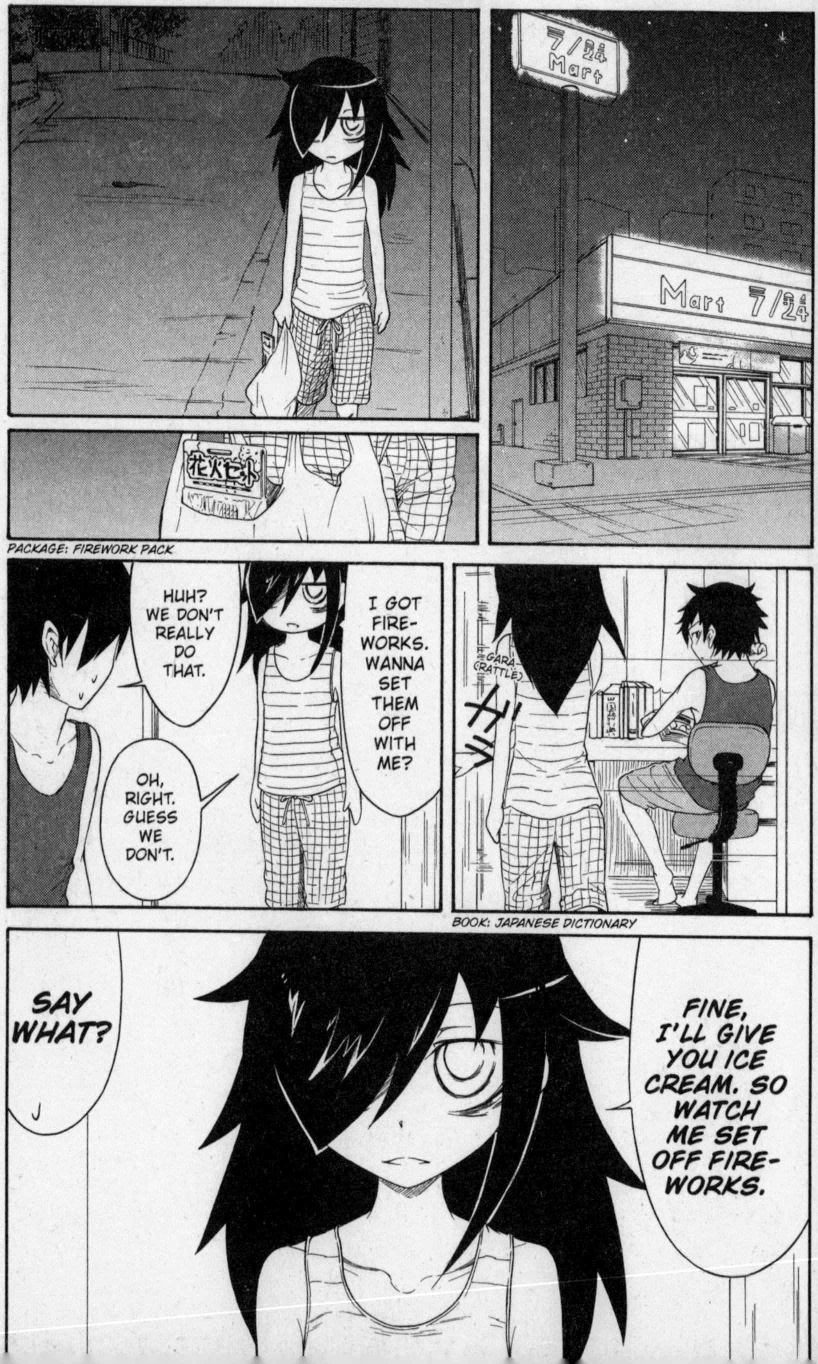
7/24 Mart
Mart 7/24
花火セット
PACKAGE: FIREWORK PACK
GARA (RATTLE)
ガラ
I GOT FIRE-WORKS. WANNA SET THEM OFF WITH ME?
HUH? WE DON'T REALLY DO THAT.
OH, RIGHT. GUESS WE DON'T.
BOOK: JAPANESE DICTIONARY
FINE, I'LL GIVE YOU ICE CREAM. SO WATCH ME SET OFF FIRE-WORKS.
SAY WHAT?

SIXTH DAY

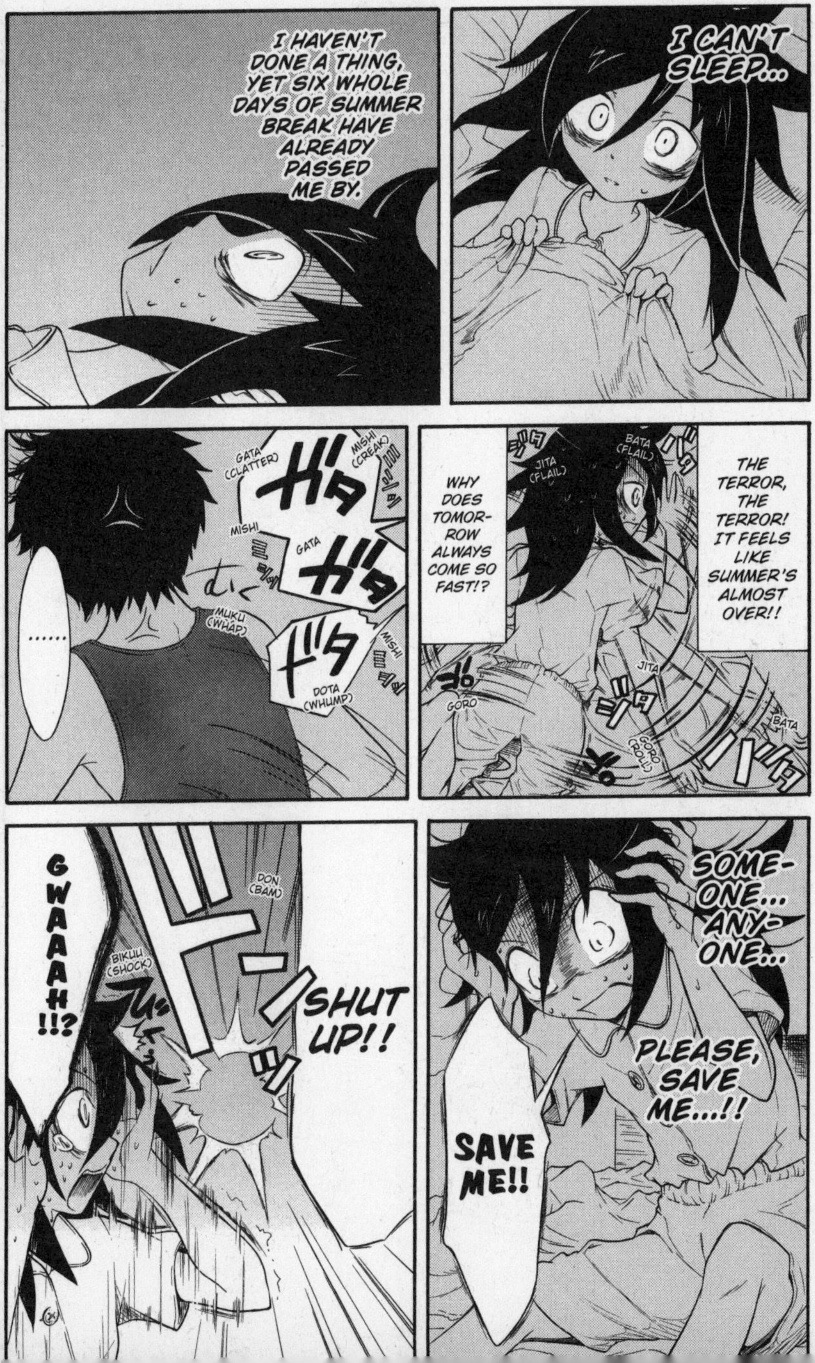
I CAN'T SLEEP...
I HAVEN'T DONE A THING, YET SIX WHOLE DAYS OF SUMMER BREAK HAVE ALREADY PASSED ME BY.
BATA (FLAIL)
JITA (FLAIL)
THE TERROR, THE TERROR! IT FEELS LIKE SUMMER'S ALMOST OVER!!
WHY DOES TOMOR-ROW ALWAYS COME SO FAST!?
JITA
BATA
GORO
GORO (ROLL)
MISHI (CREAK)
GATA (CLATTER)
MISHI
GATA
MUKU (WHAP)
MISHI
DOTA (WHUMP)
......
SOME-ONE... ANY-ONE...
PLEASE, SAVE ME...!!
SAVE ME!!
DON (BAM)
SHUT UP!!
BIKUU (SHOCK)
GWAAAAH!!?

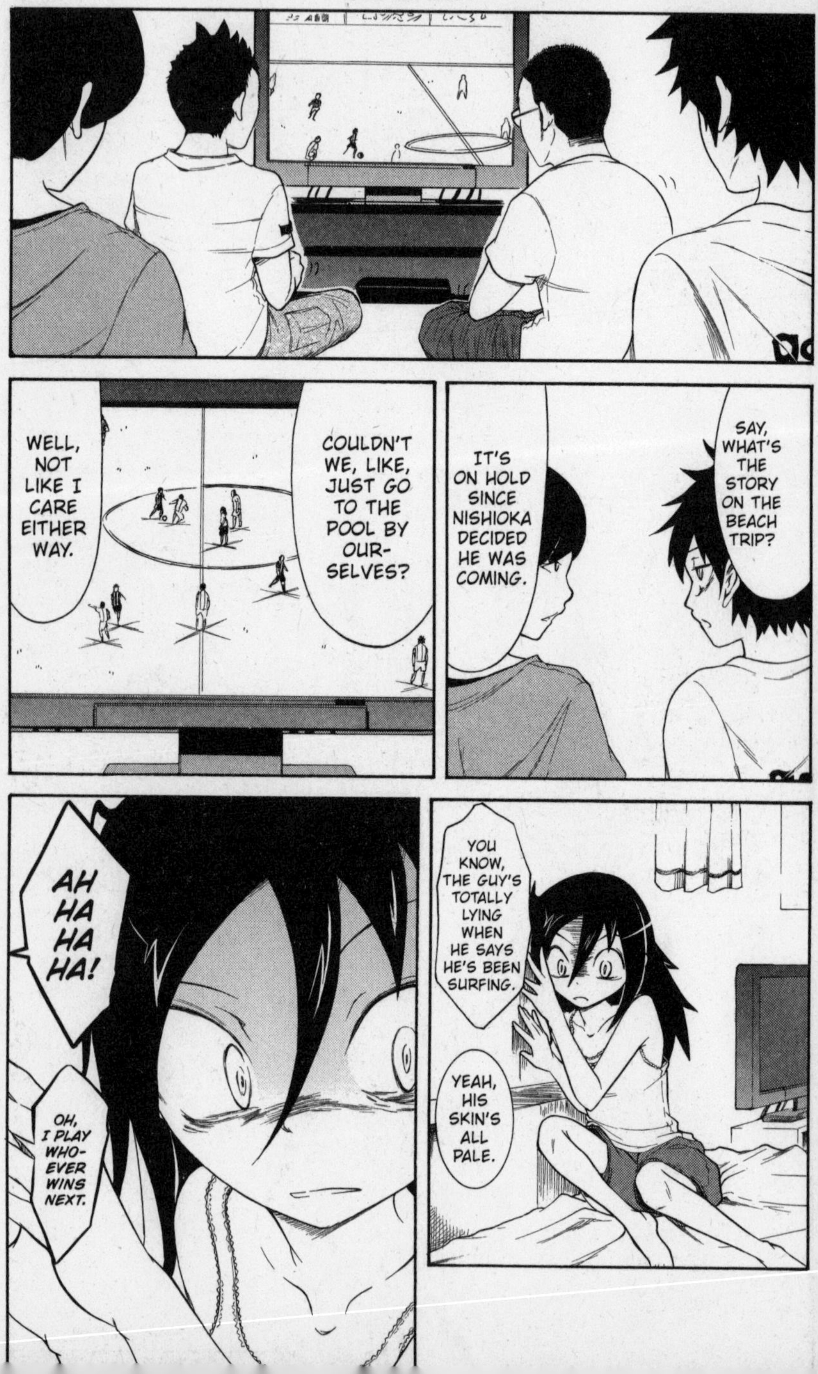
SAY, WHAT'S THE STORY ON THE BEACH TRIP?
IT'S ON HOLD SINCE NISHIOKA DECIDED HE WAS COMING.
COULDN'T WE, LIKE, JUST GO TO THE POOL BY OUR-SELVES?
WELL, NOT LIKE I CARE EITHER WAY.
YOU KNOW, THE GUY'S TOTALLY LYING WHEN HE SAYS HE'S BEEN SURFING.
YEAH, HIS SKIN'S ALL PALE.
AH HA HA HA!
OH, I PLAY WHO-EVER WINS NEXT.

FOURTH DAY

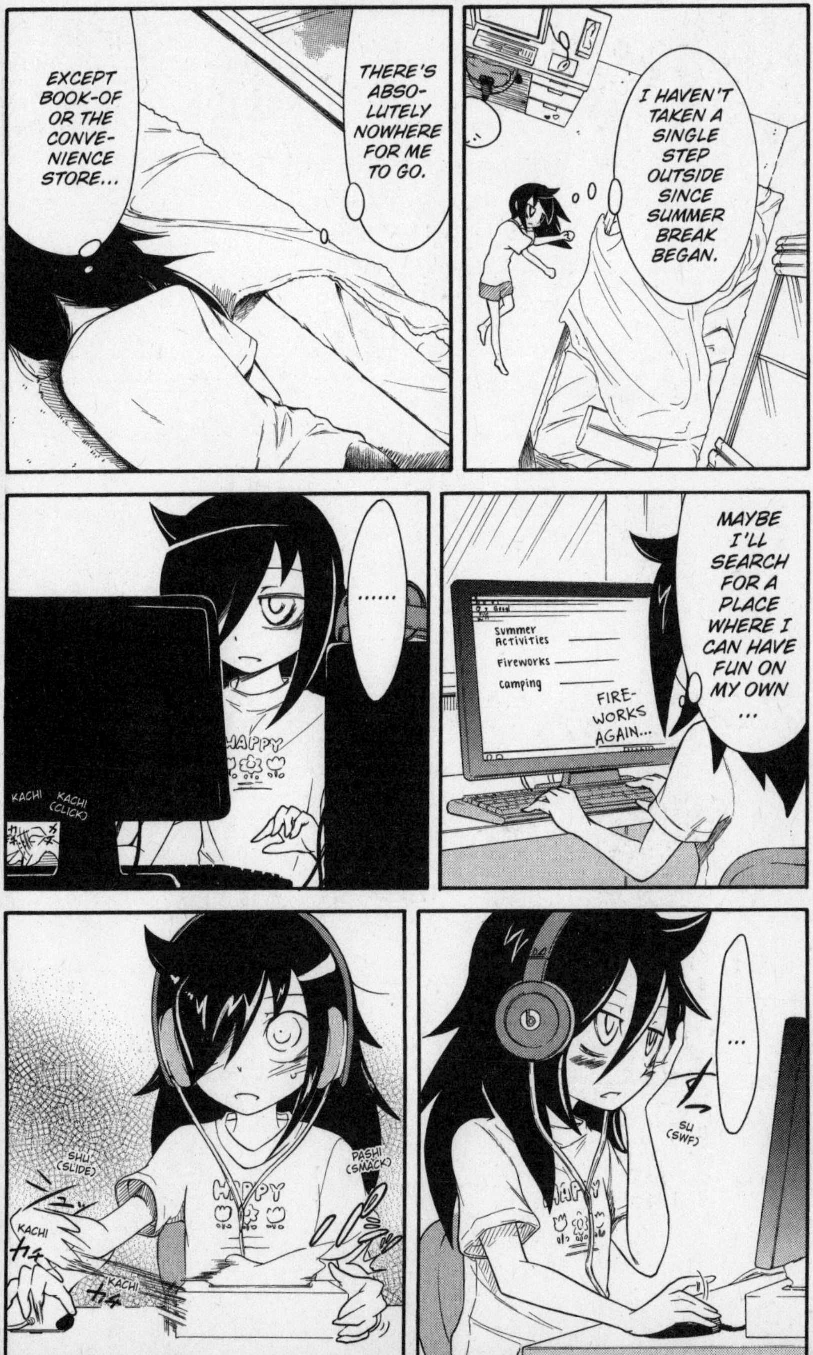
I HAVEN'T TAKEN A SINGLE STEP OUTSIDE SINCE SUMMER BREAK BEGAN.
THERE'S ABSO-LUTELY NOWHERE FOR ME TO GO.
EXCEPT BOOK-OF OR THE CONVE-NIENCE STORE...
MAYBE I'LL SEARCH FOR A PLACE WHERE I CAN HAVE FUN ON MY OWN ...
Summer Activities
Fireworks
Camping
FIRE-WORKS AGAIN...
......
KACHI
KACHI (CLICK)
...
SU (SWF)
PASHI (SMACK)
SHU (SLIDE)
KACHI
KACHI

ADMITTING

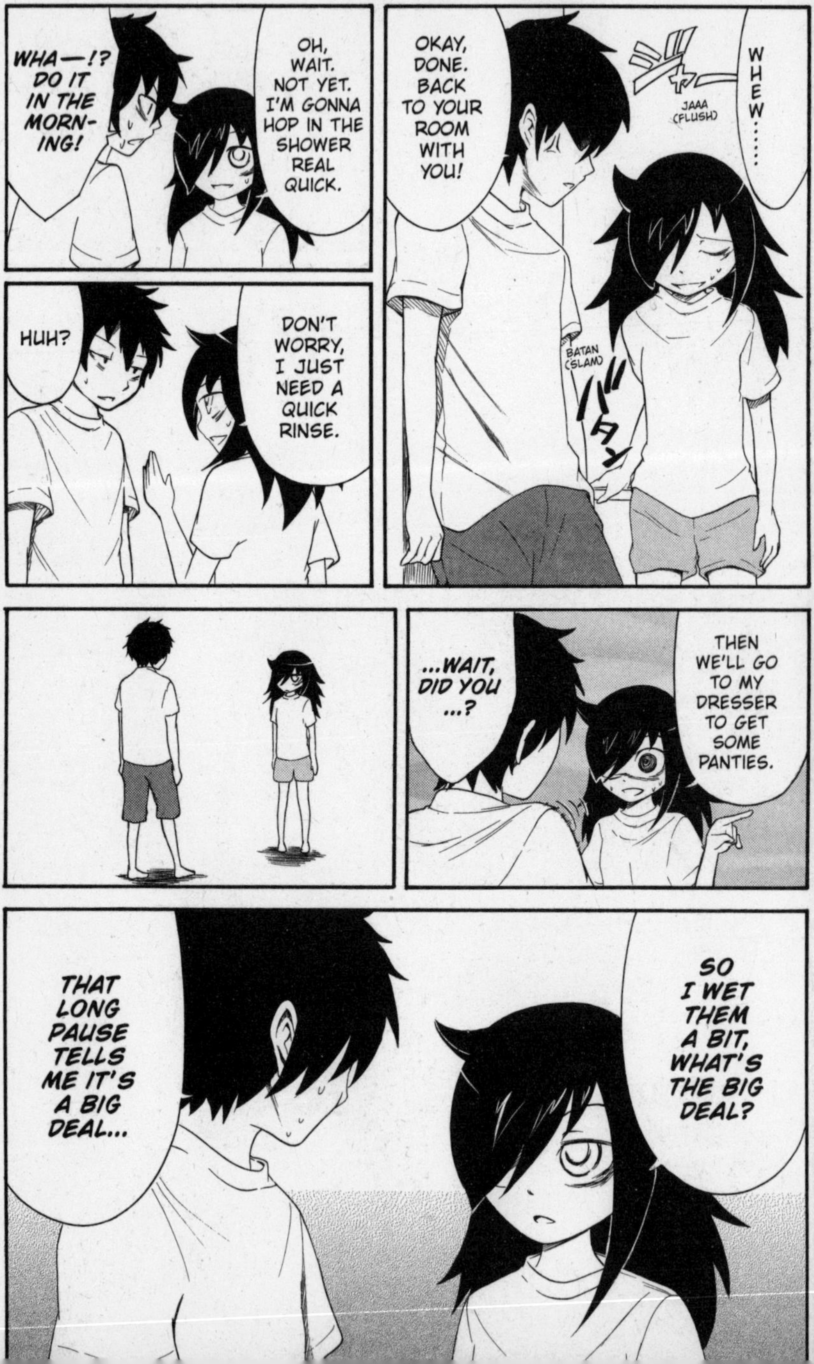
WHEW......
JAAA (FLUSH)
OKAY, DONE. BACK TO YOUR ROOM WITH YOU!
BATAN (SLAM)
OH, WAIT. NOT YET. I'M GONNA HOP IN THE SHOWER REAL QUICK.
WHA—!? DO IT IN THE MORNING!
DON'T WORRY, I JUST NEED A QUICK RINSE.
HUH?
THEN WE'LL GO TO MY DRESSER TO GET SOME PANTIES.
...WAIT, DID YOU ...?
SO I WET THEM A BIT, WHAT'S THE BIG DEAL?
THAT LONG PAUSE TELLS ME IT'S A BIG DEAL...

GIRL POWER

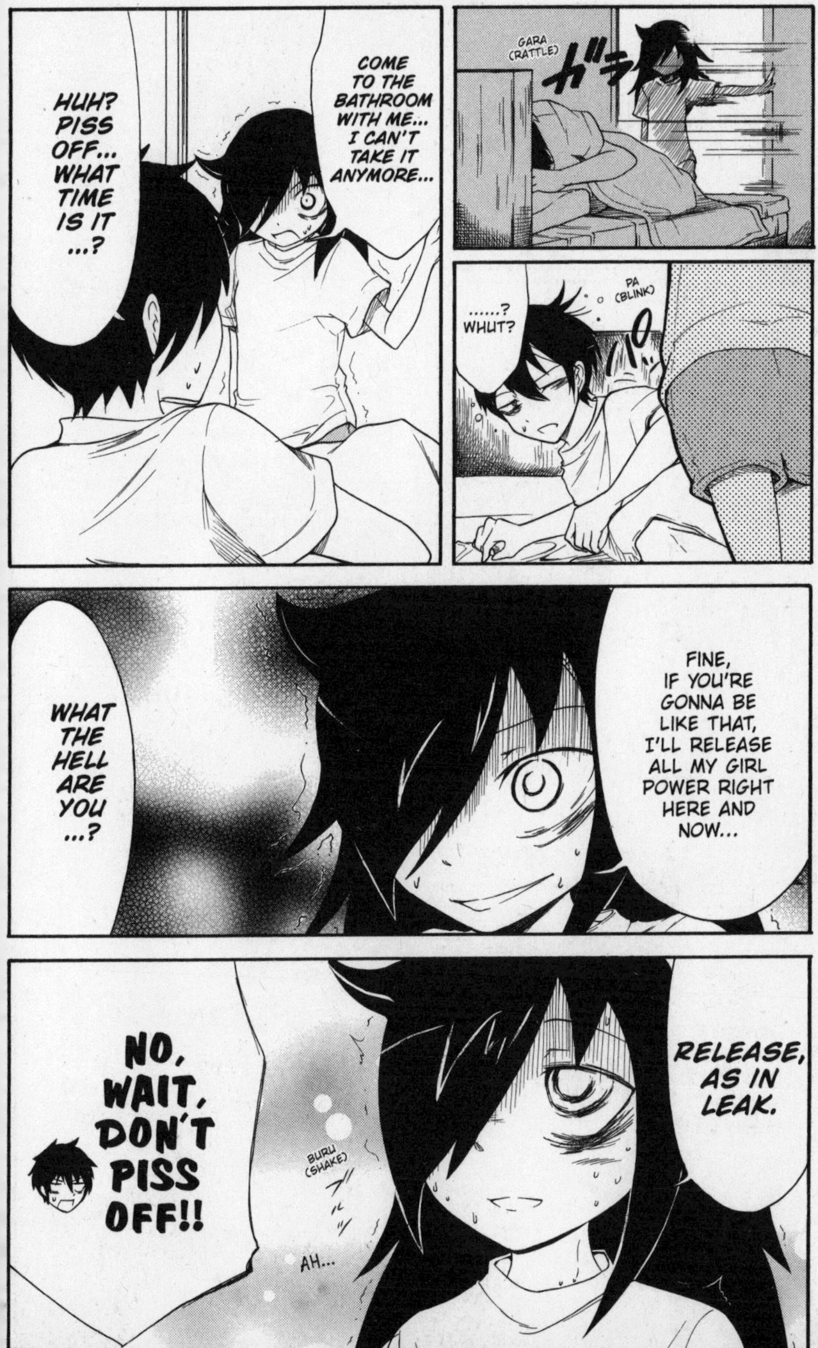
GARA (RATTLE)
PA (BLINK)
......? WHUT?
COME TO THE BATHROOM WITH ME... I CAN'T TAKE IT ANYMORE...
HUH? PISS OFF... WHAT TIME IS IT ...?
FINE, IF YOU'RE GONNA BE LIKE THAT, I'LL RELEASE ALL MY GIRL POWER RIGHT HERE AND NOW...
WHAT THE HELL ARE YOU ...?
RELEASE, AS IN LEAK.
BURU (SHAKE)
AH...
NO, WAIT, DON'T PISS OFF!!

DAY 3

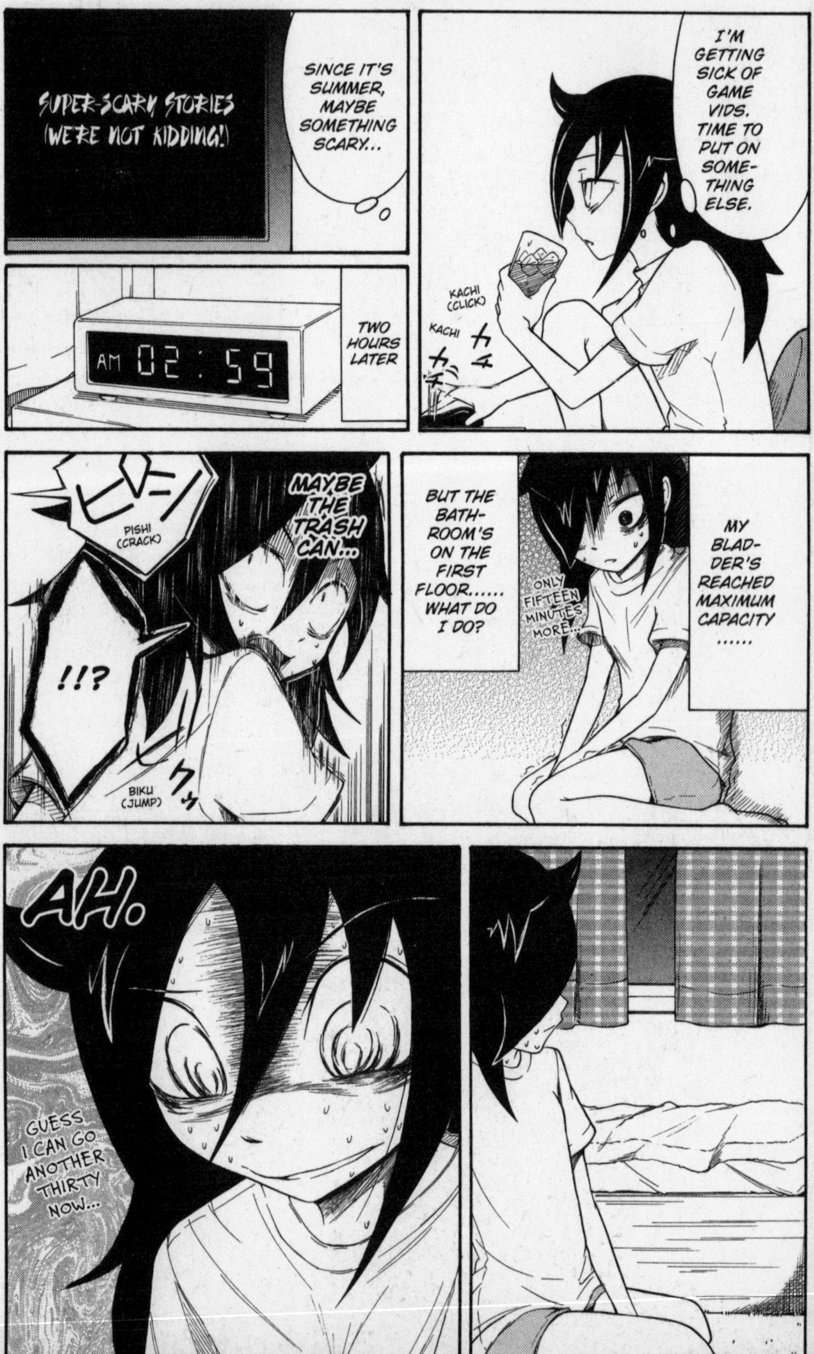
I'M GETTING SICK OF GAME VIDS. TIME TO PUT ON SOMETHING ELSE.
KACHI (CLICK)
KACHI
SINCE IT'S SUMMER, MAYBE SOMETHING SCARY...
SUPER-SCARY STORIES (WE'RE NOT KIDDING!)
TWO HOURS LATER
AM 02:59
MY BLADDER'S REACHED MAXIMUM CAPACITY ......
BUT THE BATHROOM'S ON THE FIRST FLOOR...... WHAT DO I DO?
ONLY FIFTEEN MINUTES MORE...
MAYBE THE TRASH CAN...
PISHI (CRACK)
!!?
BIKU (JUMP)
AH.
GUESS I CAN GO ANOTHER THIRTY NOW...

DAY 2

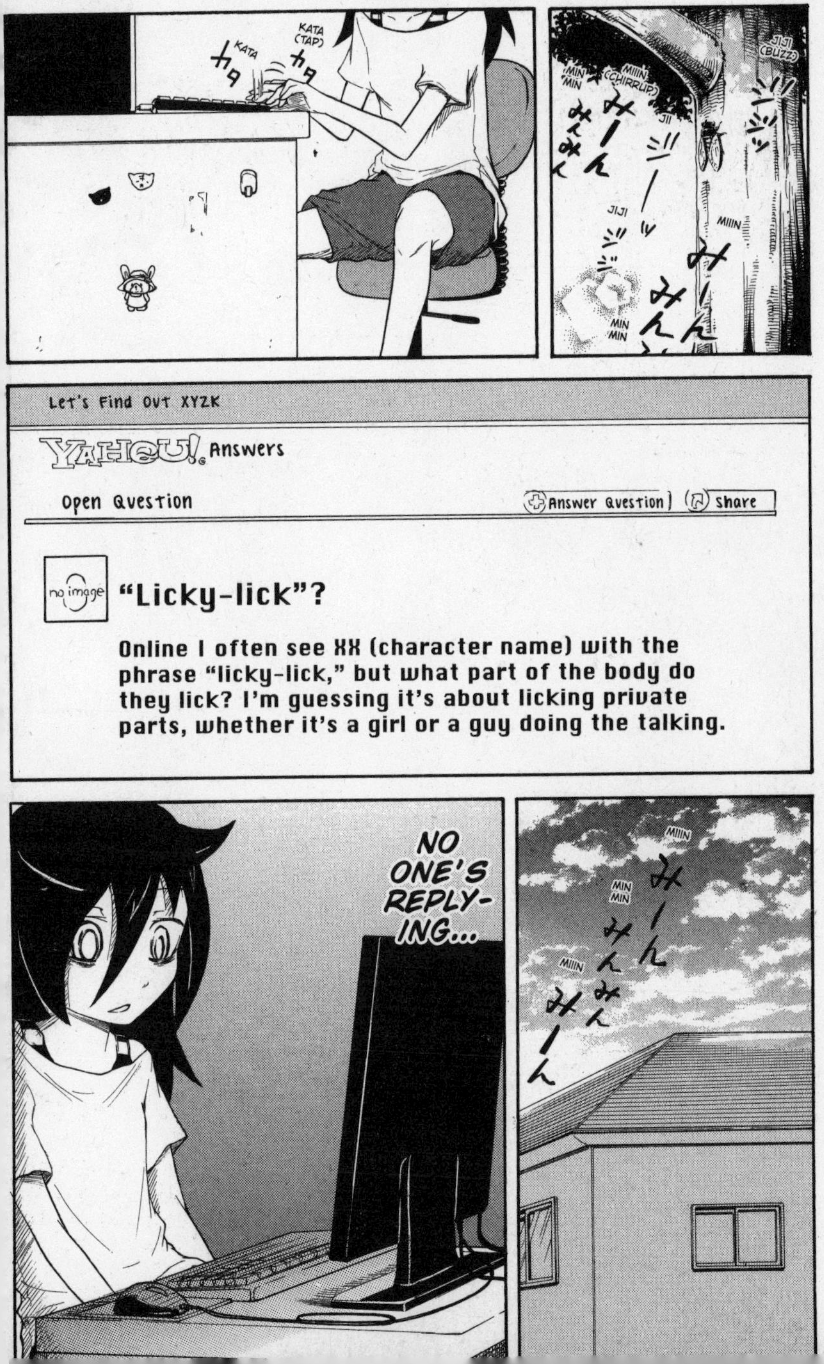
JIJI (BUZZ)
MIIN (CHIRRUP)
MIN MIN
JIJI
MIIN
JIJI
MIN MIN
KATA (TAP)
KATA
Let's Find Out XYZK
YAHOU! Answers
Open Question
Answer Question
Share
no image
"Licky-lick"?
Online I often see XX (character name) with the phrase "licky-lick," but what part of the body do they lick? I'm guessing it's about licking private parts, whether it's a girl or a guy doing the talking.
MIIN
MIN MIN
MIIN
NO ONE'S REPLY-ING...

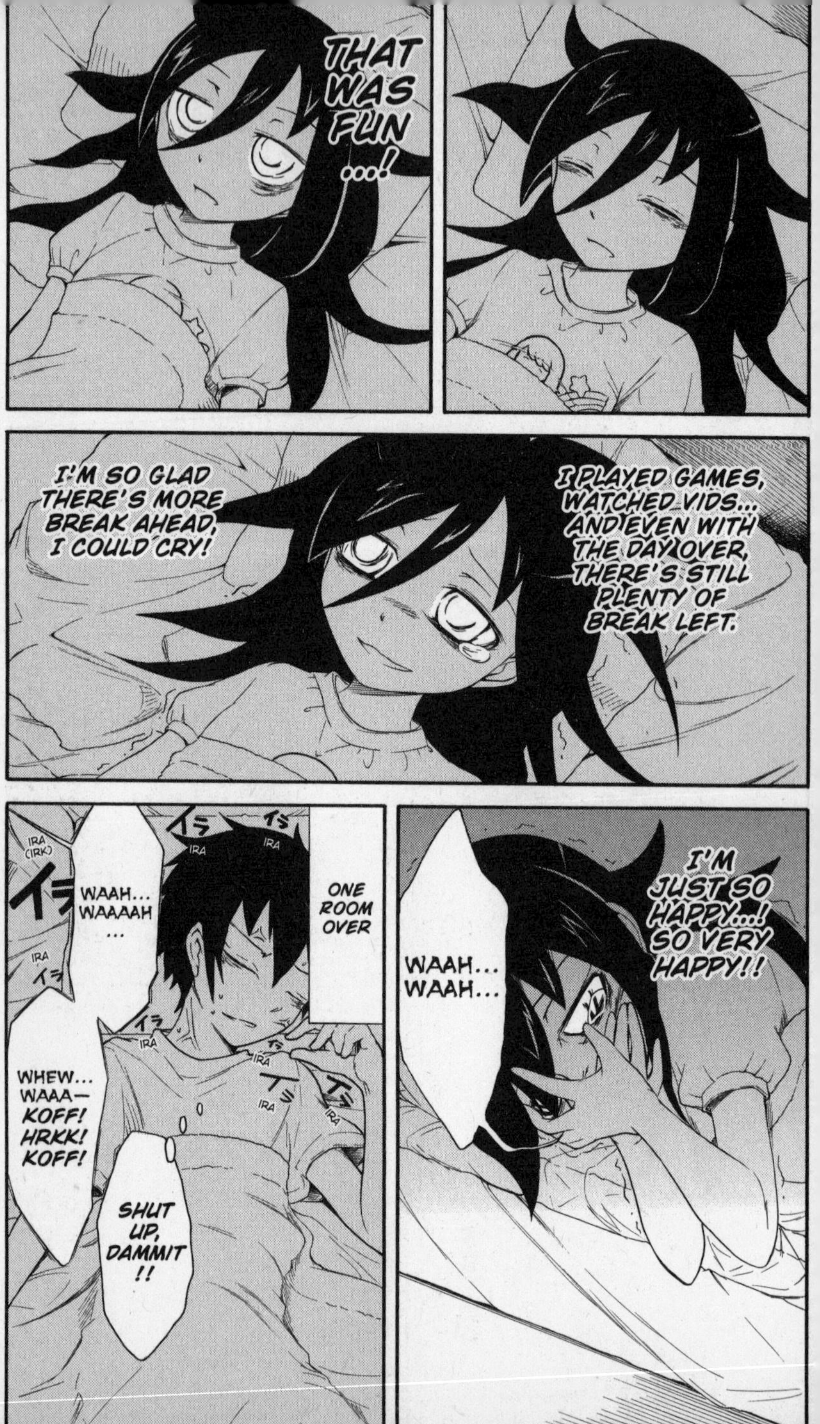
THAT WAS FUN ...!
I PLAYED GAMES, WATCHED VIDS... AND EVEN WITH THE DAY OVER, THERE'S STILL PLENTY OF BREAK LEFT.
I'M SO GLAD THERE'S MORE BREAK AHEAD, I COULD CRY!
I'M JUST SO HAPPY...! SO VERY HAPPY!!
WAAH... WAAH...
ONE ROOM OVER
IRA (IRK)
WAAH... WAAAAH ...
WHEW... WAAA—KOFF! HRKK! KOFF!
SHUT UP, DAMMIT!!

SUMMER BREAK, DAY 1

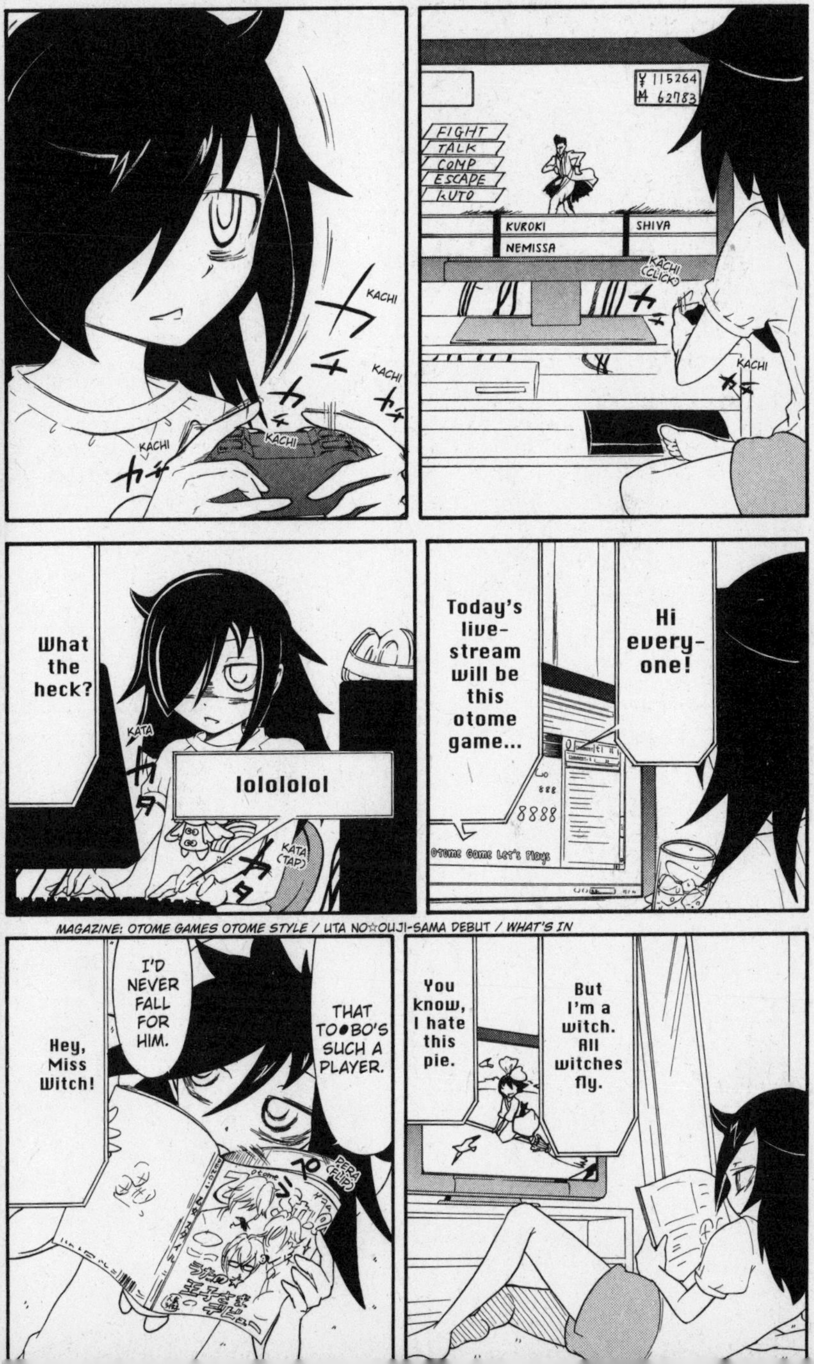
¥115264
M 62783
FIGHT
TALK
COMP
ESCAPE
KUROKI
SHIVA
NEMISSA
KACHI (CLICK)
KACHI
KACHI
KACHI
KACHI
KACHI
Hi everyone!
Today's live-stream will be this otome game...
888
8888
Otome Game Let's Plays
lolololol
What the heck?
KATA
KATA (TAP)
MAGAZINE: OTOME GAMES OTOME STYLE / UTA NO☆OUJI-SAMA DEBUT / WHAT'S IN
But I'm a witch. All witches fly.
You know, I hate this pie.
THAT TO●BO'S SUCH A PLAYER.
I'D NEVER FALL FOR HIM.
Hey, Miss Witch!
PERA (FLIP)

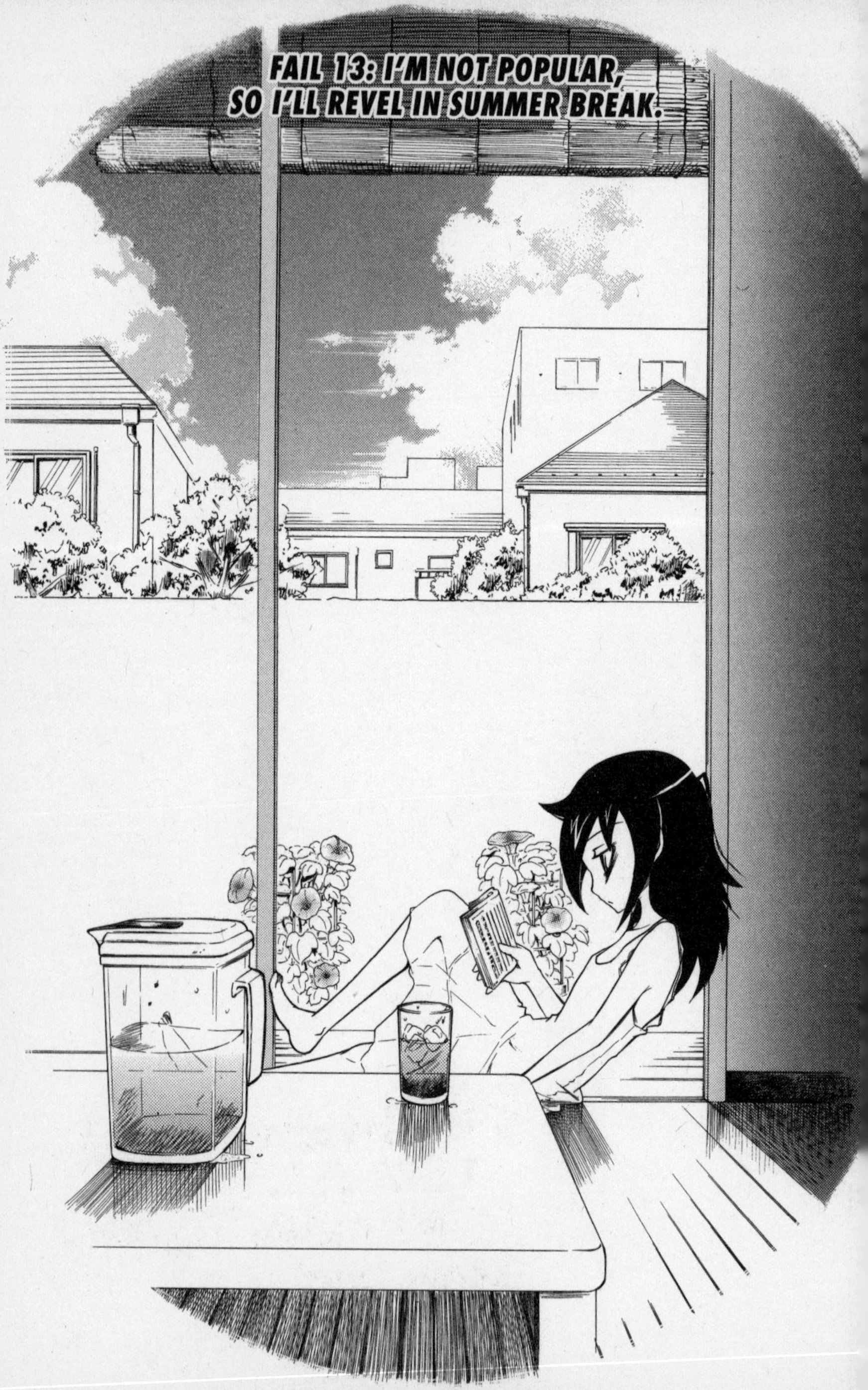
FAIL 13: I'M NOT POPULAR, SO I'LL REVEL IN SUMMER BREAK.

No Matter How I Look at It, It's You Guys' Fault I'm Not Popular!

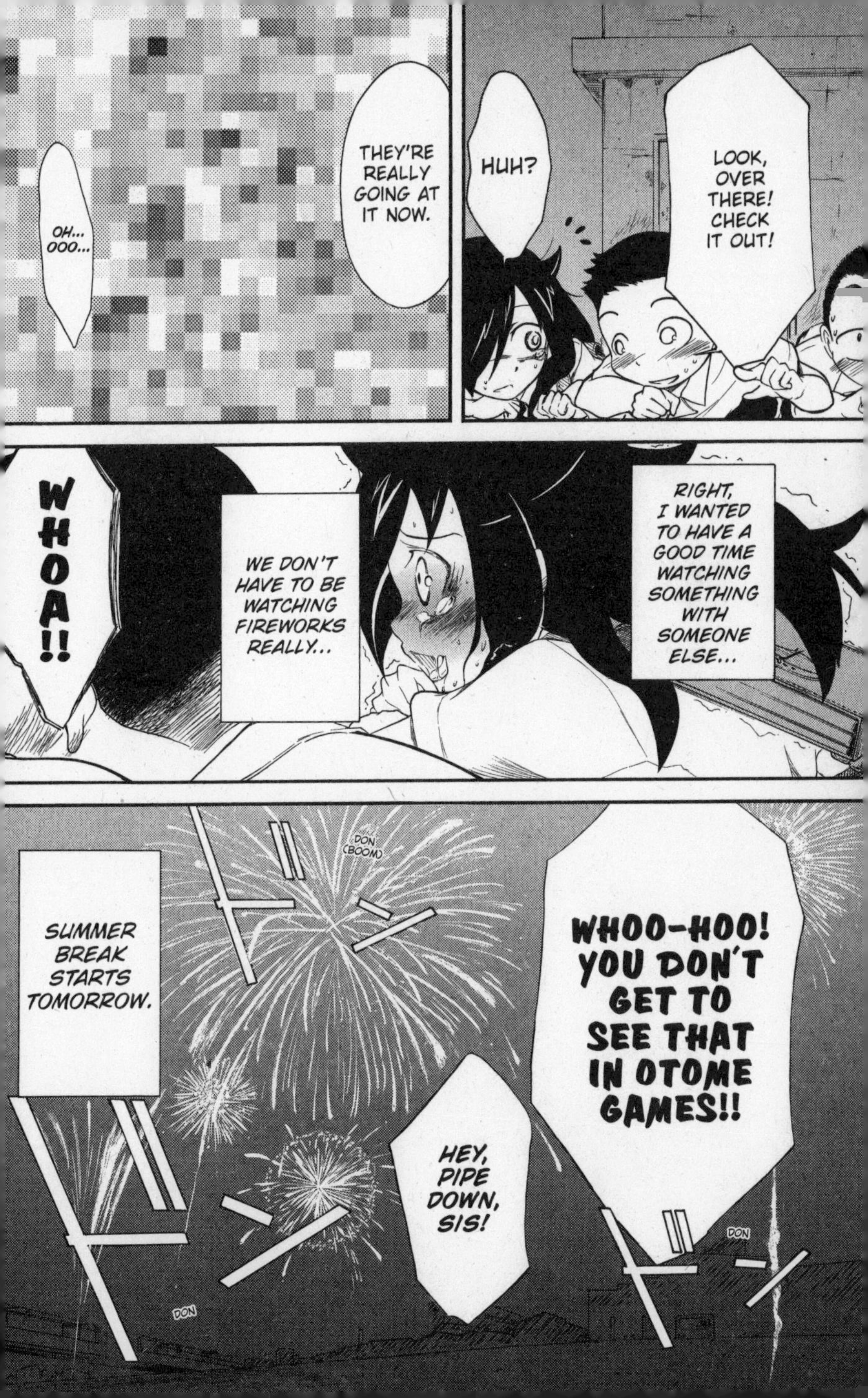
LOOK, OVER THERE! CHECK IT OUT!
HUH?
THEY'RE REALLY GOING AT IT NOW.
OH... OOO...
RIGHT, I WANTED TO HAVE A GOOD TIME WATCHING SOMETHING WITH SOMEONE ELSE...
WE DON'T HAVE TO BE WATCHING FIREWORKS REALLY...
WHOA!!
WHOO-HOO! YOU DON'T GET TO SEE THAT IN OTOME GAMES!!
DON (BOOM)
SUMMER BREAK STARTS TOMORROW.
HEY, PIPE DOWN, SIS!
DON
DON

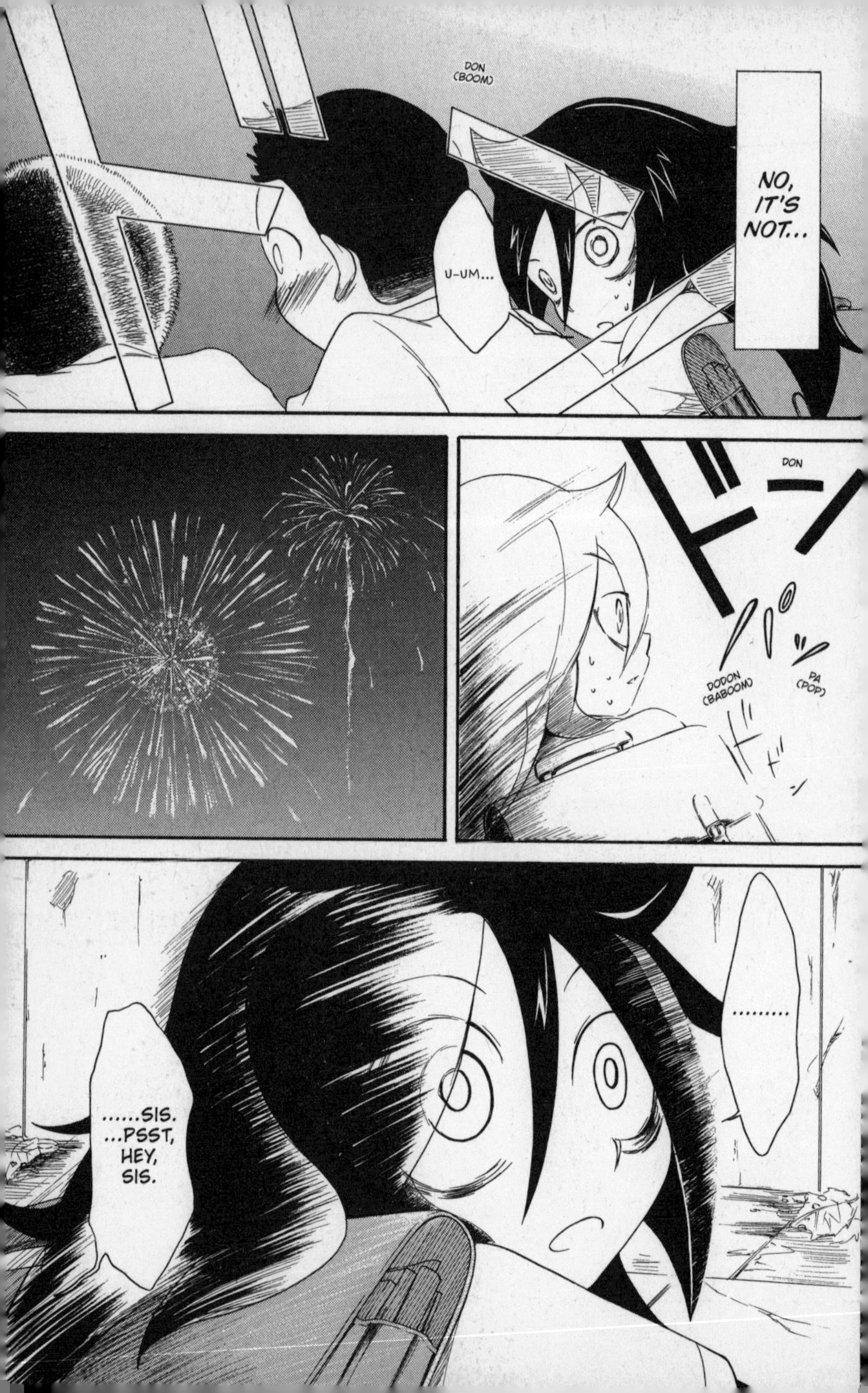
NO, IT'S NOT...
DON (BOOM)
U-UM...
DON
PA (POP)
DODON (BABOOM)
....
......SIS. ...PSST, HEY, SIS.

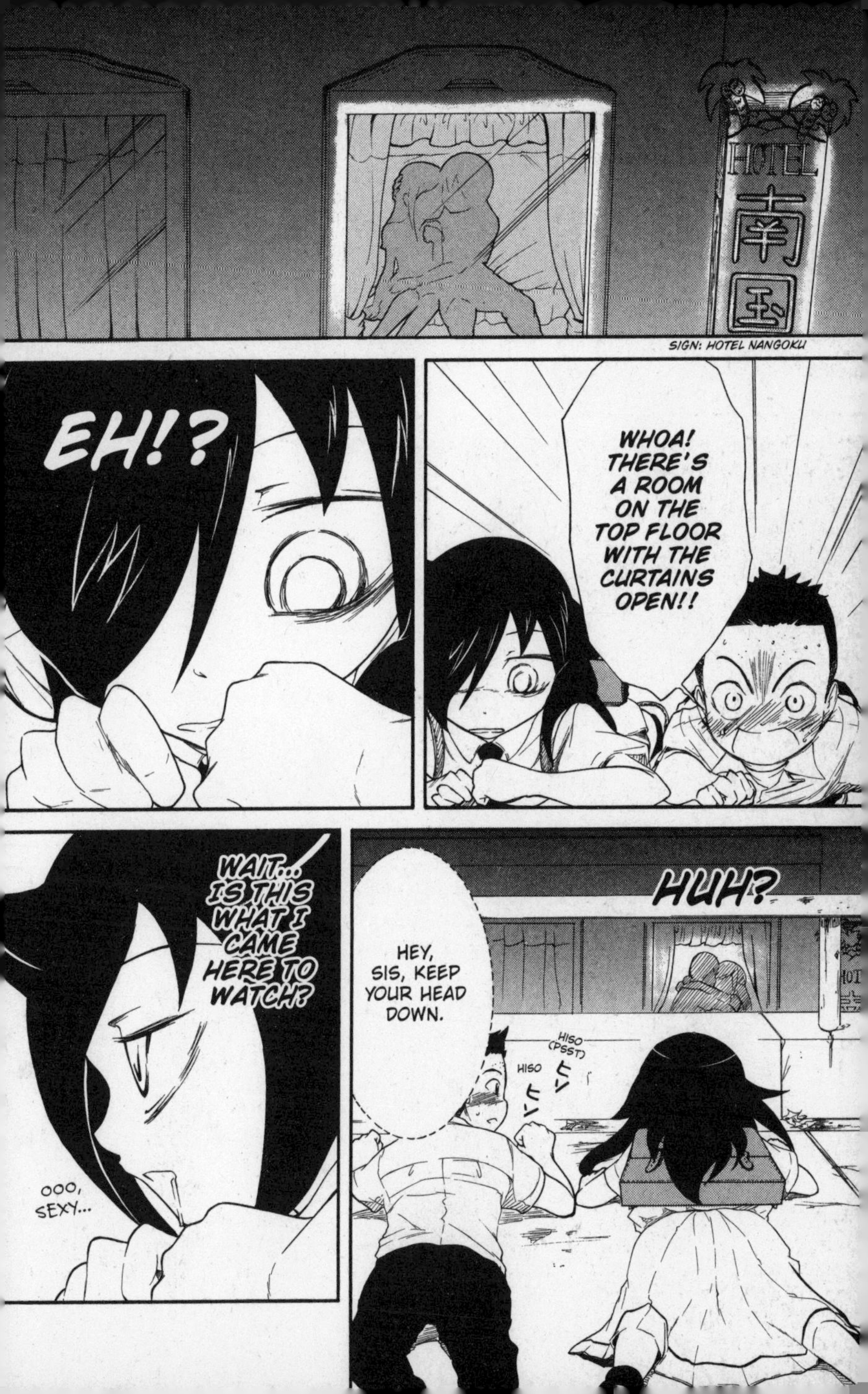
HOTEL
南国
SIGN: HOTEL NANGOKU
WHOA! THERE'S A ROOM ON THE TOP FLOOR WITH THE CURTAINS OPEN!!
EH!?
HUH?
HEY, SIS, KEEP YOUR HEAD DOWN.
HISO (PSST)
HISO
WAIT... IS THIS WHAT I CAME HERE TO WATCH?
OOO, SEXY...

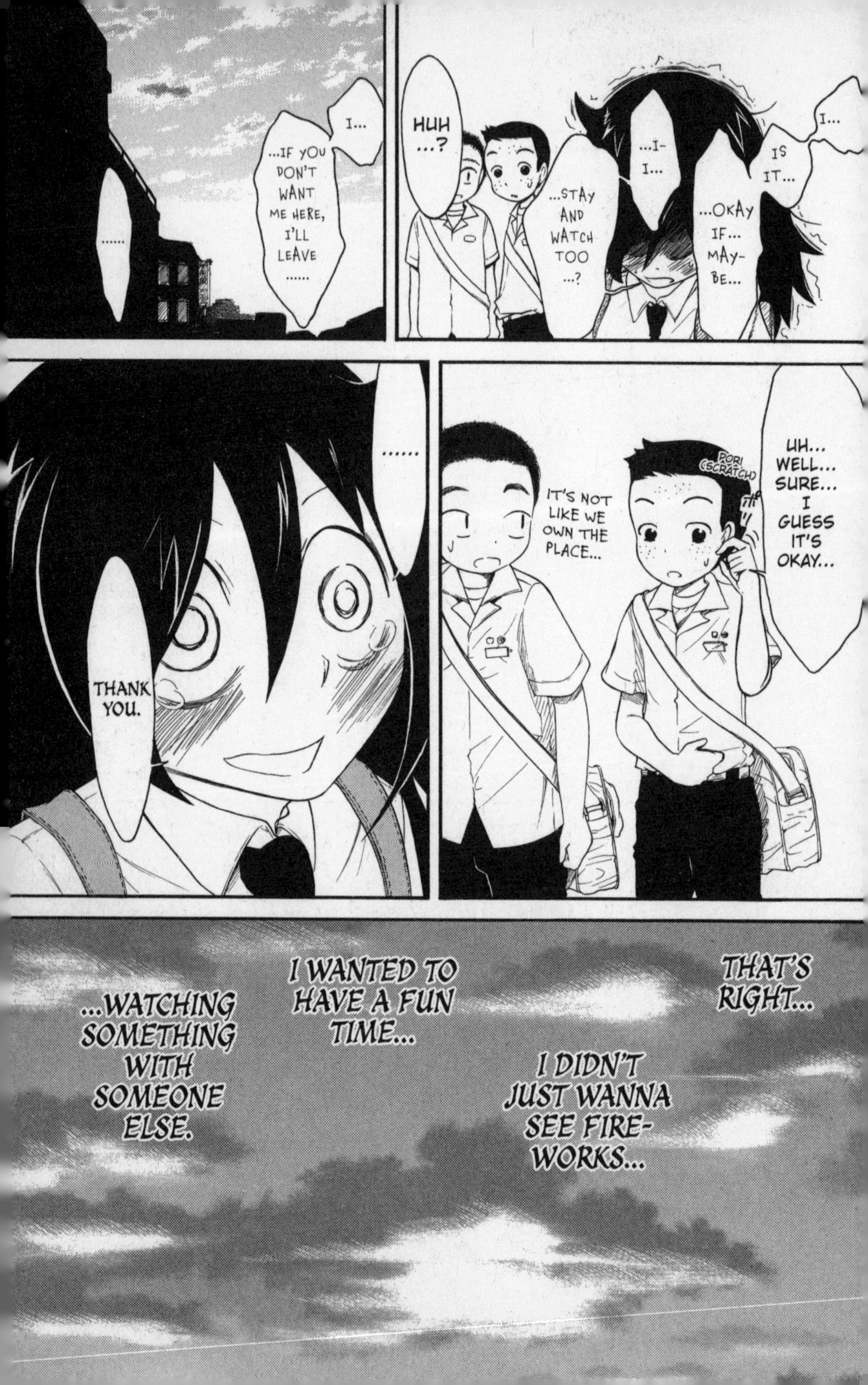
I...
IS IT...
...I- I...
...OKAY IF... MAY-BE...
...STAY AND WATCH TOO ...?
HUH ...?
I...
...IF YOU DON'T WANT ME HERE, I'LL LEAVE ......
......
UH... WELL... SURE... I GUESS IT'S OKAY...
PORI (SCRATCH)
IT'S NOT LIKE WE OWN THE PLACE...
......
THANK YOU.
THAT'S RIGHT...
I DIDN'T JUST WANNA SEE FIRE-WORKS...
I WANTED TO HAVE A FUN TIME...
...WATCHING SOMETHING WITH SOMEONE ELSE.

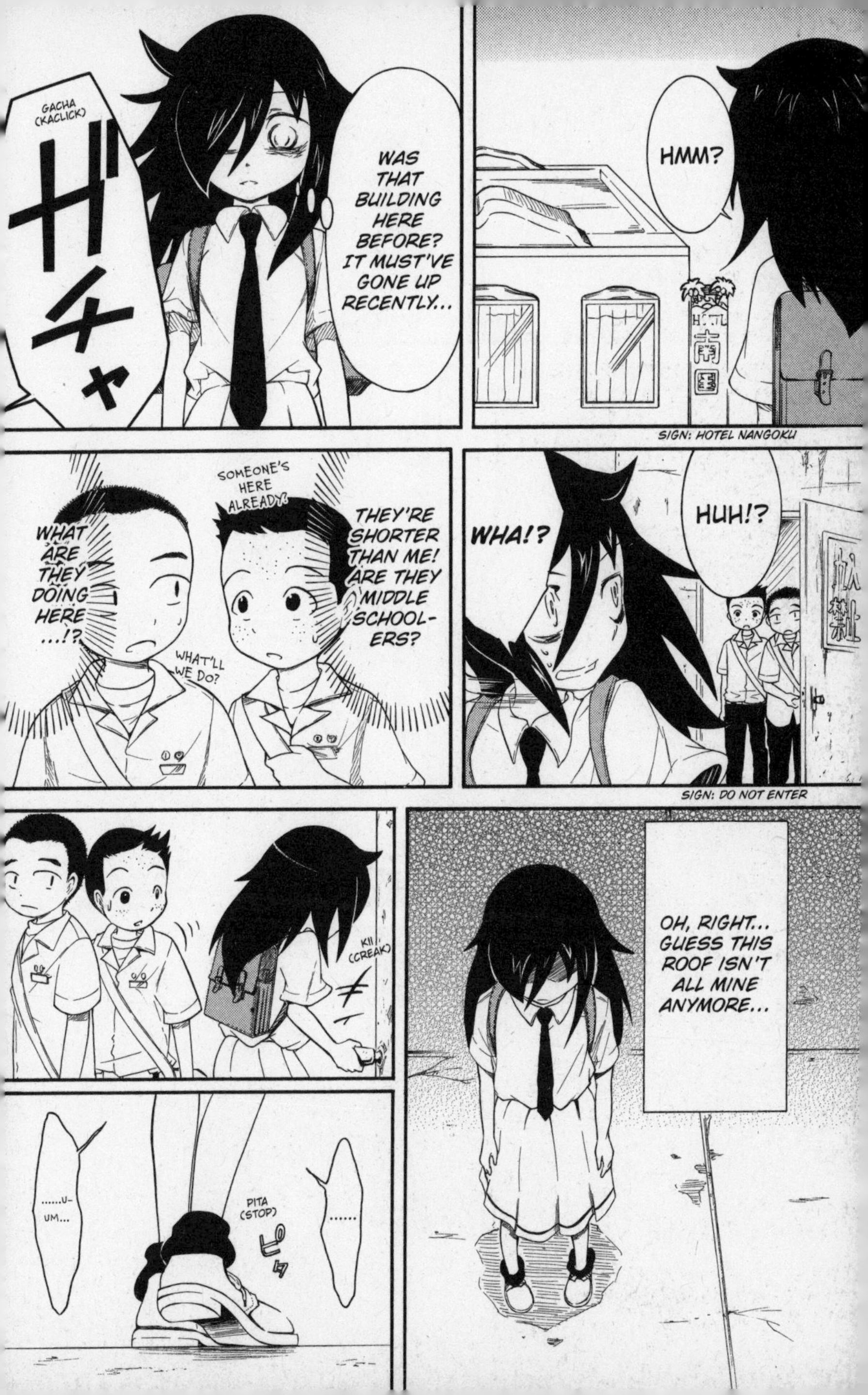
HMM?
SIGN: HOTEL NANGOKU
GACHA (KACLICK)
WAS THAT BUILDING HERE BEFORE? IT MUST'VE GONE UP RECENTLY...
HUH!?
WHA!?
SIGN: DO NOT ENTER
SOMEONE'S HERE ALREADY!?
THEY'RE SHORTER THAN ME! ARE THEY MIDDLE SCHOOLERS?
WHAT ARE THEY DOING HERE...!?
WHAT'LL WE DO?
OH, RIGHT... GUESS THIS ROOF ISN'T ALL MINE ANYMORE...
KII (CREAK)
......
PITA (STOP)
......U-UM...

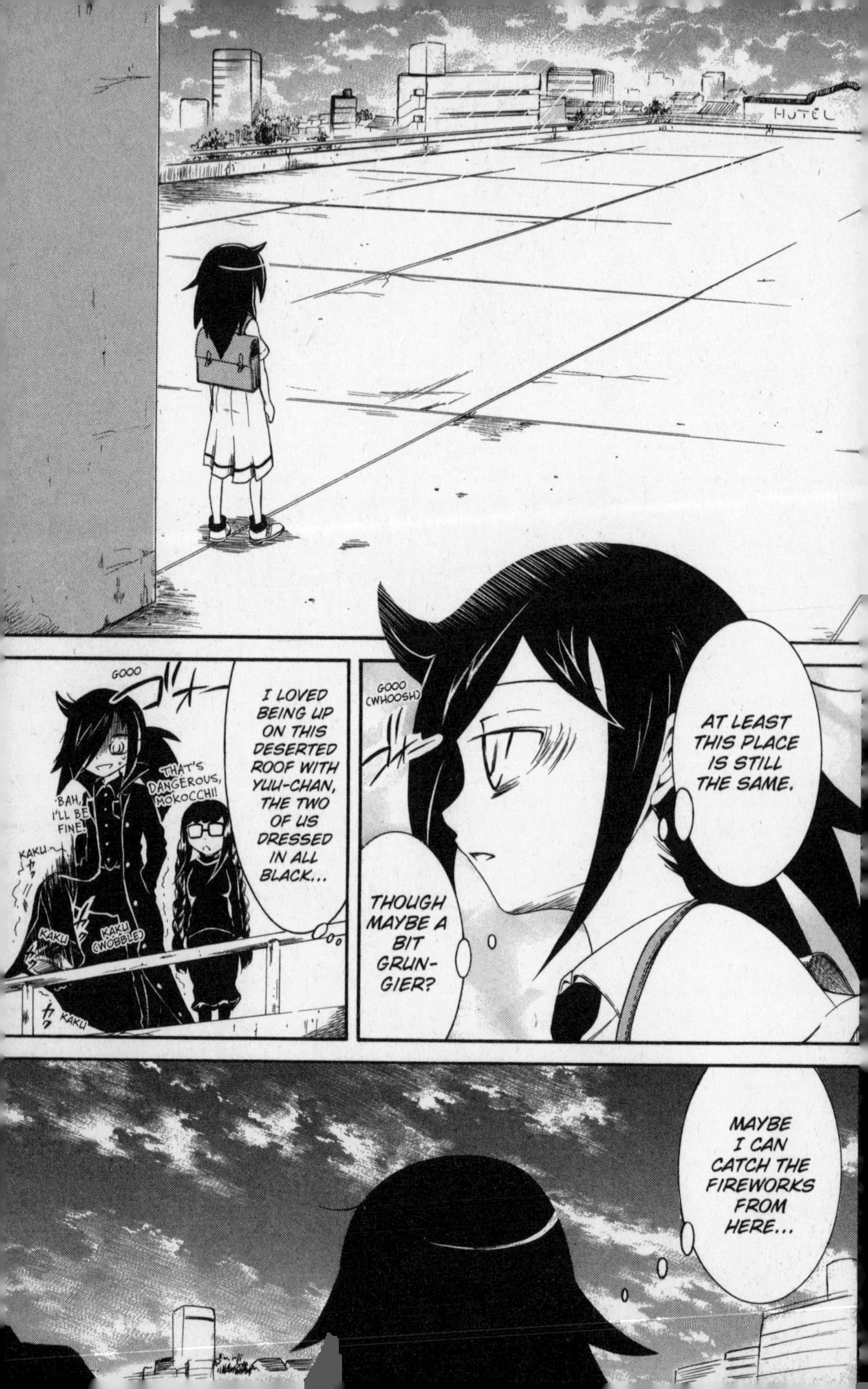
HOTEL
AT LEAST THIS PLACE IS STILL THE SAME.
THOUGH MAYBE A BIT GRUN-GIER?
GOOO (WHOOSH)
I LOVED BEING UP ON THIS DESERTED ROOF WITH YUU-CHAN, THE TWO OF US DRESSED IN ALL BLACK...
GOOO
THAT'S DANGEROUS, MOKOCCHI!
BAH, I'LL BE FINE!
KAKU
KAKU
KAKU (WOBBLE)
KAKU
MAYBE I CAN CATCH THE FIREWORKS FROM HERE...

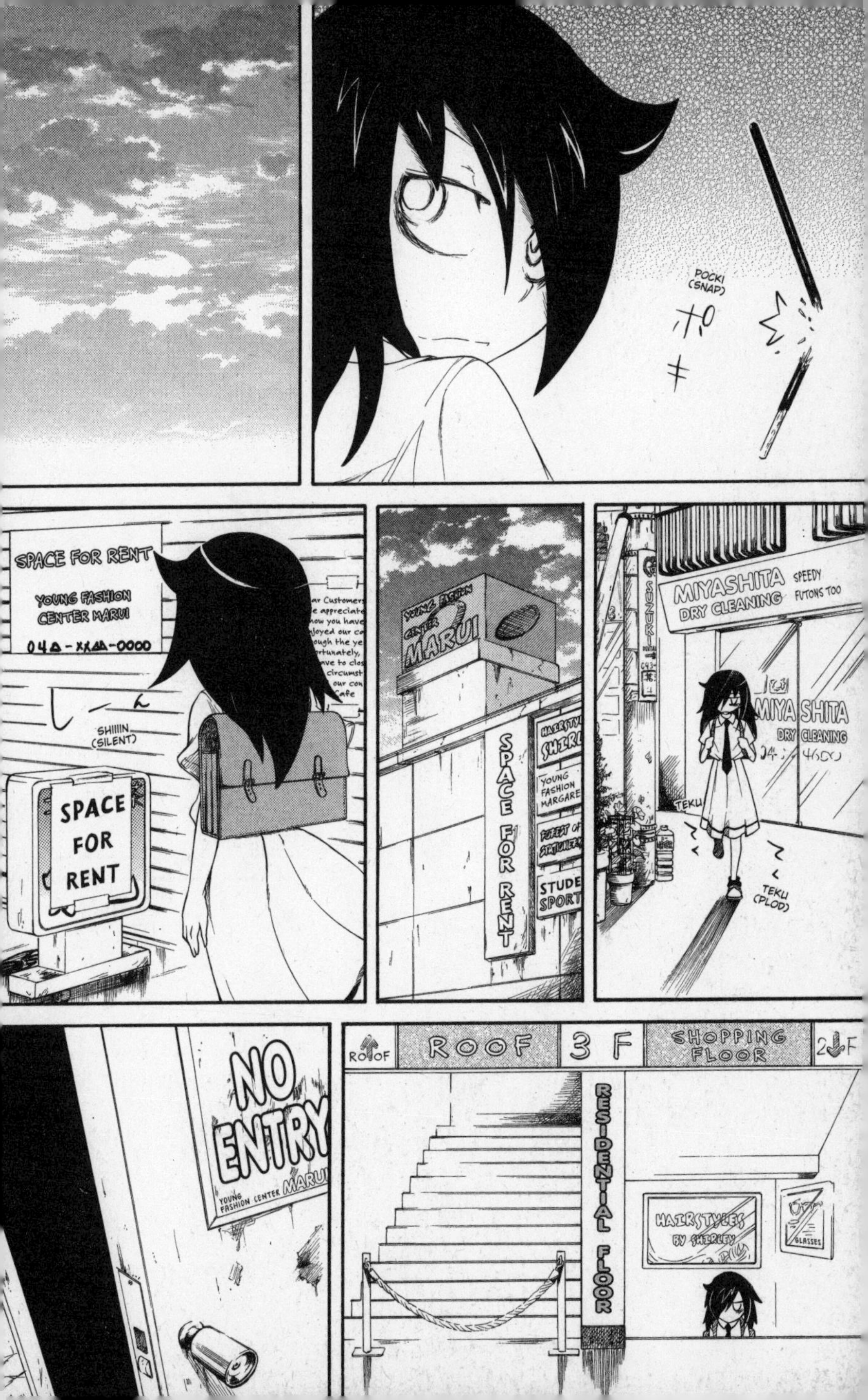
ポキッ
POCKI (SNAP)
MIYASHITA DRY CLEANING
SPEEDY FUTONS TOO
SUZUKI
MIYA SHITA
DRY CLEANING
TEKU
TEKU (PLOD)
YOUNG FASHION CENTER MARUI
SPACE FOR RENT
YOUNG FASHION MARGARE
STUDE SPORT
SPACE FOR RENT
YOUNG FASHION CENTER MARUI
04△-XX△△-0000
しーん
SHIIIIN (SILENT)
SPACE FOR RENT
ROOF
ROOF
3 F
SHOPPING FLOOR
2F
RESIDENTIAL FLOOR
HAIRSTYLES BY SHIRLEY
GLASSES
NO ENTRY
YOUNG FASHION CENTER MARUI

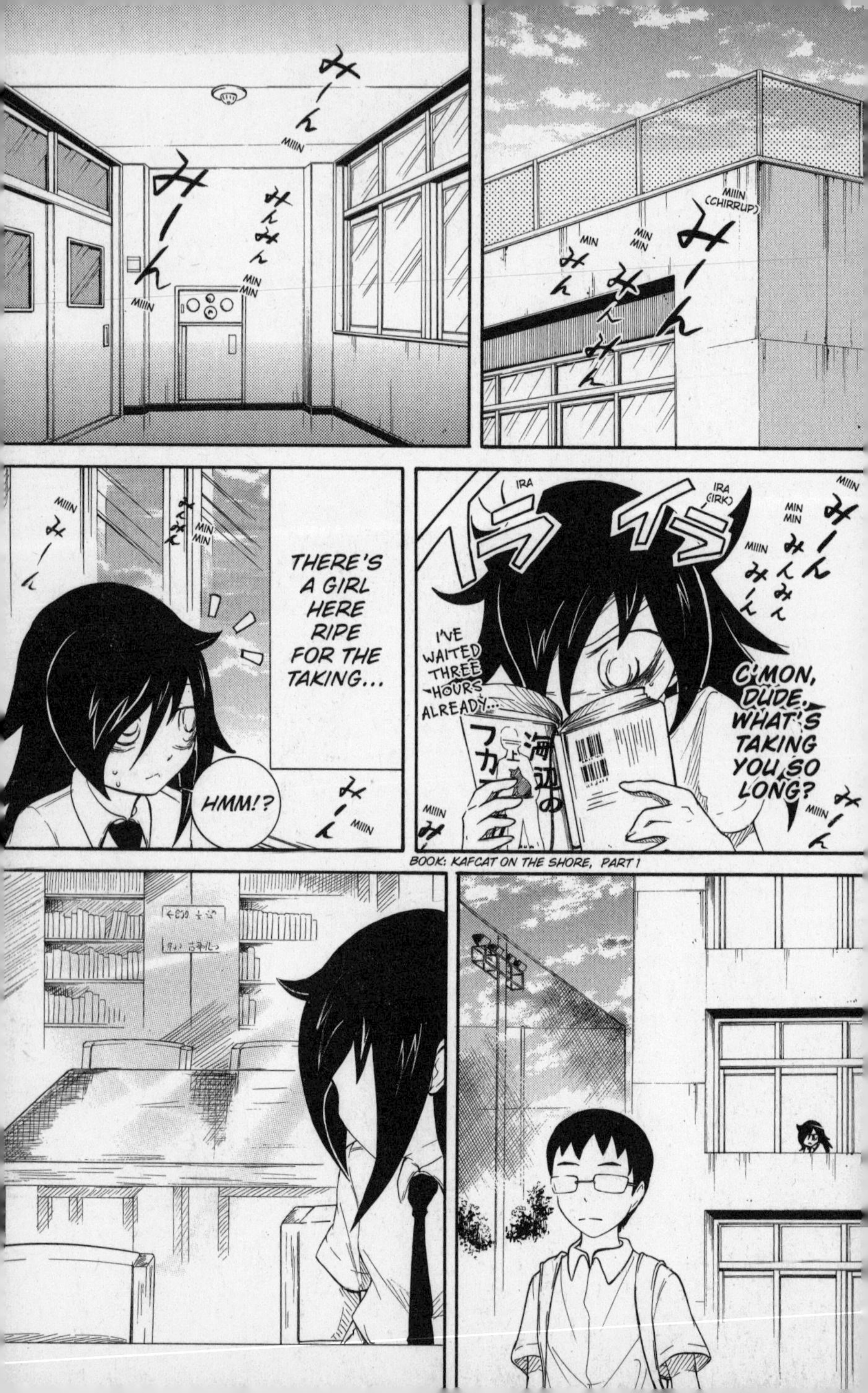
MIIN (CHIRRUP)
MIN MIN
MIN
MIIN
MIN MIN
MIIN
IRA (IRK)
IRA
MIIN
MIN MIN
MIIN
C'MON, DUDE, WHAT'S TAKING YOU SO LONG?
I'VE WAITED THREE HOURS ALREADY...
MIIN
MIIN
BOOK: KAFCAT ON THE SHORE, PART 1
THERE'S A GIRL HERE RIPE FOR THE TAKING...
MIIN
MIN MIN
HMM!?
MIIN

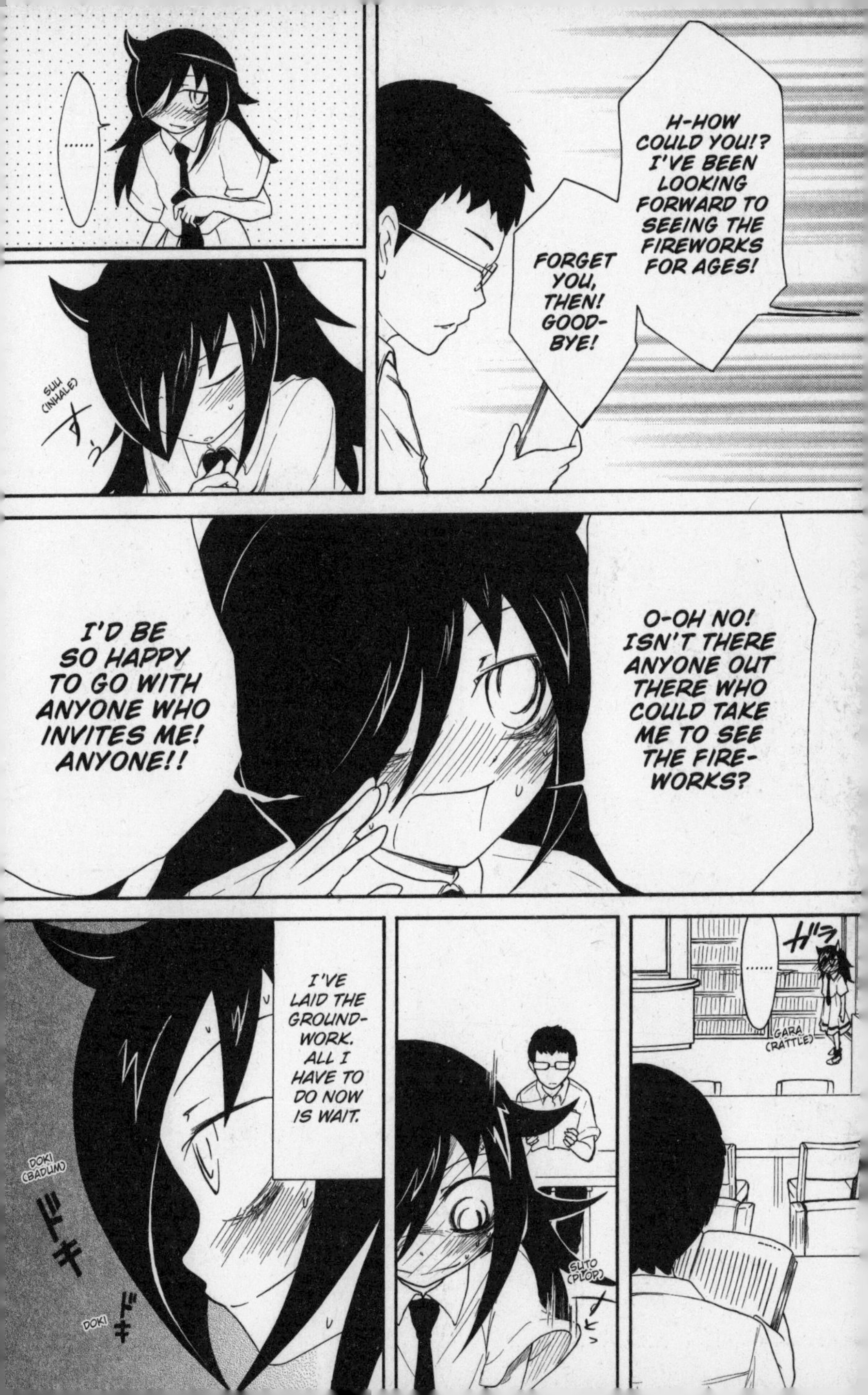
H-HOW COULD YOU!? I'VE BEEN LOOKING FORWARD TO SEEING THE FIREWORKS FOR AGES!
FORGET YOU, THEN! GOOD-BYE!
......
SUU (INHALE)
O-OH NO! ISN'T THERE ANYONE OUT THERE WHO COULD TAKE ME TO SEE THE FIRE-WORKS?
I'D BE SO HAPPY TO GO WITH ANYONE WHO INVITES ME! ANYONE!!
......
GARA (RATTLE)
SUTO (PLOP)
I'VE LAID THE GROUND-WORK. ALL I HAVE TO DO NOW IS WAIT.
DOKI (BADUM)
DOKI

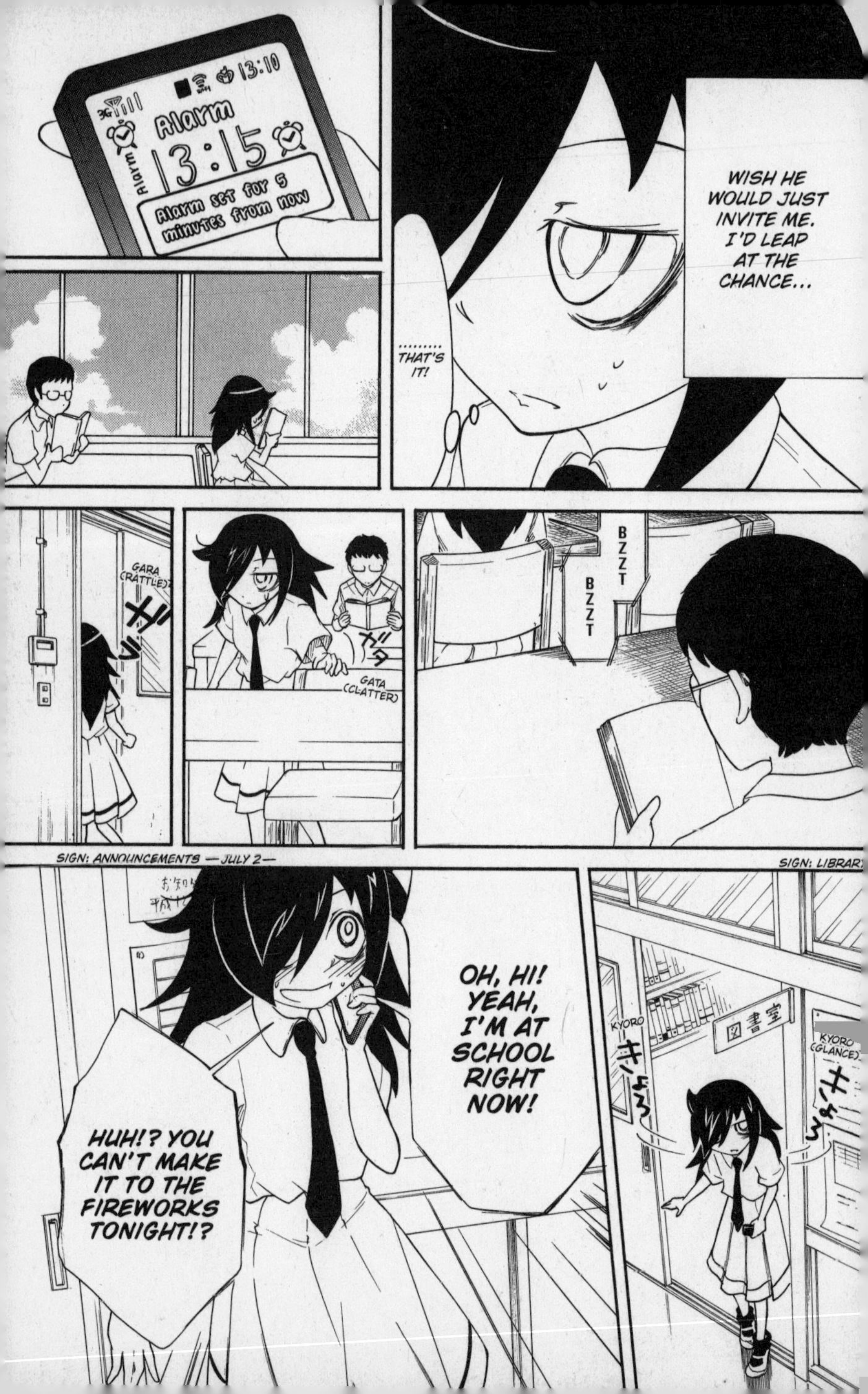
WISH HE WOULD JUST INVITE ME. I'D LEAP AT THE CHANCE...
....
THAT'S IT!
13:10
Alarm
13:15
Alarm
Alarm set for 5 minutes from now
BZZT
BZZT
GATA (CLATTER)
GARA (RATTLE)
SIGN: LIBRARY
SIGN: ANNOUNCEMENTS —JULY 2—
KYORO (GLANCE)
図書室
KYORO
OH, HI! YEAH, I'M AT SCHOOL RIGHT NOW!
HUH!? YOU CAN'T MAKE IT TO THE FIREWORKS TONIGHT!?

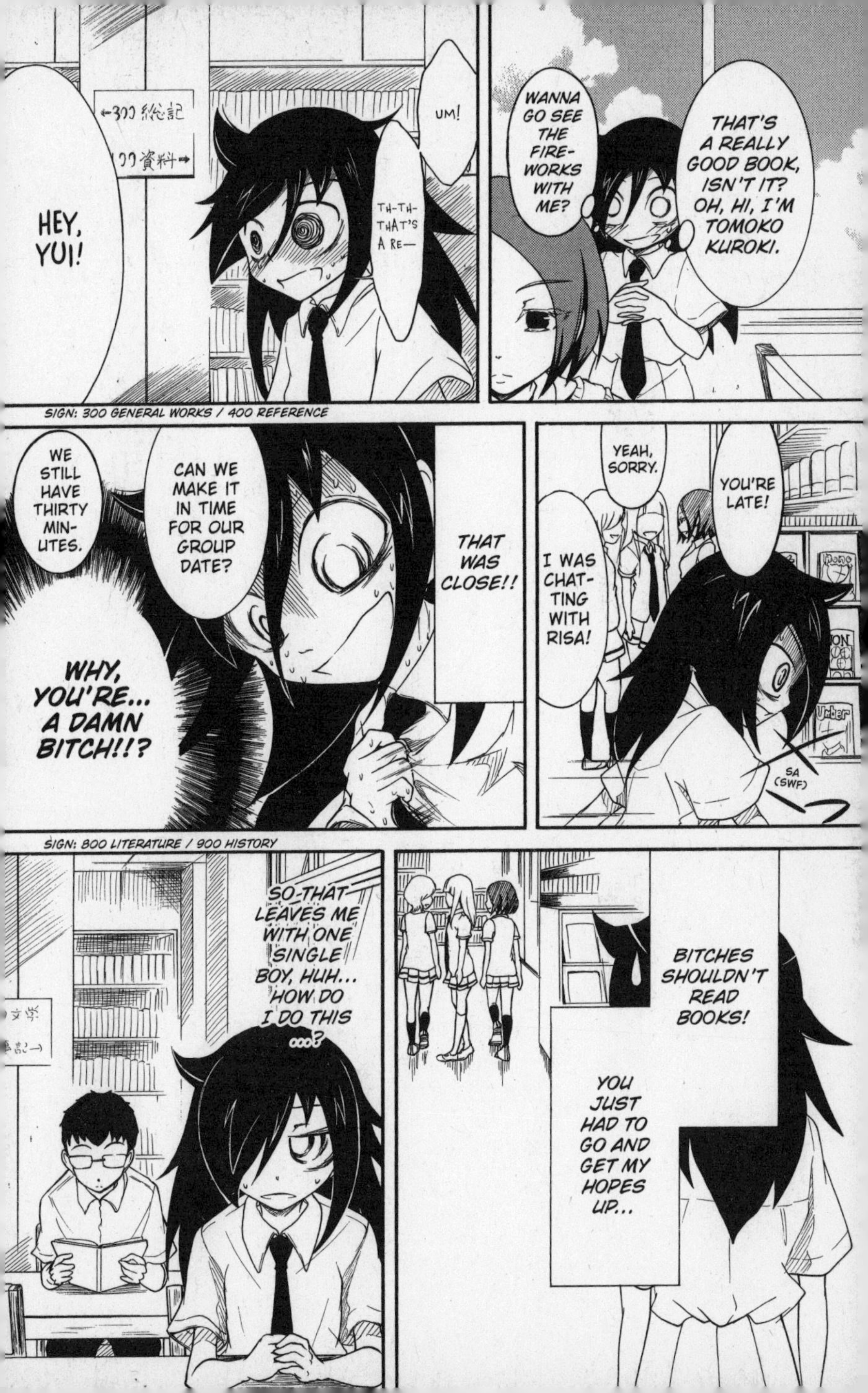
THAT'S A REALLY GOOD BOOK, ISN'T IT? OH, HI, I'M TOMOKO KUROKI.
WANNA GO SEE THE FIRE-WORKS WITH ME?
UM!
TH-TH-THAT'S A RE—
HEY, YUI!
SIGN: 300 GENERAL WORKS / 400 REFERENCE
YOU'RE LATE!
YEAH, SORRY.
I WAS CHAT-TING WITH RISA!
SA (SWF)
THAT WAS CLOSE!!
CAN WE MAKE IT IN TIME FOR OUR GROUP DATE?
WE STILL HAVE THIRTY MIN-UTES.
WHY, YOU'RE... A DAMN BITCH!!?
SIGN: 800 LITERATURE / 900 HISTORY
BITCHES SHOULDN'T READ BOOKS!
YOU JUST HAD TO GO AND GET MY HOPES UP...
SO THAT LEAVES ME WITH ONE SINGLE BOY, HUH... HOW DO I DO THIS ...?

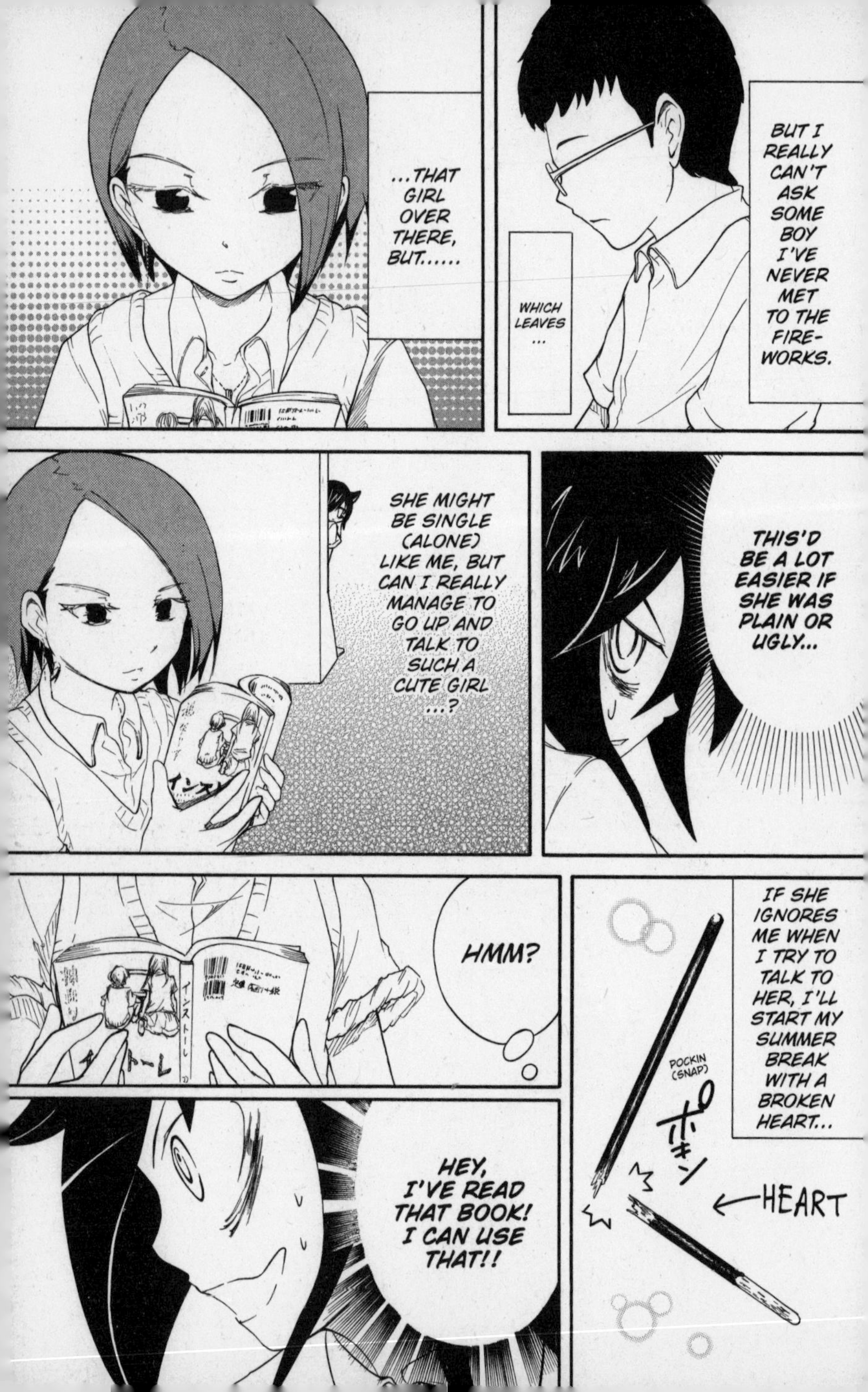
BUT I REALLY CAN'T ASK SOME BOY I'VE NEVER MET TO THE FIRE-WORKS.
WHICH LEAVES ...
...THAT GIRL OVER THERE, BUT......
THIS'D BE A LOT EASIER IF SHE WAS PLAIN OR UGLY...
SHE MIGHT BE SINGLE (ALONE) LIKE ME, BUT CAN I REALLY MANAGE TO GO UP AND TALK TO SUCH A CUTE GIRL ...?
IF SHE IGNORES ME WHEN I TRY TO TALK TO HER, I'LL START MY SUMMER BREAK WITH A BROKEN HEART...
ポキン
POCKIN (SNAP)
HEART
HMM?
HEY, I'VE READ THAT BOOK! I CAN USE THAT!!

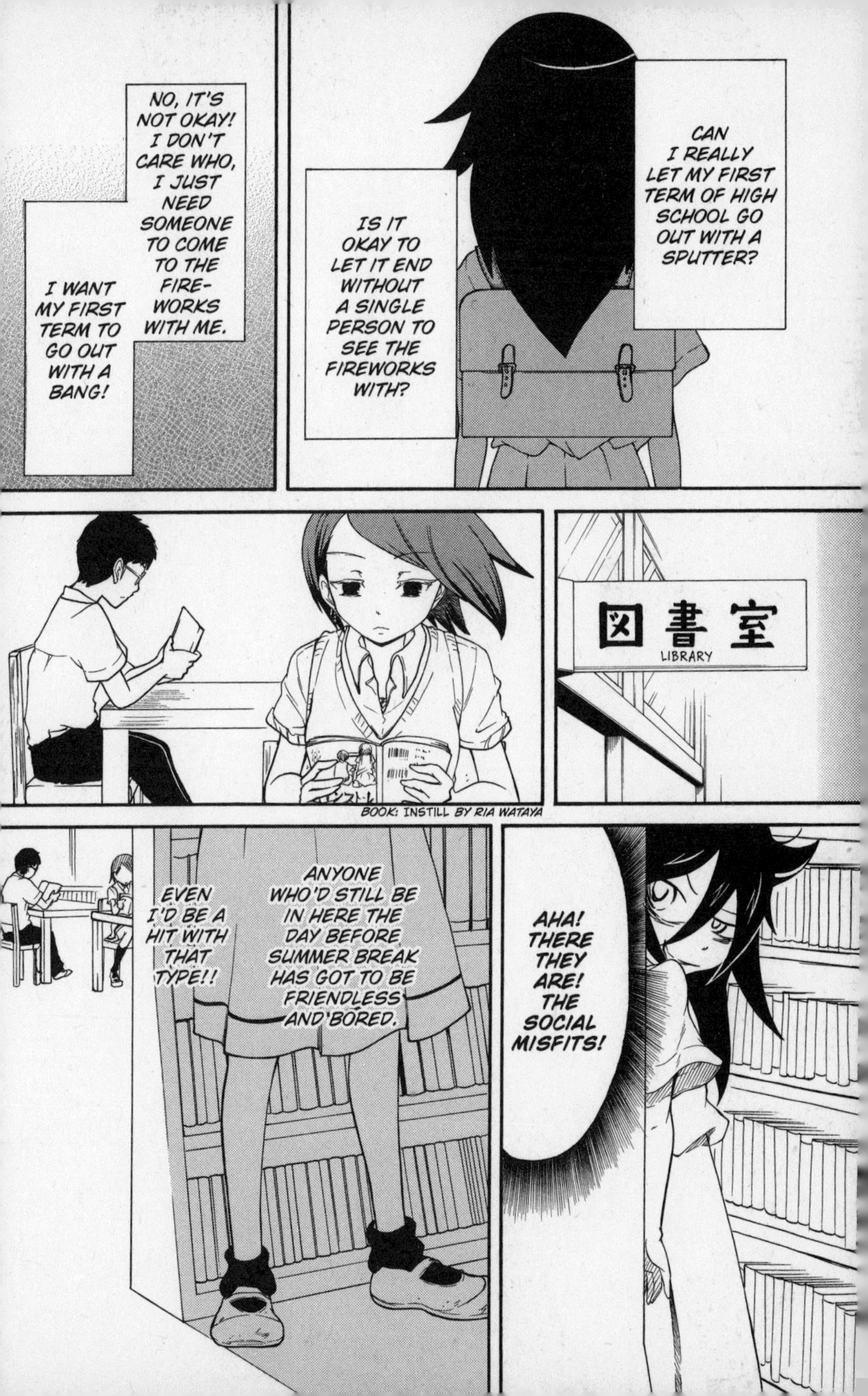
CAN I REALLY LET MY FIRST TERM OF HIGH SCHOOL GO OUT WITH A SPUTTER?
IS IT OKAY TO LET IT END WITHOUT A SINGLE PERSON TO SEE THE FIREWORKS WITH?
NO, IT'S NOT OKAY! I DON'T CARE WHO, I JUST NEED SOMEONE TO COME TO THE FIRE-WORKS WITH ME.
I WANT MY FIRST TERM TO GO OUT WITH A BANG!
図書室
LIBRARY
BOOK: INSTILL BY RIA WATAYA
AHA! THERE THEY ARE! THE SOCIAL MISFITS!
ANYONE WHO'D STILL BE IN HERE THE DAY BEFORE SUMMER BREAK HAS GOT TO BE FRIENDLESS AND BORED.
EVEN I'D BE A HIT WITH THAT TYPE!!

FAIL 12: I'M NOT POPULAR, SO I'LL GO SEE THE FIREWORKS.

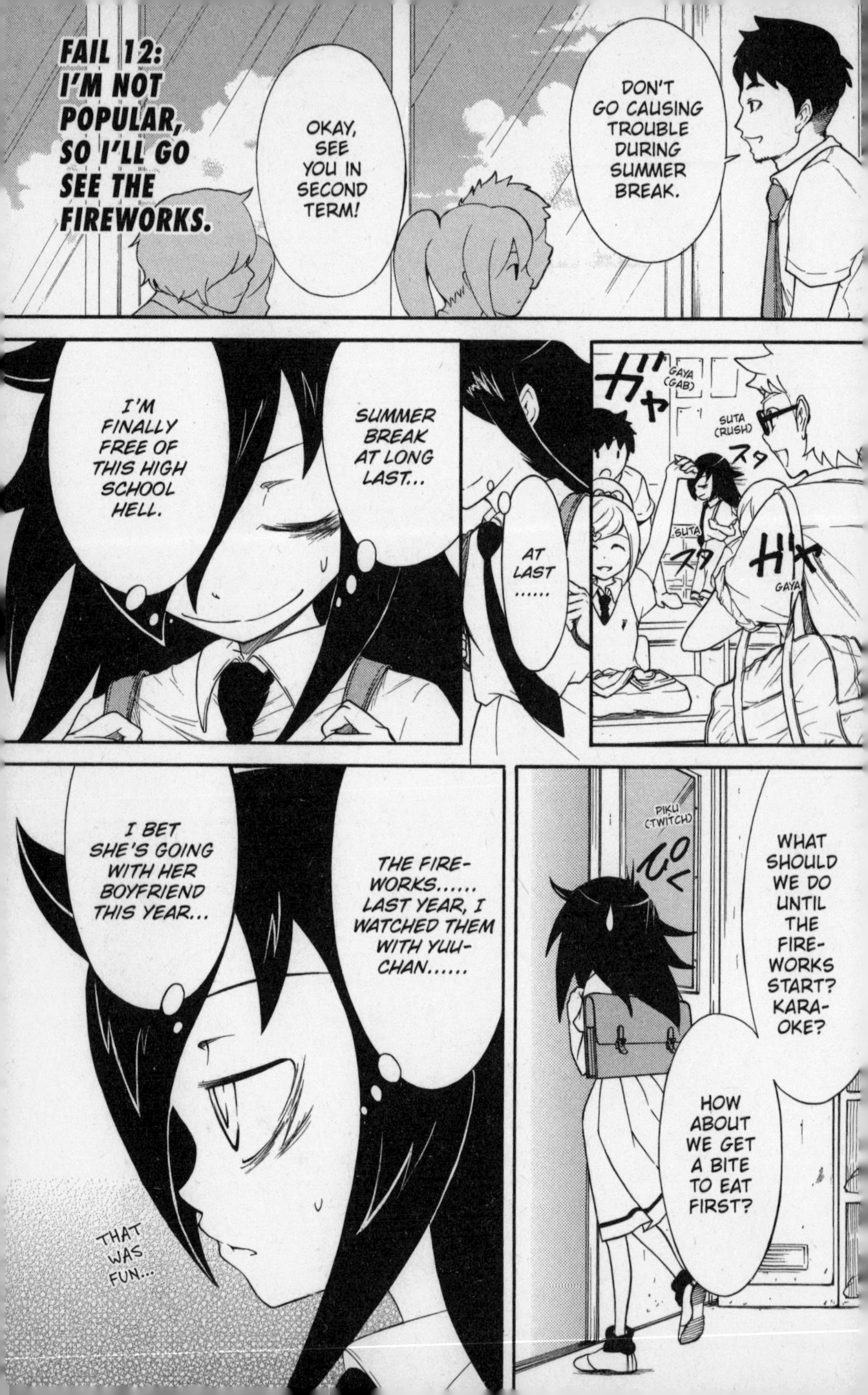
DON'T GO CAUSING TROUBLE DURING SUMMER BREAK.
OKAY, SEE YOU IN SECOND TERM!
GAYA (GAB)
SUTA (RUSH)
SUTA
GAYA
AT LAST......
SUMMER BREAK AT LONG LAST...
I'M FINALLY FREE OF THIS HIGH SCHOOL HELL.
PIKU (TWITCH)
WHAT SHOULD WE DO UNTIL THE FIRE-WORKS START? KARA-OKE?
HOW ABOUT WE GET A BITE TO EAT FIRST?
THE FIRE-WORKS...... LAST YEAR, I WATCHED THEM WITH YUU-CHAN......
I BET SHE'S GOING WITH HER BOYFRIEND THIS YEAR...
THAT WAS FUN...

No Matter How I Look at It, It's You Guys' Fault I'm Not Popular!

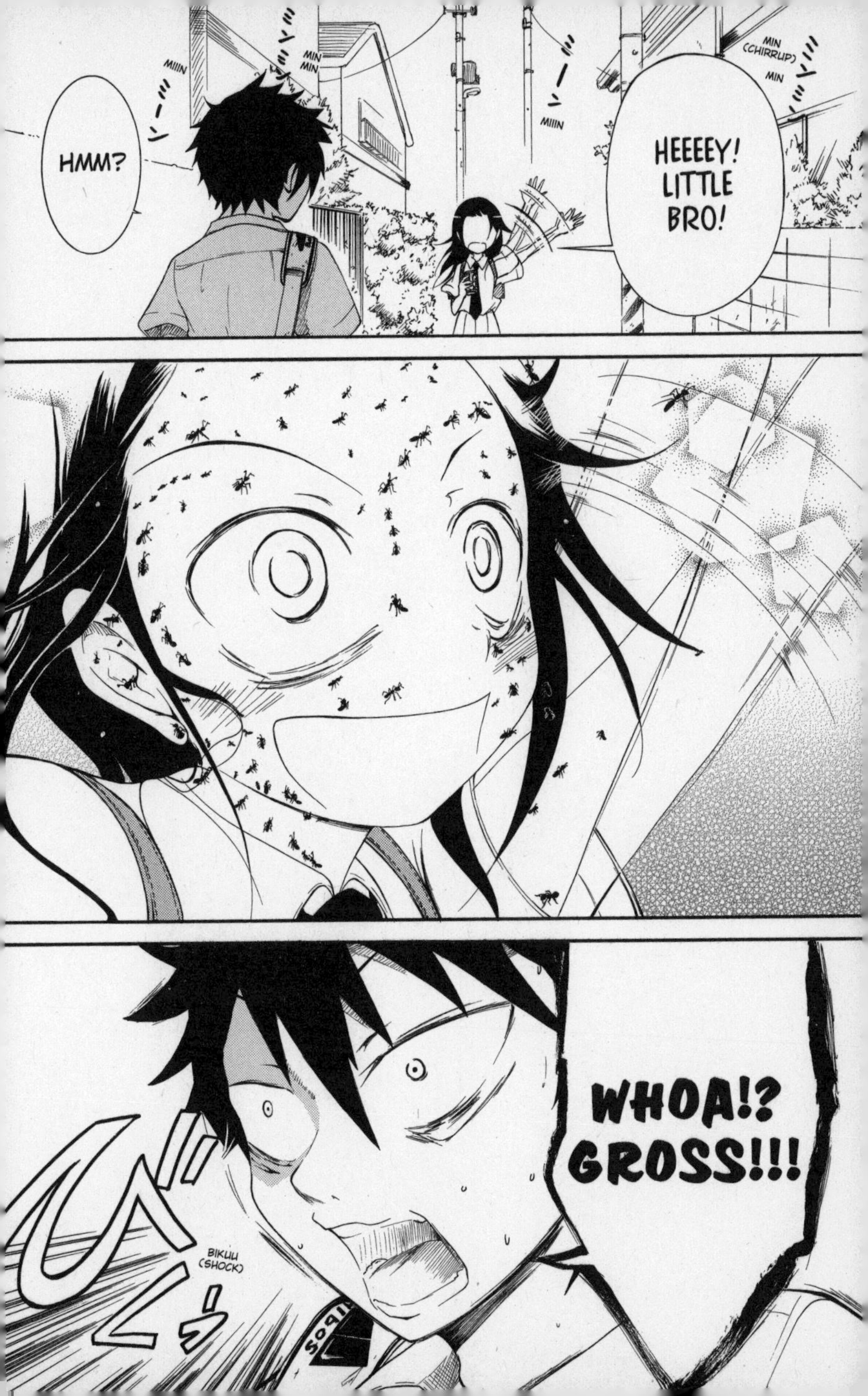
MIN (CHIRRUP) MIN
HEEEEY! LITTLE BRO!
MIIN
MIN MIN
MIIN
HMM?
WHOA!? GROSS!!!
BIKUU (SHOCK)

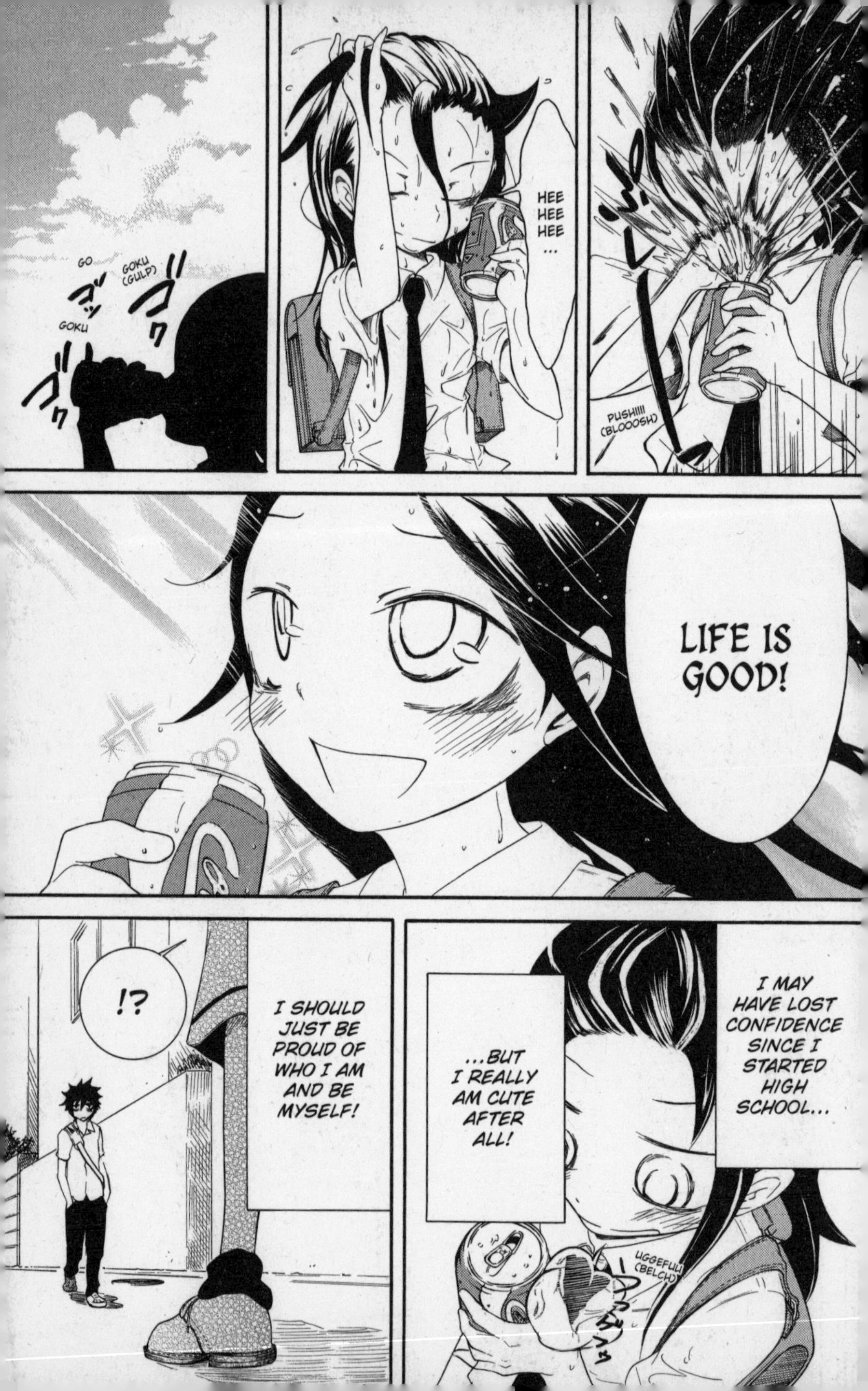
PUSH!!!! (BLOOOSH)
HEE HEE HEE ...
GOKU (GULP)
GO
GOKU
LIFE IS GOOD!
I MAY HAVE LOST CONFIDENCE SINCE I STARTED HIGH SCHOOL...
...BUT I REALLY AM CUTE AFTER ALL!
UGGEFUU (BELCH)
I SHOULD JUST BE PROUD OF WHO I AM AND BE MYSELF!
!?

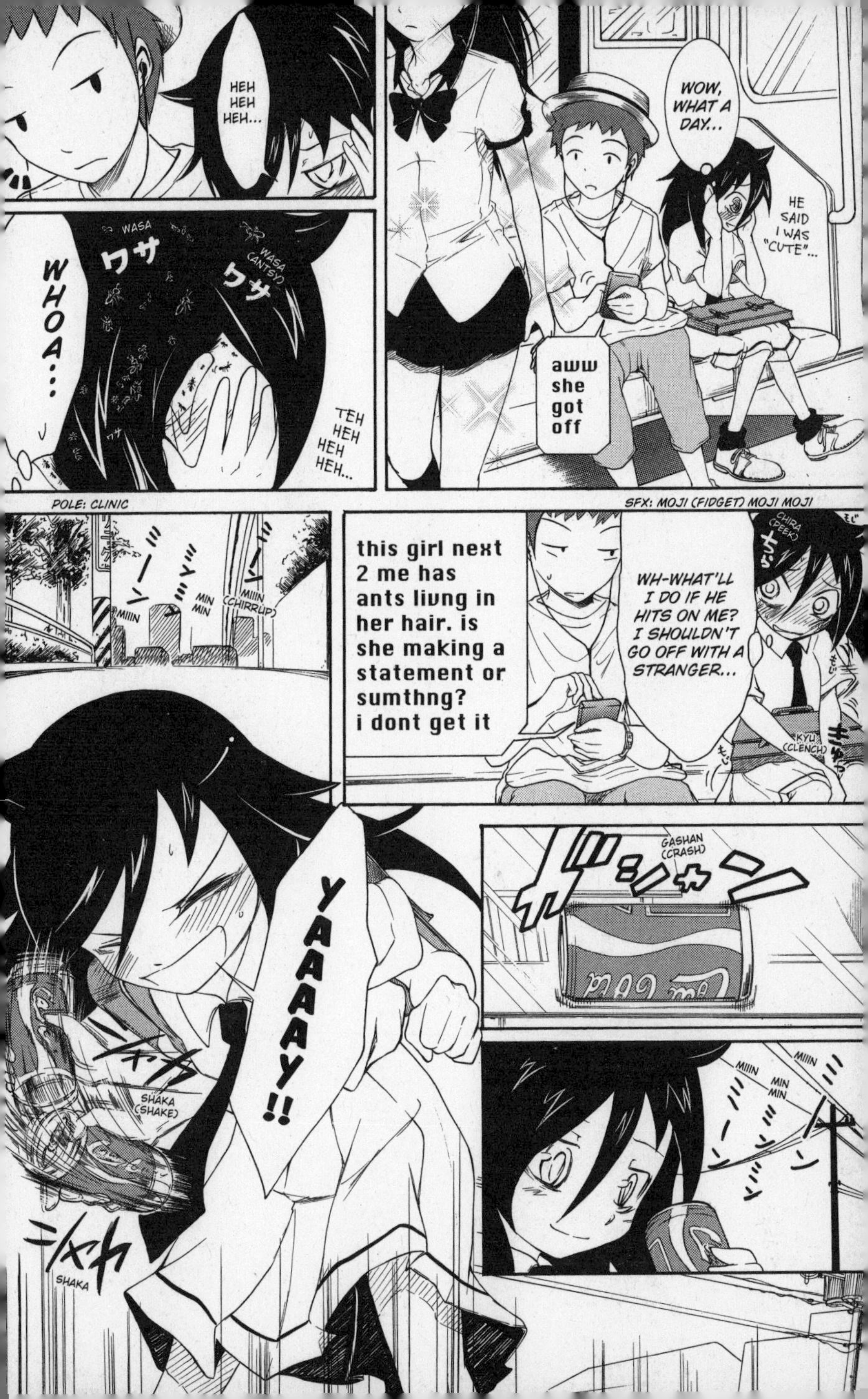
WOW, WHAT A DAY...
HE SAID I WAS "CUTE"...
aww she got off
HEH HEH HEH...
WASA
ワサ
WASA (ANTSY)
ワサ
WHOA...
TEH HEH HEH HEH...
SFX: MOJI (FIDGET) MOJI MOJI
POLE: CLINIC
CHIRA (PEEK)
WH-WHAT'LL I DO IF HE HITS ON ME? I SHOULDN'T GO OFF WITH A STRANGER...
this girl next 2 me has ants livng in her hair. is she making a statement or sumthng? i dont get it
KYU (CLENCH)
MIIIN (CHIRRUP)
MIN MIN
MIIIN
GASHAN (CRASH)
MIIIN
MIN MIN
MIIIN
YAAAAAY!!
SHAKA (SHAKE)
SHAKA

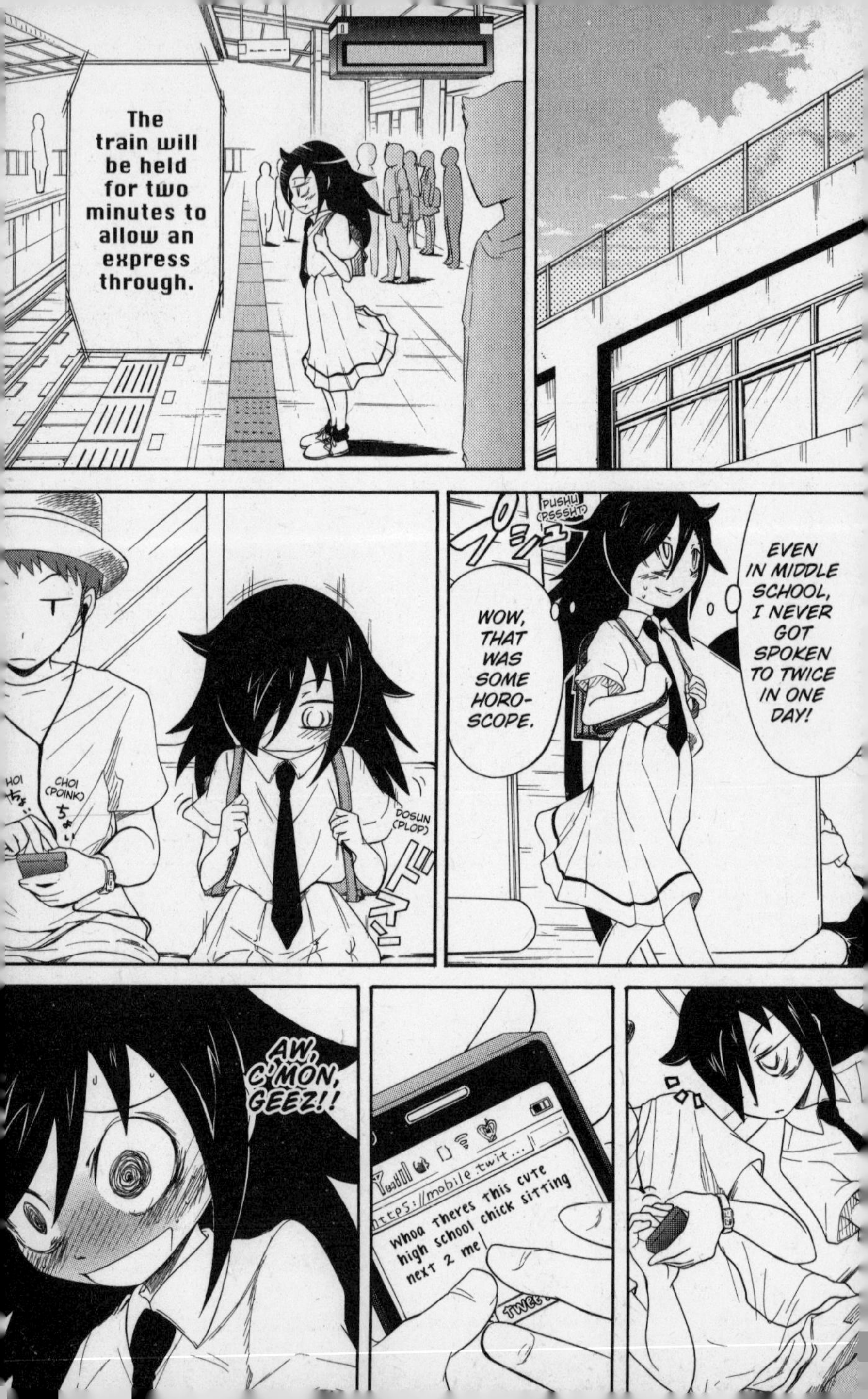
The train will be held for two minutes to allow an express through.
PUSHU (PSSSHT)
EVEN IN MIDDLE SCHOOL, I NEVER GOT SPOKEN TO TWICE IN ONE DAY!
WOW, THAT WAS SOME HOROSCOPE.
DOSUN (PLOP)
CHOI (POINK)
HOI
https://mobile.twit...
whoa theres this cute high school chick sitting next 2 me
AW, C'MON, GEEZ!!

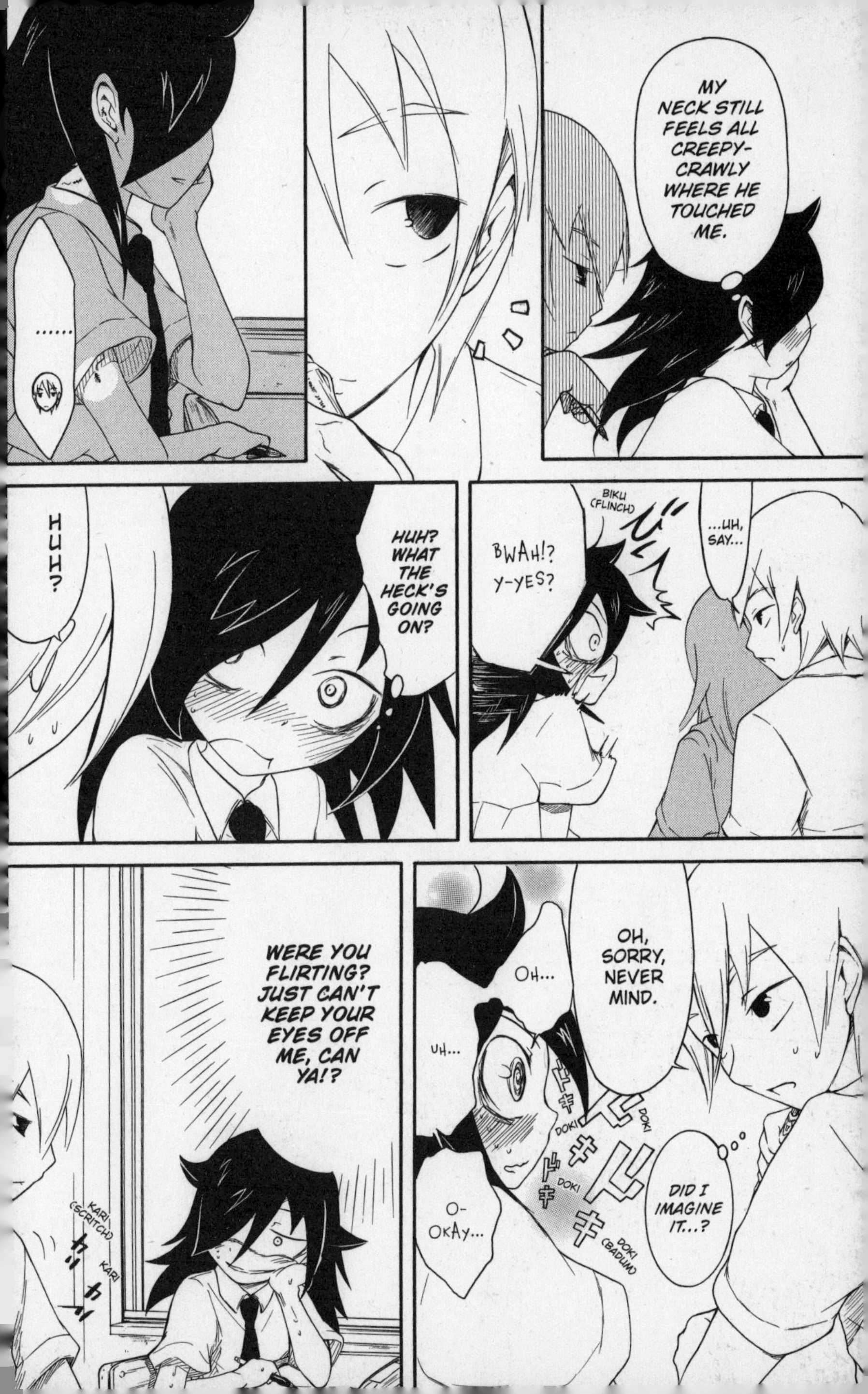
MY NECK STILL FEELS ALL CREEPY-CRAWLY WHERE HE TOUCHED ME.
......
...UH, SAY...
BIKU (FLINCH)
BWAH!? Y-YES?
HUH? WHAT THE HECK'S GOING ON?
HUH?
OH, SORRY, NEVER MIND.
OH...
UH...
DOKI DOKI DOKI DOKI (BADUM)
DID I IMAGINE IT...?
O- OKAY...
WERE YOU FLIRTING? JUST CAN'T KEEP YOUR EYES OFF ME, CAN YA!?
KARI (SCRITCH) KARI

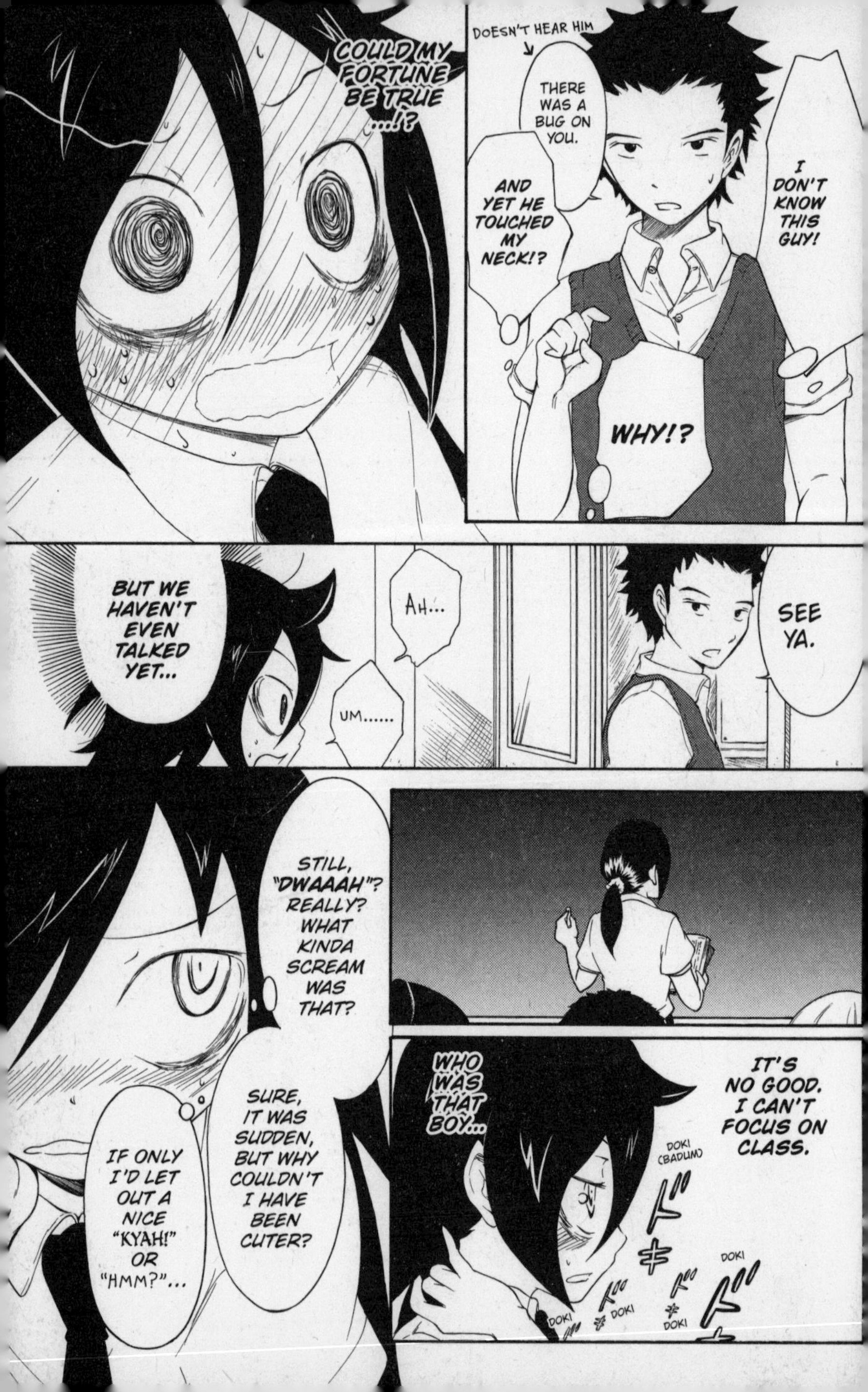
DOESN'T HEAR HIM
THERE WAS A BUG ON YOU.
I DON'T KNOW THIS GUY!
AND YET HE TOUCHED MY NECK!?
WHY!?
COULD MY FORTUNE BE TRUE ...!?
SEE YA.
AH...
UM......
BUT WE HAVEN'T EVEN TALKED YET...
IT'S NO GOOD. I CAN'T FOCUS ON CLASS.
DOKI (BADUM)
DOKI
WHO WAS THAT BOY...
DOKI
DOKI
DOKI
STILL, "DWAAAH"? REALLY? WHAT KINDA SCREAM WAS THAT?
SURE, IT WAS SUDDEN, BUT WHY COULDN'T I HAVE BEEN CUTER?
IF ONLY I'D LET OUT A NICE "KYAH!" OR "HMM?"...

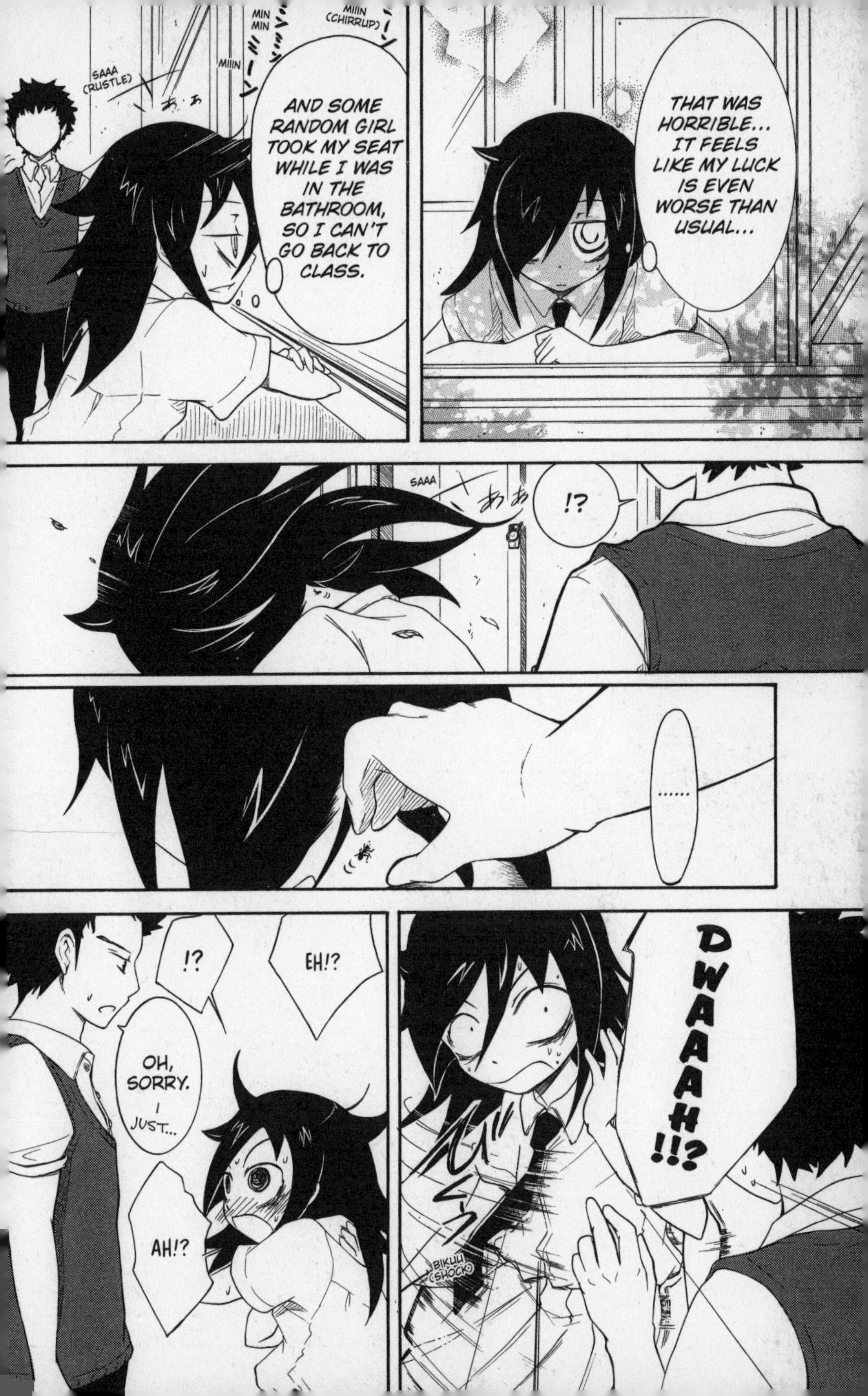
THAT WAS HORRIBLE... IT FEELS LIKE MY LUCK IS EVEN WORSE THAN USUAL...
MIIN (CHIRRUP)
MIN MIN
MIIN
SAAA (RUSTLE)
AND SOME RANDOM GIRL TOOK MY SEAT WHILE I WAS IN THE BATHROOM, SO I CAN'T GO BACK TO CLASS.
!?
SAAA
......
DWAAAAH!!?
BIKUU (SHOCK)
EH!?
!?
OH, SORRY. I JUST...
AH!?

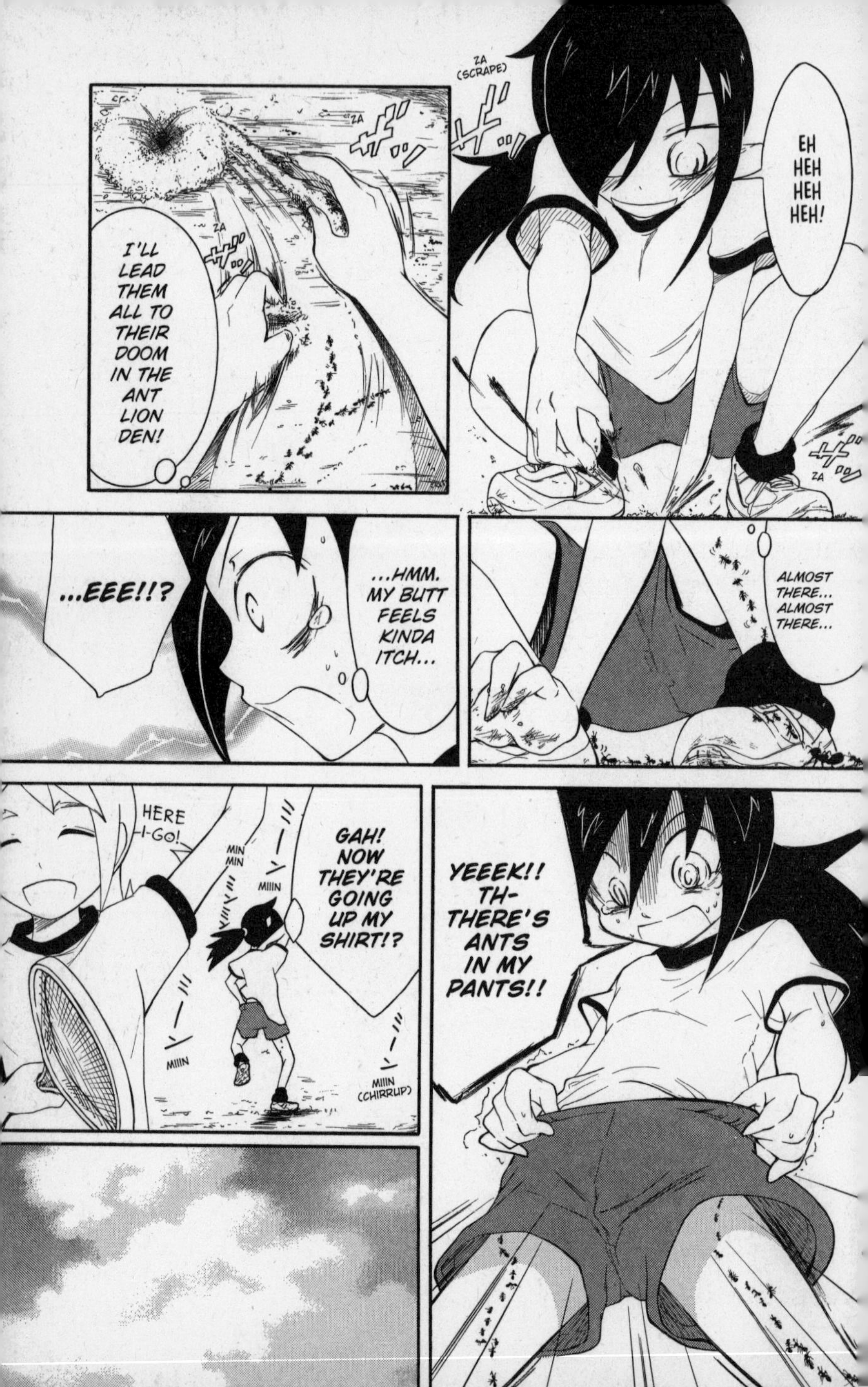
ZA (SCRAPE)
EH HEH HEH HEH!
ZA
ZA
ZA
I'LL LEAD THEM ALL TO THEIR DOOM IN THE ANT LION DEN!
ALMOST THERE... ALMOST THERE...
...HMM. MY BUTT FEELS KINDA ITCH...
...EEE!!?
YEEEK!! TH-THERE'S ANTS IN MY PANTS!!
GAH! NOW THEY'RE GOING UP MY SHIRT!?
MIN MIN
MIIIN
HERE I-GO!
MIIIN
MIIIN (CHIRRUP)

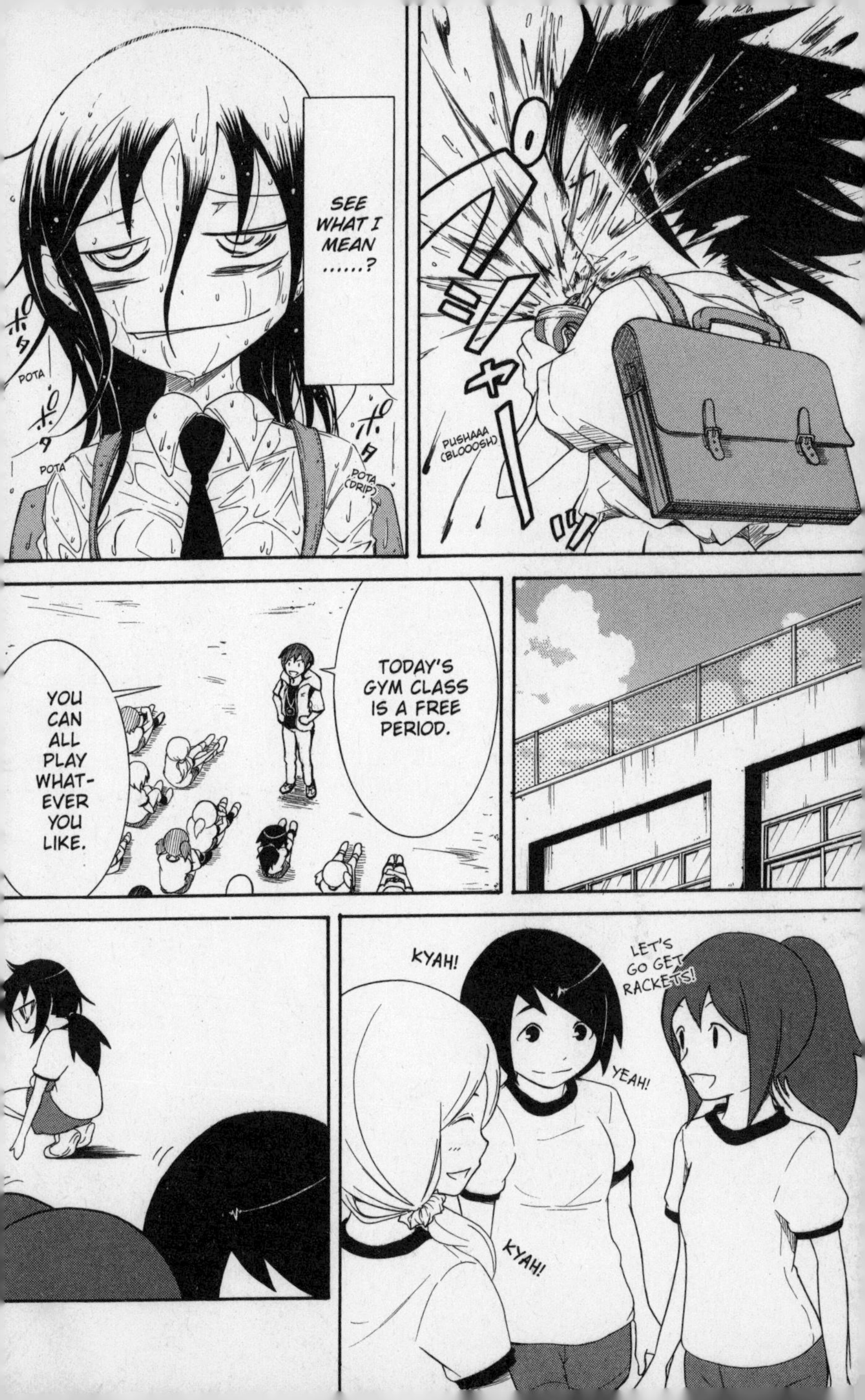
PUSHAAA (BLOOOSH)
SEE WHAT I MEAN ......?
POTA
POTA
POTA (DRIP)
TODAY'S GYM CLASS IS A FREE PERIOD.
YOU CAN ALL PLAY WHAT-EVER YOU LIKE.
LET'S GO GET RACKETS!
KYAH!
YEAH!
KYAH!

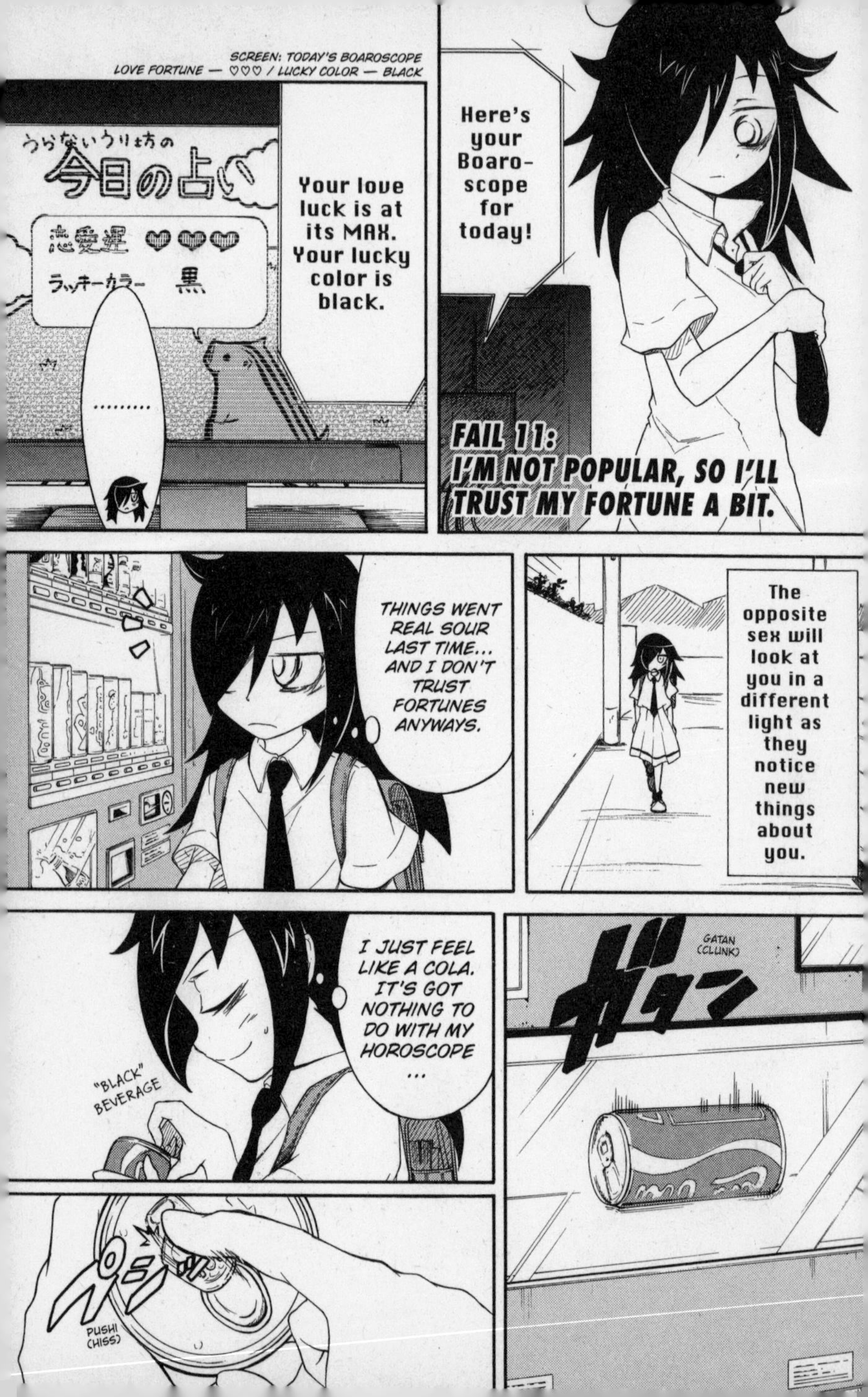
Here's your Boaroscope for today!
FAIL 11:
I'M NOT POPULAR, SO I'LL TRUST MY FORTUNE A BIT.
SCREEN: TODAY'S BOAROSCOPE
LOVE FORTUNE — ♡♡♡ / LUCKY COLOR — BLACK
うらないウリ坊の
今日の占い
恋愛運 ♡♡♡
ラッキーカラー 黒
Your love luck is at its MAX. Your lucky color is black.
....
The opposite sex will look at you in a different light as they notice new things about you.
THINGS WENT REAL SOUR LAST TIME... AND I DON'T TRUST FORTUNES ANYWAYS.
GATAN (CLUNK)
I JUST FEEL LIKE A COLA. IT'S GOT NOTHING TO DO WITH MY HOROSCOPE ...
"BLACK" BEVERAGE
PUSHI (HISS)

No Matter How I Look at It, It's You Guys' Fault I'm Not Popular!

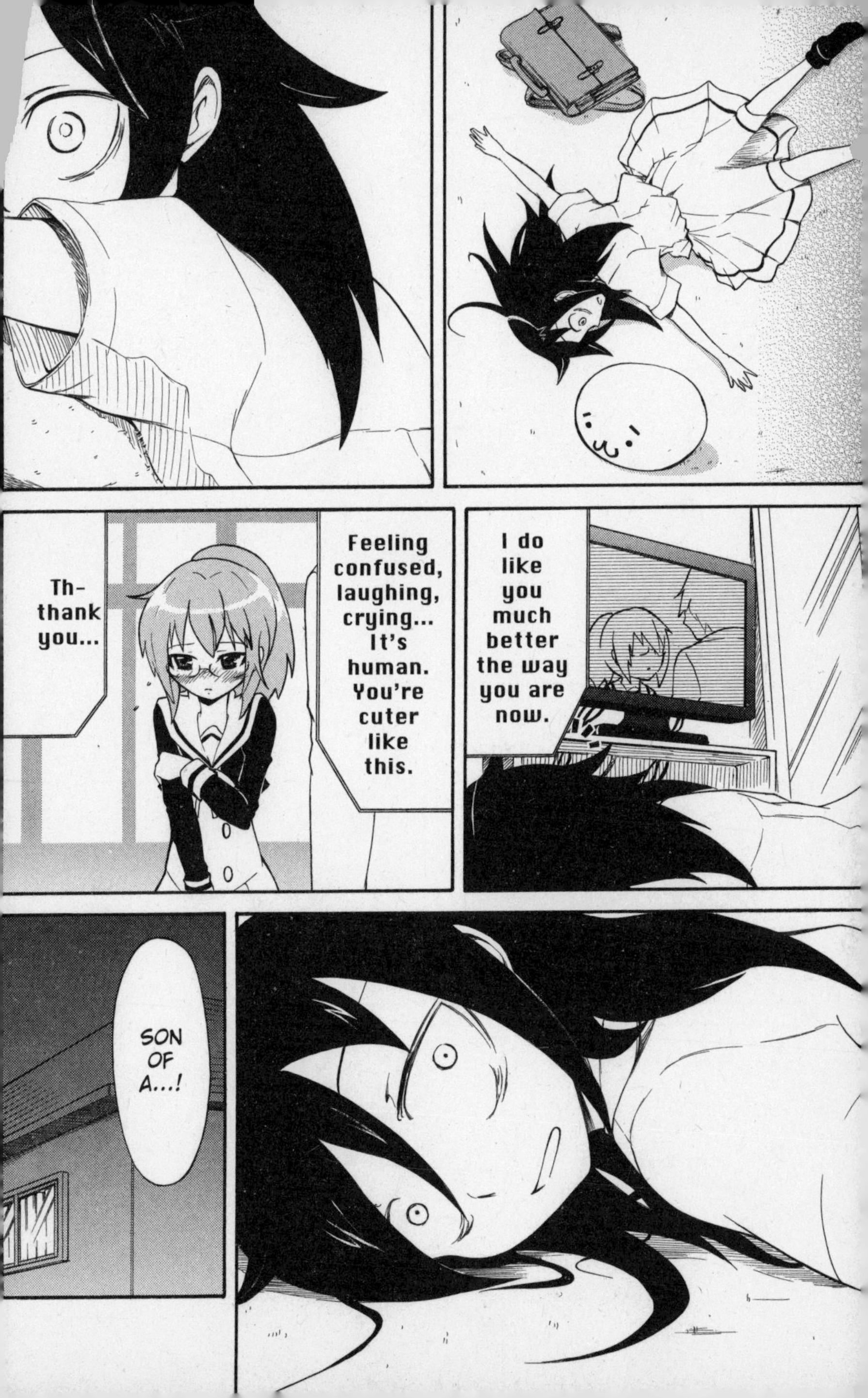
I do like you much better the way you are now.
Feeling confused, laughing, crying... It's human. You're cuter like this.
Th-thank you...
SON OF A...!

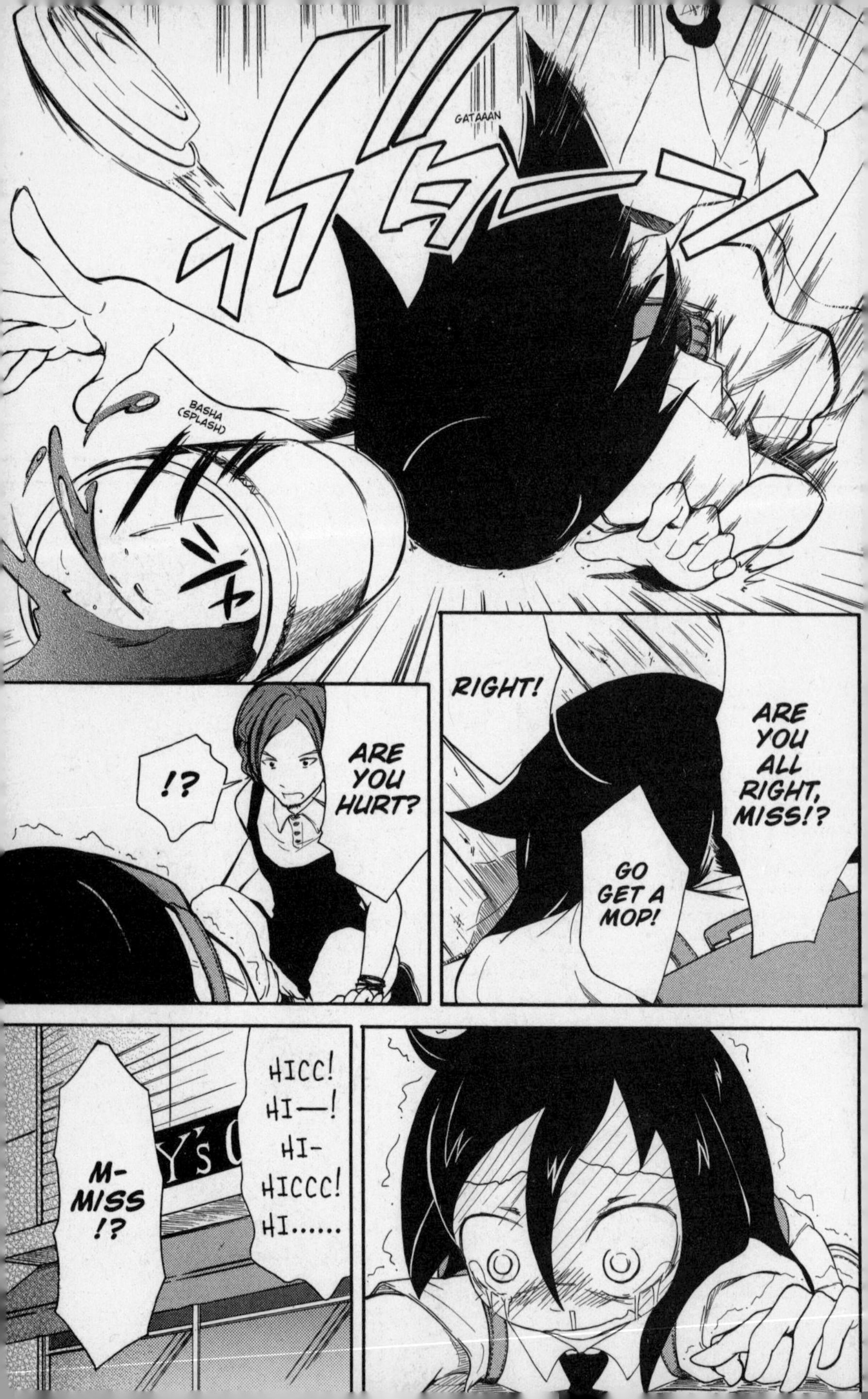
GATAAAN
BASHA (SPLASH)
ARE YOU ALL RIGHT, MISS!?
GO GET A MOP!
RIGHT!
ARE YOU HURT?
!?
HICC! HI—! HI-HICCC! HI......
M-MISS!?

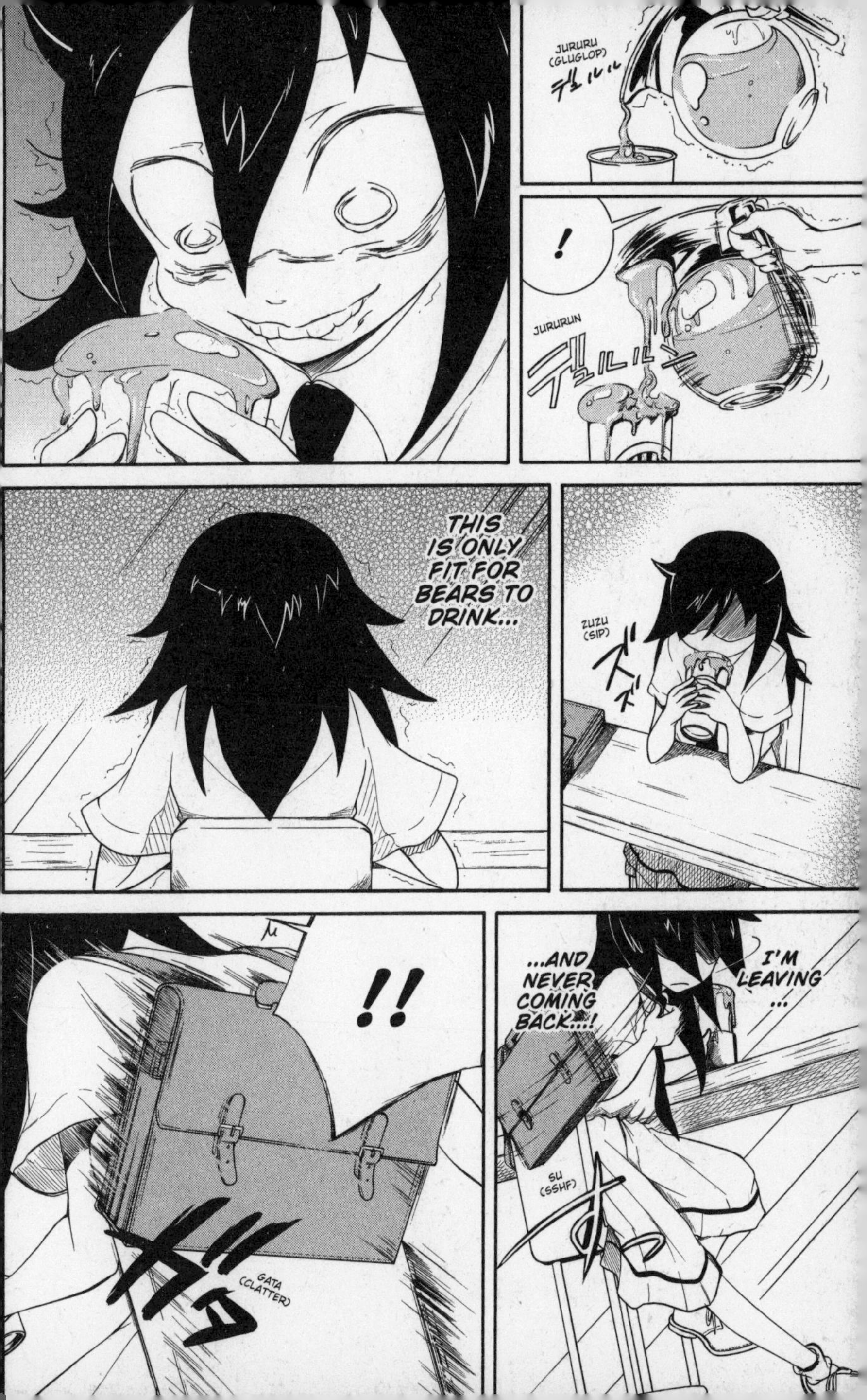
JURURU (GLUGLOP)
デュルル
!
JURURUN
デュルルン
ZUZU (SIP)
ズズ
THIS IS ONLY FIT FOR BEARS TO DRINK...
I'M LEAVING...
...AND NEVER COMING BACK...!
SU (SSHF)
!!
GATA (CLATTER)

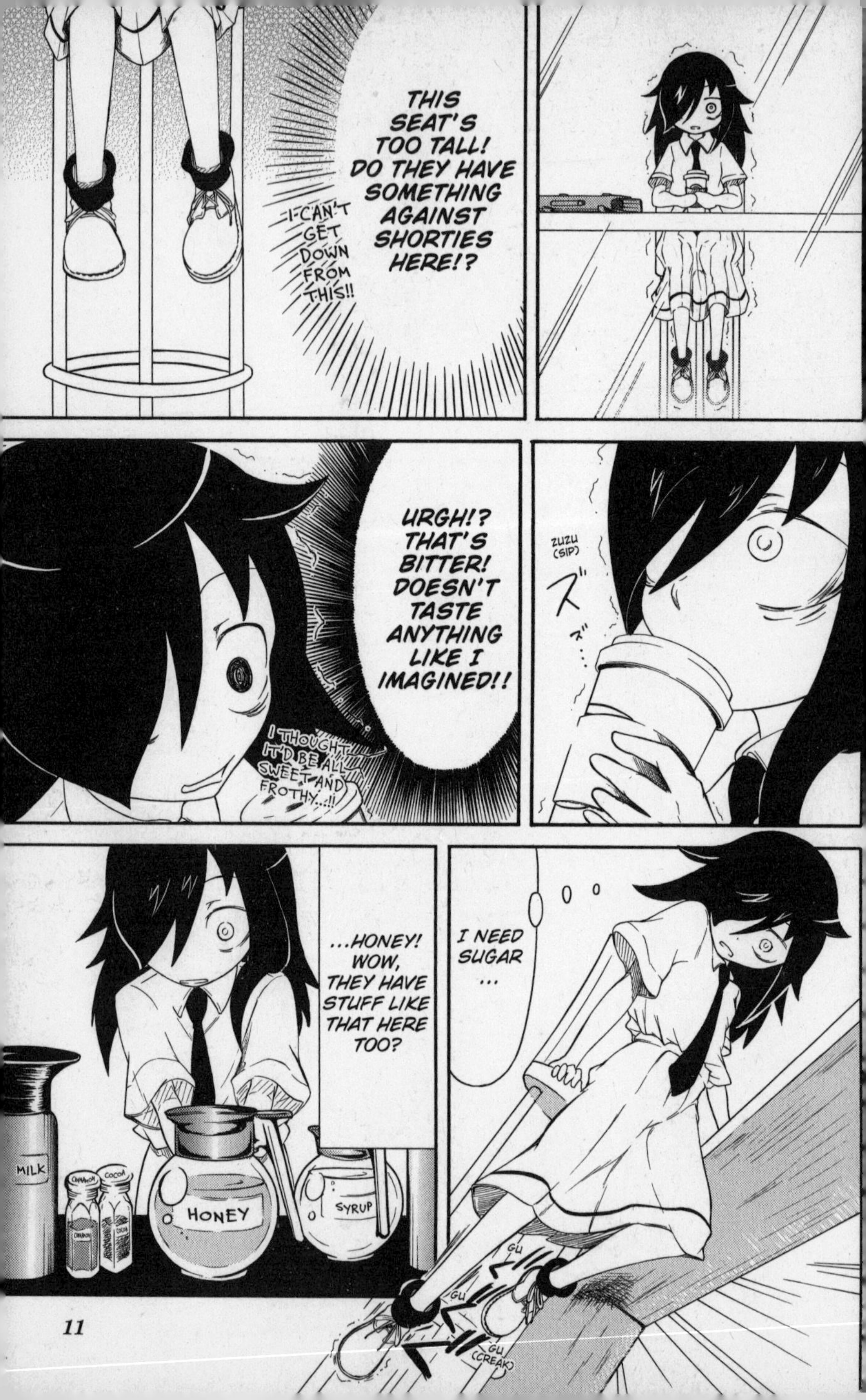
THIS SEAT'S TOO TALL! DO THEY HAVE SOMETHING AGAINST SHORTIES HERE!?
I CAN'T GET DOWN FROM THIS!!
ZUZU (SIP)
URGH!? THAT'S BITTER! DOESN'T TASTE ANYTHING LIKE I IMAGINED!!
I THOUGHT IT'D BE ALL SWEET AND FROTHY...!!
I NEED SUGAR ...
GU
GU
GU (CREAK)
...HONEY! WOW, THEY HAVE STUFF LIKE THAT HERE TOO?
MILK
CINNAMON
COCOA
HONEY
SYRUP

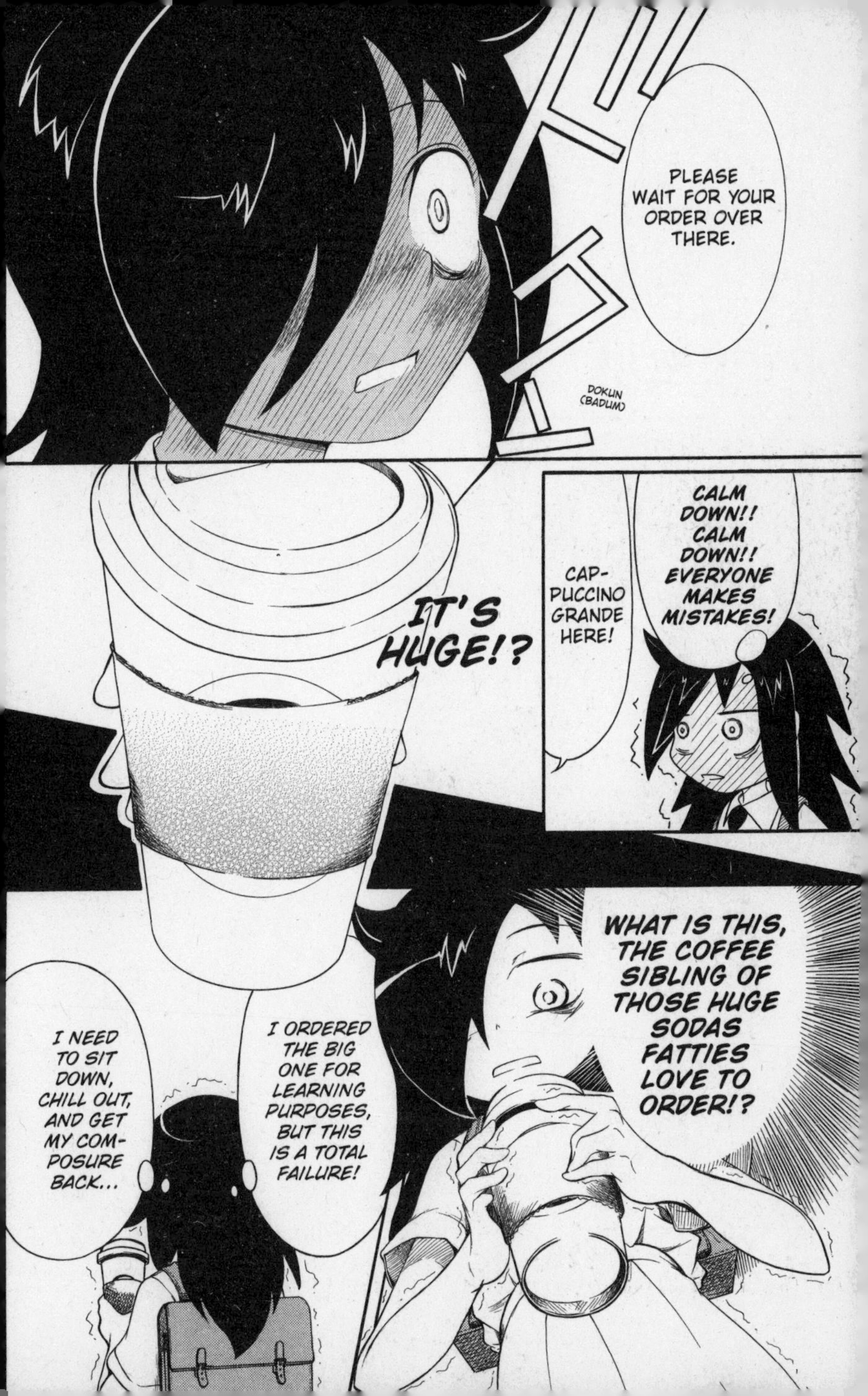
PLEASE WAIT FOR YOUR ORDER OVER THERE.
DOKUN (BADUM)
CALM DOWN!! CALM DOWN!! EVERYONE MAKES MISTAKES!
CAP-PUCCINO GRANDE HERE!
IT'S HUGE!?
WHAT IS THIS, THE COFFEE SIBLING OF THOSE HUGE SODAS FATTIES LOVE TO ORDER!?
I ORDERED THE BIG ONE FOR LEARNING PURPOSES, BUT THIS IS A TOTAL FAILURE!
I NEED TO SIT DOWN, CHILL OUT, AND GET MY COM-POSURE BACK...

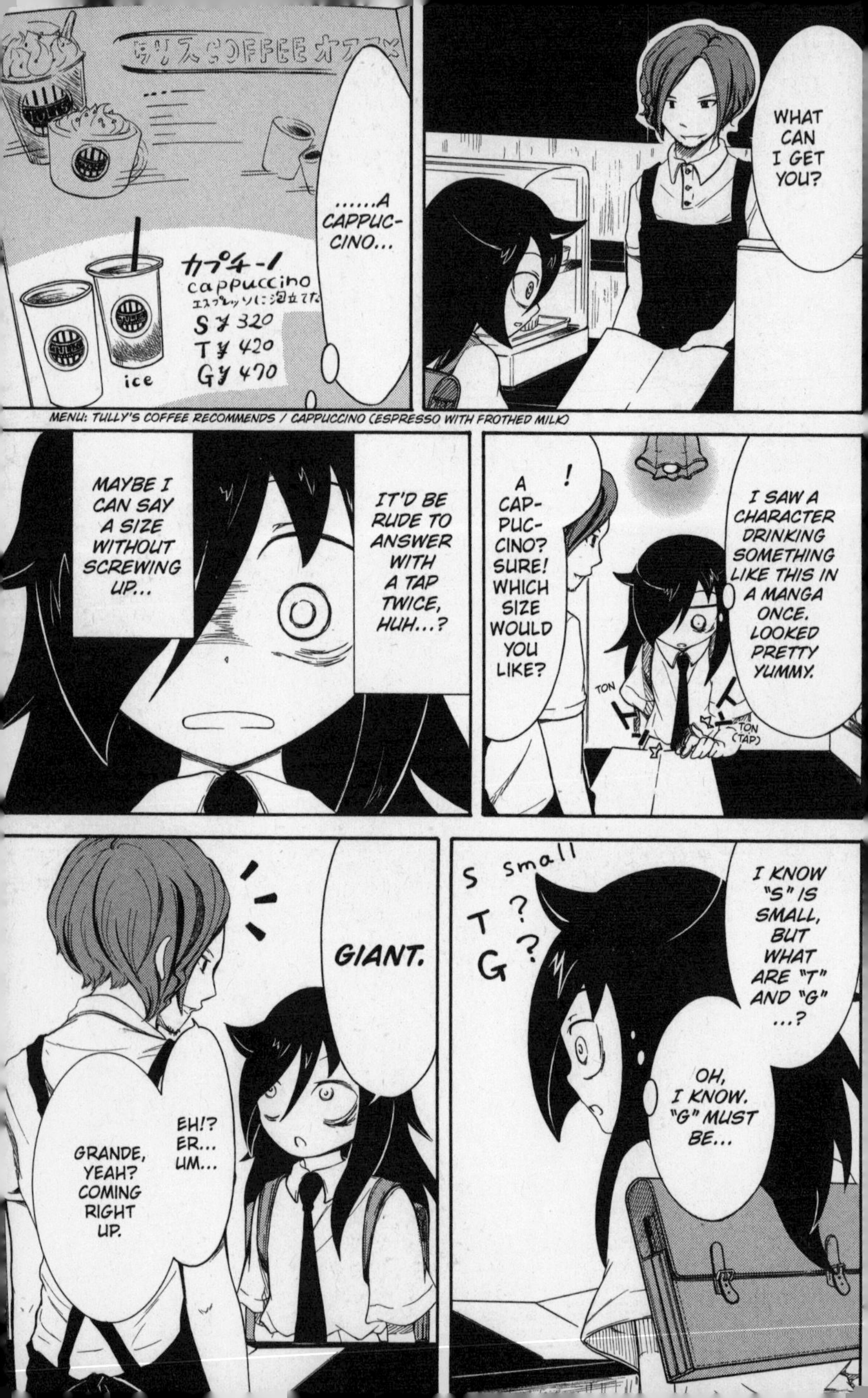
WHAT CAN I GET YOU?
......A CAPPUCCINO...
カプチーノ
cappuccino
エスプレッソに泡立てた
S ¥320
T ¥420
G ¥470
ice
MENU: TULLY'S COFFEE RECOMMENDS / CAPPUCCINO (ESPRESSO WITH FROTHED MILK)
I SAW A CHARACTER DRINKING SOMETHING LIKE THIS IN A MANGA ONCE. LOOKED PRETTY YUMMY.
TON
TON (TAP)
!
A CAPPUCCINO? SURE! WHICH SIZE WOULD YOU LIKE?
IT'D BE RUDE TO ANSWER WITH A TAP TWICE, HUH...?
MAYBE I CAN SAY A SIZE WITHOUT SCREWING UP...
I KNOW "S" IS SMALL, BUT WHAT ARE "T" AND "G"...?
S small
T ?
G ?
OH, I KNOW. "G" MUST BE...
GIANT.
EH!? ER... UM...
GRANDE, YEAH? COMING RIGHT UP.

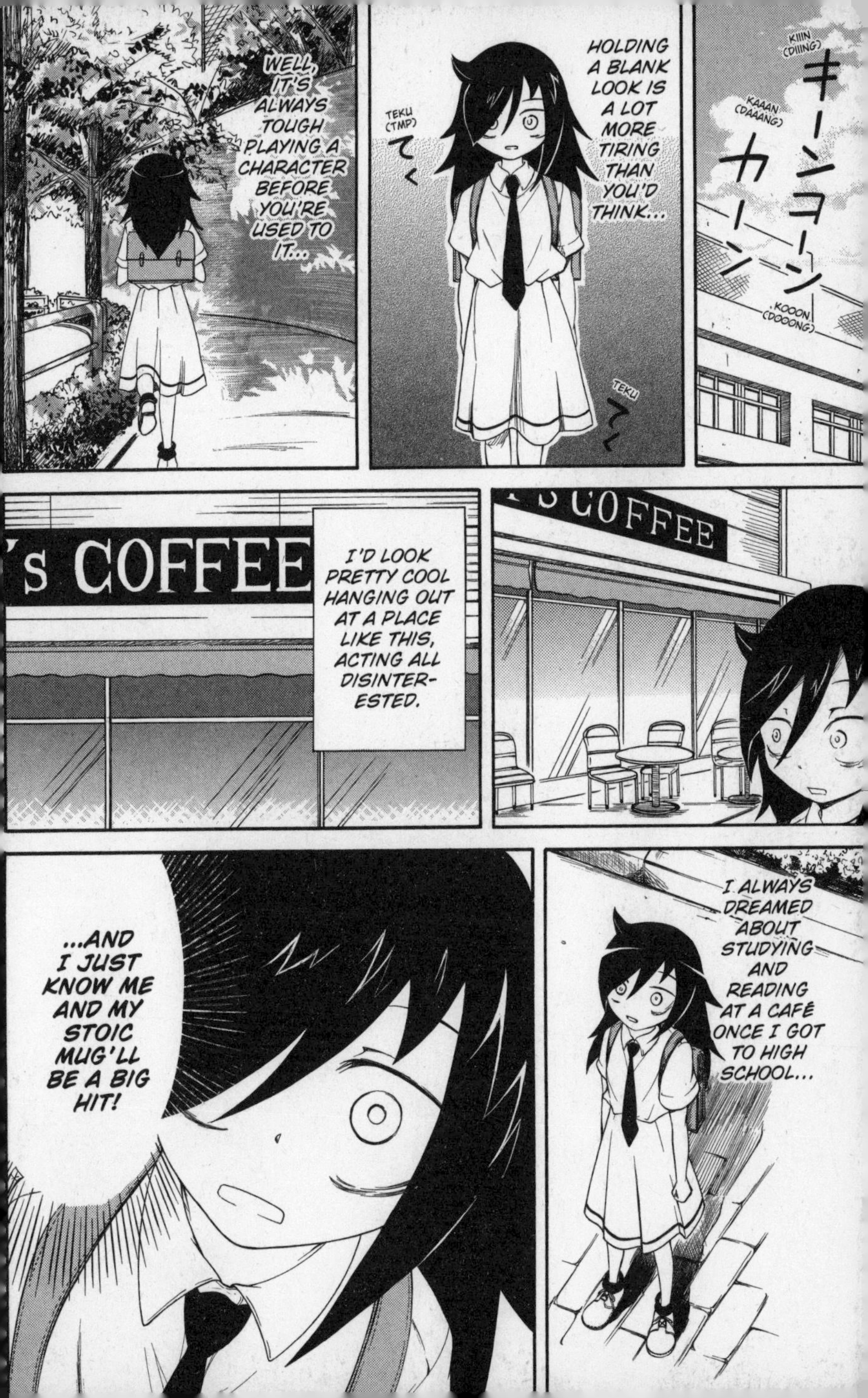
キーンコーン
KIIIN (DIIING)
KAAAN (DAAANG)
カーン
KOOON (DOOONG)
TEKU (TMP)
てく
HOLDING A BLANK LOOK IS A LOT MORE TIRING THAN YOU'D THINK...
TEKU
てく
WELL, IT'S ALWAYS TOUGH PLAYING A CHARACTER BEFORE YOU'RE USED TO IT...
S COFFEE
'S COFFEE
I'D LOOK PRETTY COOL HANGING OUT AT A PLACE LIKE THIS, ACTING ALL DISINTER-ESTED.
I ALWAYS DREAMED ABOUT STUDYING AND READING AT A CAFÉ ONCE I GOT TO HIGH SCHOOL...
...AND I JUST KNOW ME AND MY STOIC MUG'LL BE A BIG HIT!

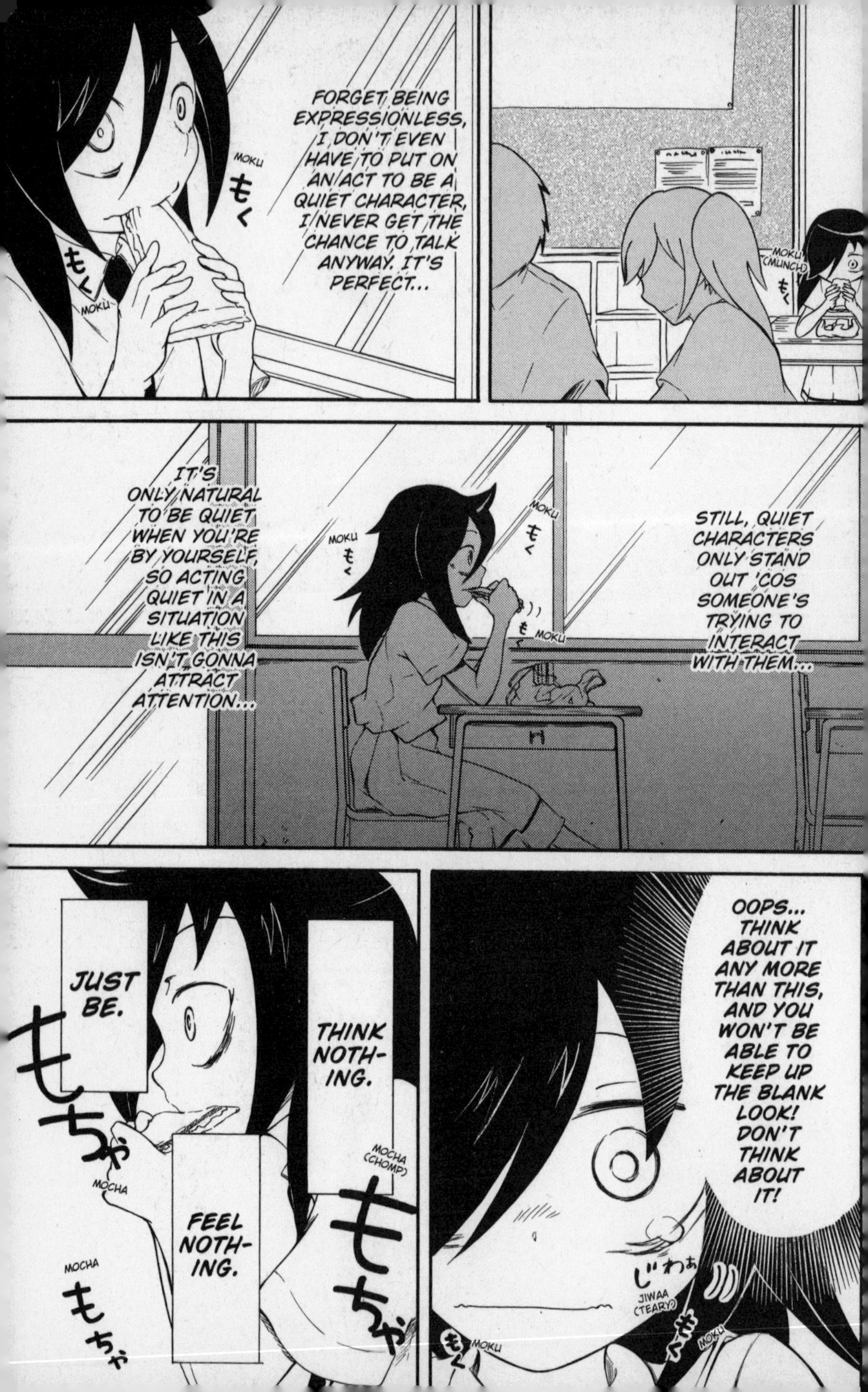
MOKU (MUNCH)
もく
FORGET BEING EXPRESSIONLESS, I DON'T EVEN HAVE TO PUT ON AN ACT TO BE A QUIET CHARACTER, I NEVER GET THE CHANCE TO TALK ANYWAY. IT'S PERFECT...
MOKU
もく
もく
MOKU
STILL, QUIET CHARACTERS ONLY STAND OUT 'COS SOMEONE'S TRYING TO INTERACT WITH THEM...
MOKU
もく
MOKU
もく
も
MOKU
IT'S ONLY NATURAL TO BE QUIET WHEN YOU'RE BY YOURSELF, SO ACTING QUIET IN A SITUATION LIKE THIS ISN'T GONNA ATTRACT ATTENTION...
OOPS... THINK ABOUT IT ANY MORE THAN THIS, AND YOU WON'T BE ABLE TO KEEP UP THE BLANK LOOK! DON'T THINK ABOUT IT!
じわぁ
JIWAA (TEARY)
MOKU
もく
もく
MOKU
THINK NOTHING.
MOCHA (CHOMP)
もちゃ
JUST BE.
もちゃ
MOCHA
FEEL NOTHING.
MOCHA
もちゃ

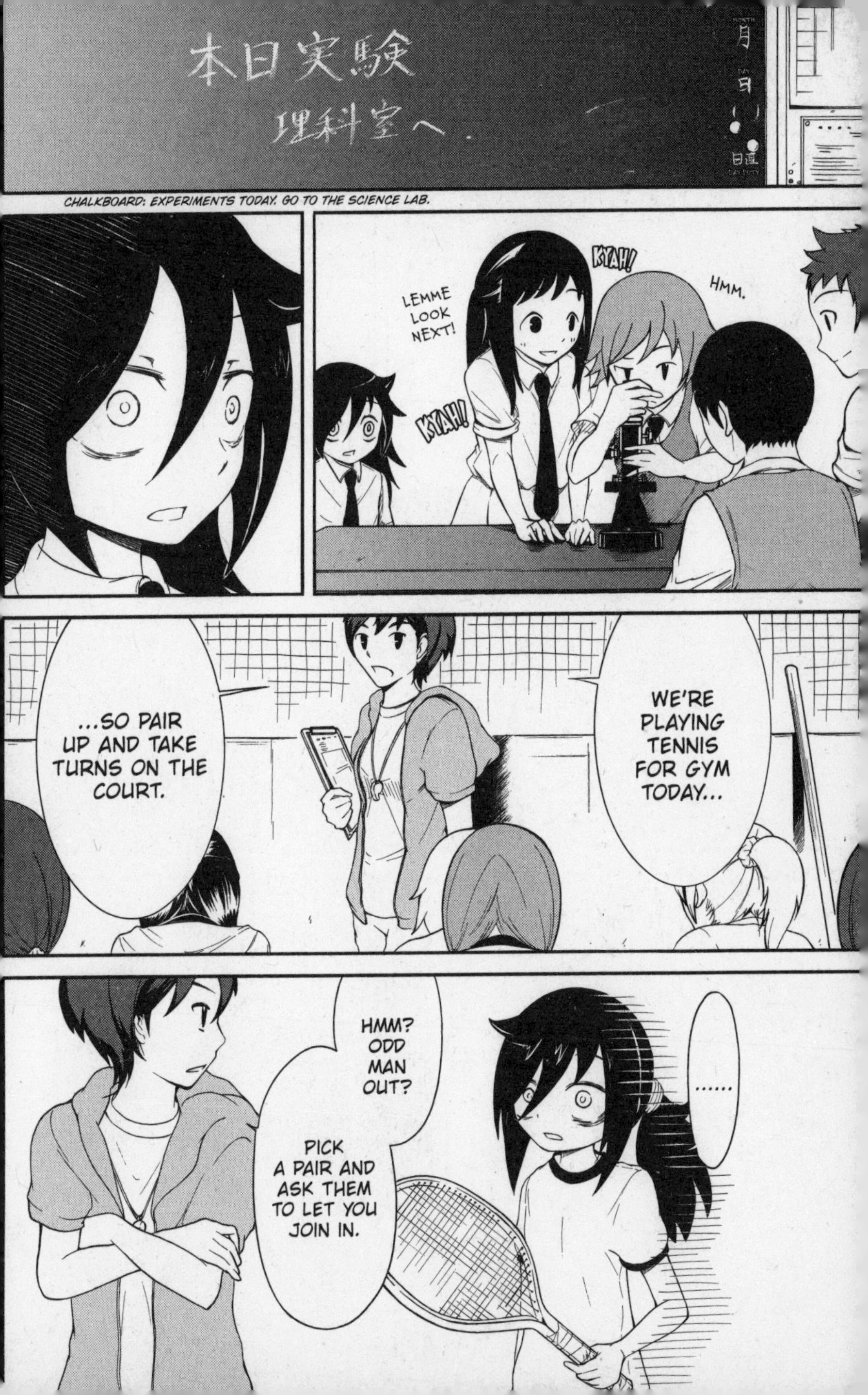
本日実験
理科室へ
月
日
日直
CHALKBOARD: EXPERIMENTS TODAY. GO TO THE SCIENCE LAB.
HMM.
KYAH!
LEMME LOOK NEXT!
KYAH!
WE'RE PLAYING TENNIS FOR GYM TODAY...
...SO PAIR UP AND TAKE TURNS ON THE COURT.
......
HMM? ODD MAN OUT?
PICK A PAIR AND ASK THEM TO LET YOU JOIN IN.

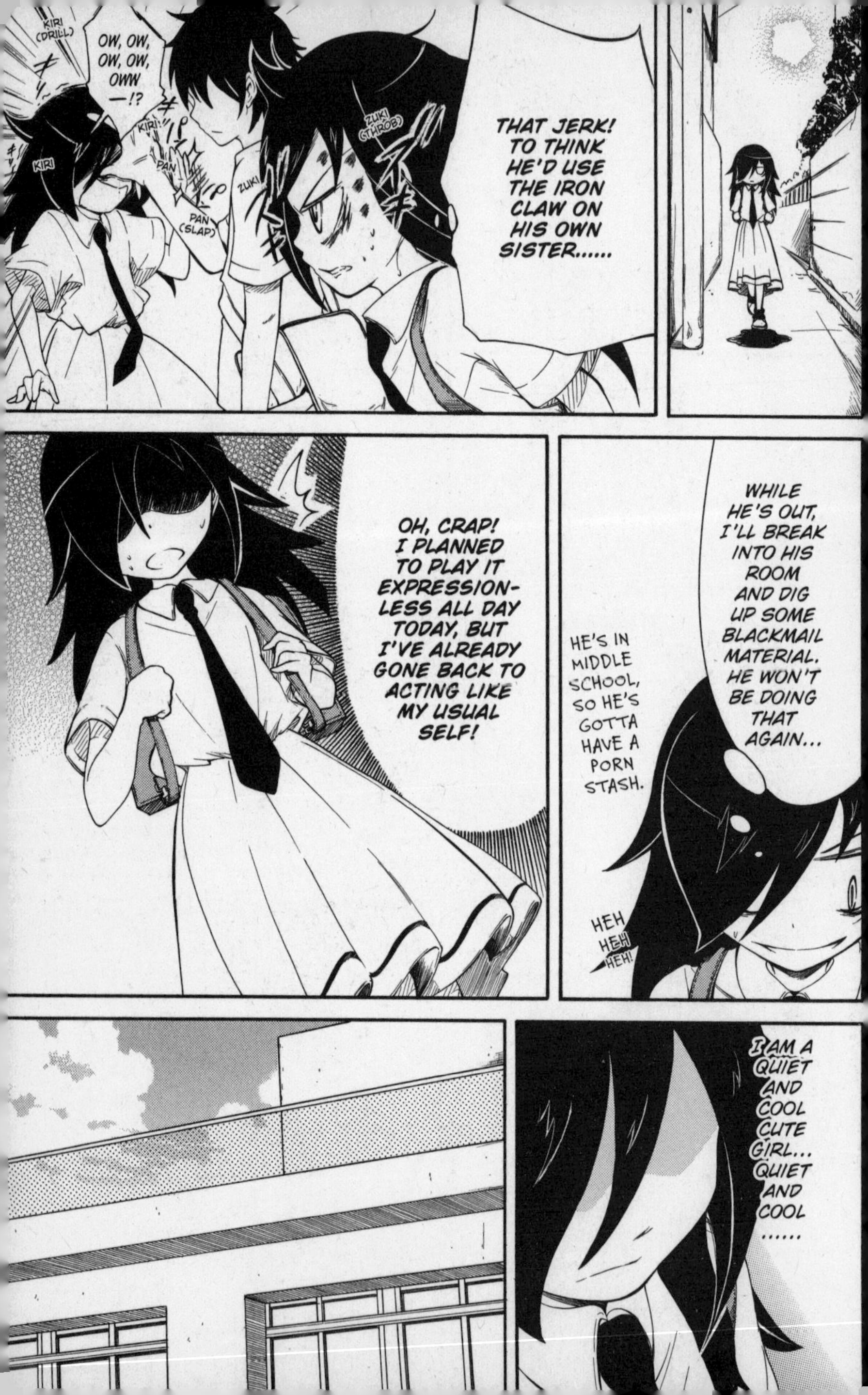
THAT JERK! TO THINK HE'D USE THE IRON CLAW ON HIS OWN SISTER......
ZUKI (THROB)
ZUKI
OW, OW, OW, OW, OWW —!?
KIRI (DRILL)
KIRI
PAN
PAN (SLAP)
KIRI
WHILE HE'S OUT, I'LL BREAK INTO HIS ROOM AND DIG UP SOME BLACKMAIL MATERIAL. HE WON'T BE DOING THAT AGAIN...
HE'S IN MIDDLE SCHOOL, SO HE'S GOTTA HAVE A PORN STASH.
HEH HEH HEH!
OH, CRAP! I PLANNED TO PLAY IT EXPRESSION-LESS ALL DAY TODAY, BUT I'VE ALREADY GONE BACK TO ACTING LIKE MY USUAL SELF!
I AM A QUIET AND COOL CUTE GIRL... QUIET AND COOL ......

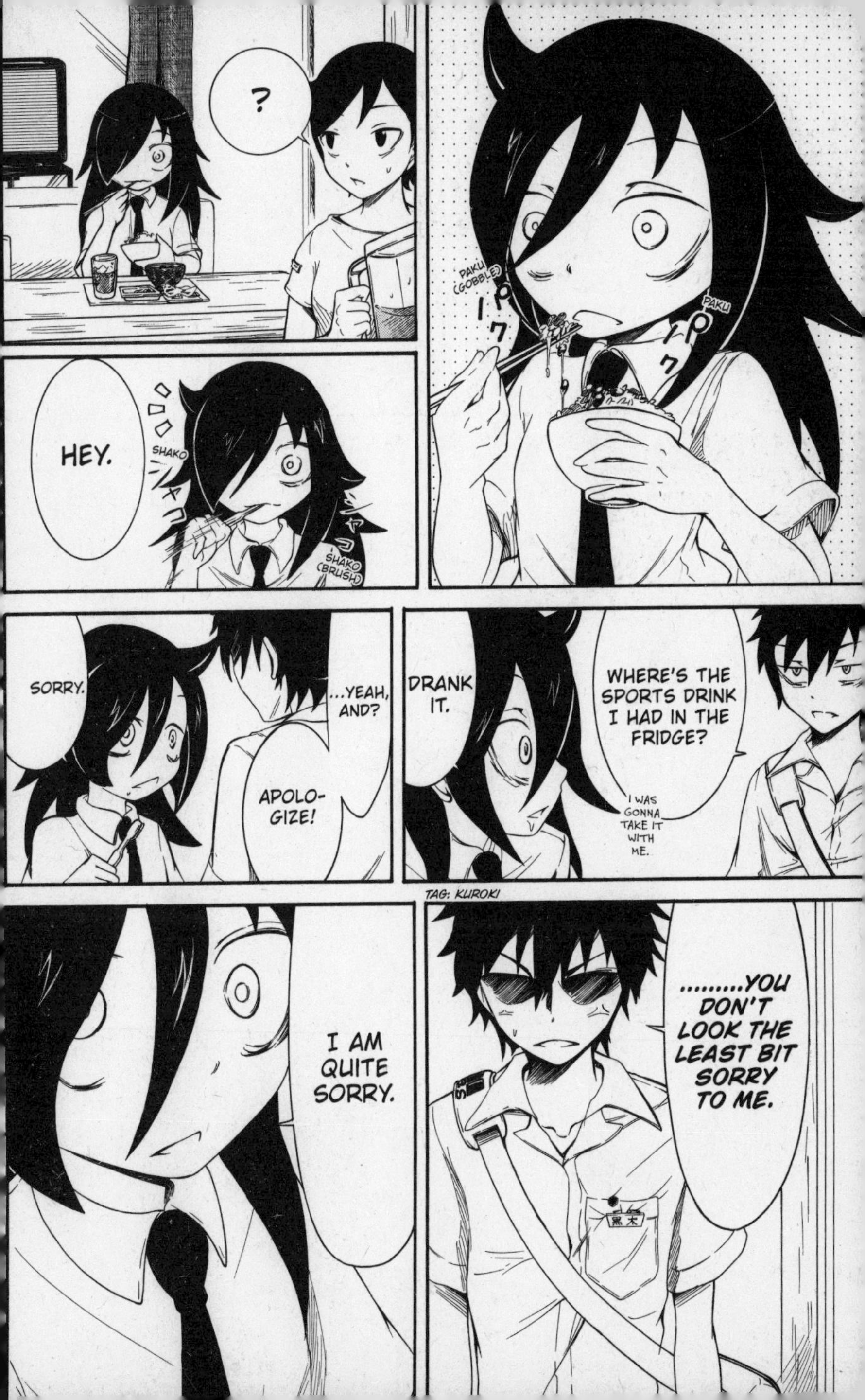
PAKU (GOBBLE)
PAKU
?
HEY.
SHAKO
SHAKO (BRUSH)
WHERE'S THE SPORTS DRINK I HAD IN THE FRIDGE?
I WAS GONNA TAKE IT WITH ME.
DRANK IT.
...YEAH, AND?
APOLO-GIZE!
SORRY.
TAG: KUROKI
.........YOU DON'T LOOK THE LEAST BIT SORRY TO ME.
I AM QUITE SORRY.

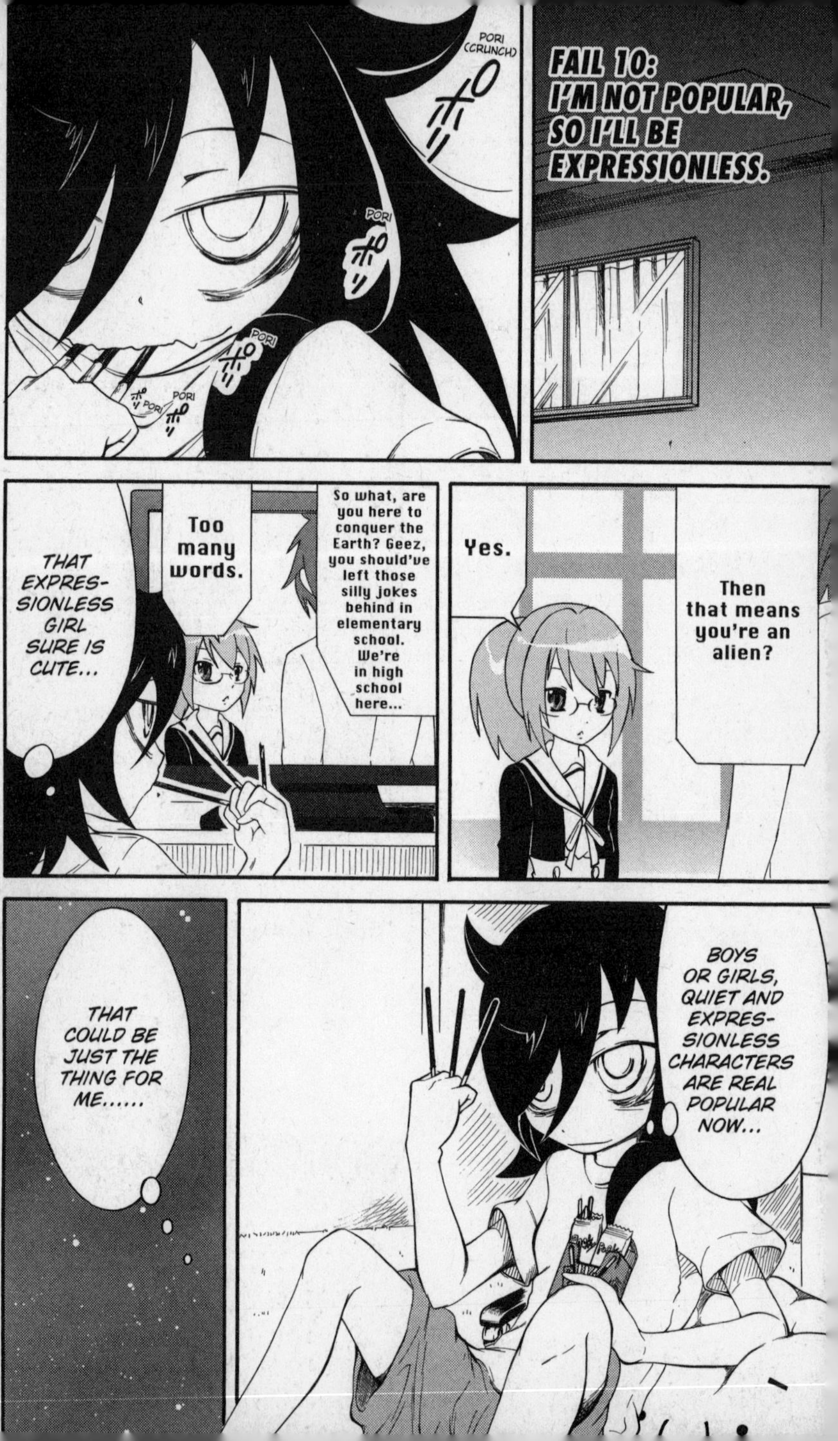
FAIL 10:
I'M NOT POPULAR, SO I'LL BE EXPRESSIONLESS.
PORI (CRUNCH)
PORI
PORI
PORI
PORI
Then that means you're an alien?
Yes.
So what, are you here to conquer the Earth? Geez, you should've left those silly jokes behind in elementary school. We're in high school here...
Too many words.
THAT EXPRES-SIONLESS GIRL SURE IS CUTE...
BOYS OR GIRLS, QUIET AND EXPRES-SIONLESS CHARACTERS ARE REAL POPULAR NOW...
THAT COULD BE JUST THE THING FOR ME......

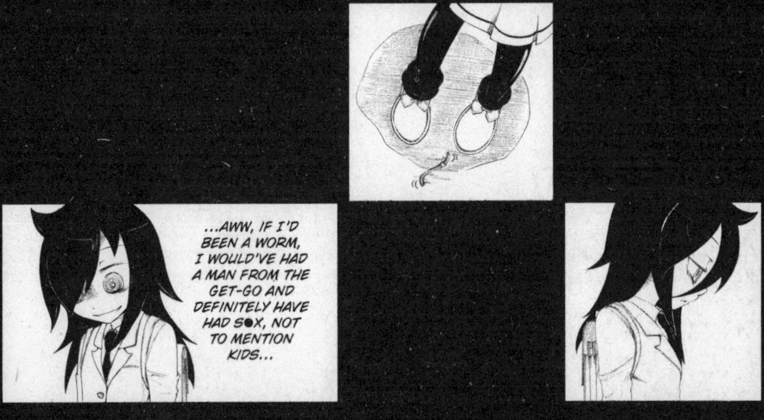
...AWW, IF I'D BEEN A WORM, I WOULD'VE HAD A MAN FROM THE GET-GO AND DEFINITELY HAVE HAD S●X, NOT TO MENTION KIDS...

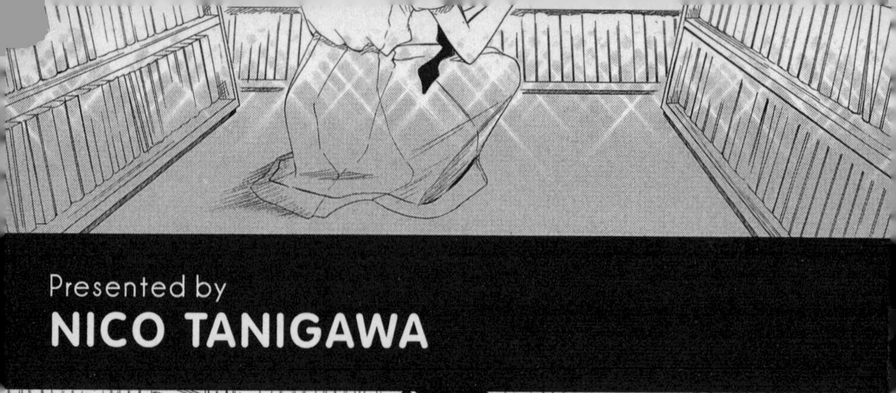

Presented by

NICO TANIGAWA

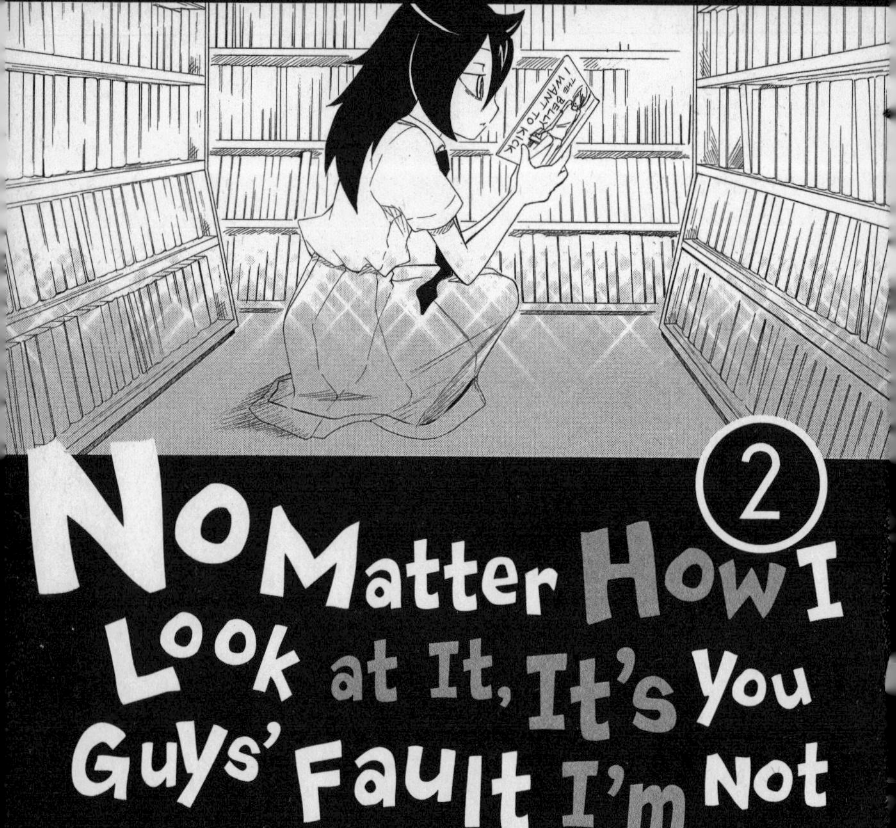

No Matter How I Look at It, It's You Guys' Fault I'm Not Popular!

2

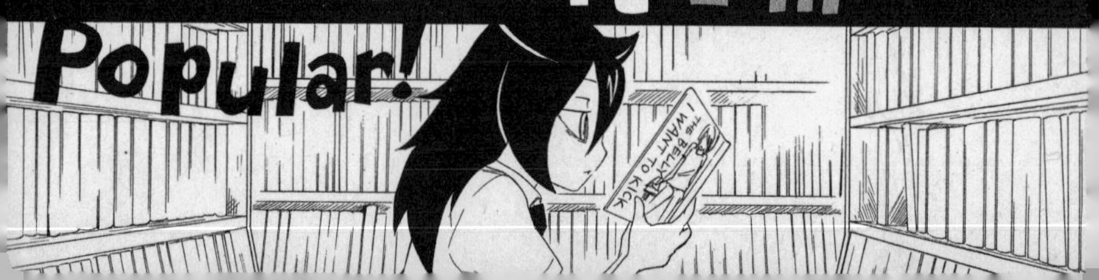